Anglais 3[e]

New Live

Odile Plays Martin-Cocher
Collège Rives du Léman, Évian
Académie de Grenoble

Michèle Meyer
Collège Mentel, Sélestat
Académie de Strasbourg

Catherine Marcangeli
Maître de conférences
Université de Paris VII-Denis Diderot

Jean-Pierre Gabilan
Maître de conférences
Université de Savoie
Chambéry

Avec la collaboration de
Elizabeth Coates-Raphoz

Didier
13, rue de l'Odéon - 75006 Paris

Remerciements

Les auteurs remercient Richard Boyce, Elisabeth Milleret, Sylvie Nacache et Virginie Rousseau pour leurs précieux conseils. Merci aussi pour leur soutien à Yves Bénéfice et Maryvonne Chéron, ainsi qu'à tous les professeurs qui nous ont communiqué leur témoignage d'utilisateur.

Illustrations : Marie-Anne Abesdris (pp. 26, 38)
Melanie Barnes (pp. 21, 33, 61)
Eric Battut (pp. 109, 110, 111, 112, 113)
Manu Boisteau (pp. 20, 34, 35, 101)
Marc Daniau (p. 62)
Antoine Déprez (pp. 10, 48, 116, 118)
Franz No (pp. 74, 75)
Marie-Noëlle Pichard (p. 12)
Fabrice Turrier (p. 92, 93)
Cartes : Graffito (pp. 205, 206, 207)

Mise en page et photogravure : AlphaStudio
Conception maquette : Véronique Lefebvre
Conception et réalisation des pages Guided Tour : Marie-Anne Abesdris
Couverture : Véronique Lefebvre - David Bart

ISBN 2 - 278 - 05350 - 7
Achevé d'imprimer en avril 2003 - Dépot Légal 5350/01

Imprimé en Italie

Avant-propos

La classe de troisième est une année charnière qui réunit des élèves dont les projets personnels, le niveau en anglais et la motivation pour cette matière peuvent être extrêmement différents.

*New Live 3e* prend en compte la spécificité de cette classe d'orientation. La méthode a été conçue pour encourager, soutenir et (re)motiver les élèves grâce à :

• des thèmes en rapport avec les intérêts et la maturité des élèves de 3e, pour que tous se sentent concernés quel que soit leur niveau scolaire,

• de nombreuses révisions au début et tout au long de l'année pour consolider les bases,

• des documents audios ou écrits courts et proches du niveau de production des élèves ; des activités guidées pour que tous puissent participer,

• des leçons à "géométrie variable" que chaque enseignant pourra adapter en fonction de son groupe,

• des tâches claires pour aider l'élève à réfléchir sur la langue et des exercices de phonologie intégrés à chaque leçon,

• des aides à l'élève lors de son travail à la maison, au moment où il a le plus besoin de soutien.

New Live 3e permet une solide préparation à la classe de seconde grâce à :

• des documents proches de l'authentique pour développer la compréhension orale ou écrite,

• un accent mis sur la production écrite, de la tâche très guidée à l'expression personnelle,

• un travail systématique pour favoriser la mémorisation et l'enrichissement du vocabulaire,

• une découverte guidée et réfléchie de quelques aspects essentiels de l'histoire et de la culture des pays anglophones.

Pour élaborer ce manuel de 3e très largement renouvelé, nous avons pris en compte l'expérience de nombreux collègues ainsi que l'évolution du public et des programmes.

Nous vous souhaitons une excellente année avec *New Live 3e*.

Les auteurs

FILES Pages	NOTIONS / FONCTIONS	GRAMMAIRE	RHYTHM'N SOUNDS
1 pages 9-22 **Celtic connections**	Présenter quelqu'un, le décrire Parler de sa personnalité, de ses habitudes Raconter des événements du passé Évoquer des contraintes du passé	Présent simple / *Wh- questions* Adverbes de fréquence *See / hear* + V-*ing* Prétérit simple + *ago - for* Prétérit *Be* + *-ing* *Had to* *Whereas / both*	Intonations des questions *Are* Les exclamatives *Was* Prononciation de *-ng*
2 pages 23-36 **Keep the cool in school**	Parler de l'influence exercée sur autrui Donner des conseils Exprimer la possibilité Faire des suppositions et des prédictions Comparer	*Make / Let someone do something* Modaux : *should - may* [*When / If* + Présent], [*will* + V] Le comparatif Présent *Be* + *-ing* *by - instead of* + V-*ing* Relatifs : *who, what*	/iː/ ou /ɪ/ Voyelles accentuées Lettres non prononcées Lire à voix haute Opérateurs et négation Syllabes accentuées
3 pages 37-50 **Science or fiction?**	Parler de ses expériences Faire un bilan maintenant d'événements passés Rapporter des propos Exprimer la possibilité	*Present perfect* + *ever, never, already, yet...* *Present perfect* + *for / since* Questions avec *Who*-sujet Discours indirect (V. introducteurs au Présent) Modaux : *might, could*	*Have* Chiffres, etc Le son /əʊ/ Questions au *Present perfect* Syllabes accentuées
4 pages 51-64 **Cowboys and Indians revisited**	Choisir le sujet d'un énoncé en fonction du contexte Rapporter des ordres Rendre compte d'évolutions Exprimer la quantité	Le passif Enoncés passifs avec: *give, offer...* Discours indirect : *ask, forbid, tell* + *to* + V Accroissement progressif Quantifieurs *Although / By* + date	*Was / were* Lire à voix haute Voix passive Syllabes accentuées
5 pages 65-78 **Young and rebellious**	Raconter des événements du passé, avec des points de repère passés Rapporter des propos	*Pluperfect* *Pluperfect* + *when, already, ever, before that* Discours indirect (V. introducteurs au Prétérit) Les numéraux	*Pluperfect : had* /ʌ/ ou /æ/ Formes faibles Lettres non prononcées Mots de plusieurs syllabes
6 pages 79-94 **Being or buying?**	Comparer une situation présente à ses expériences passées Imaginer une réalité différente Émettre des jugements sur le passé Comparer des quantités	*Present perfect* + *it's the first time* / superlatif *Present perfect Be* + *-ing* avec *for/since* [*If* + prétérit], [*would* + V] Modal + *Have* + participe passé Quantifieurs au comparatif	*Have been* V-*ing* <th> Accent de phrase Modal + *have* + participe passé
7 pages 95-114 **Commonwealth connections**	Imaginer un passé différent Insister sur un fait et en donner la conséquence Regretter d'avoir/de ne pas avoir fait quelque chose. Souhaiter que quelque chose se produise.	[*If* + *pluperfect*], [*would* + *have* + participe passé] *Such ... that / So ... that* *I wish ... / If only ...* *Regret / remember* + V-*ing*	*So* et *such* Mots de plusieurs syllabes

Précis grammatical (pages 124-167) • Liste des verbes irréguliers (pages 168-169) • Liste des expressions courantes (pages 170-171)

GUIDED TOURS	STRATEGIES	CREATIVE WRITING EXTRA READING / FUN PAGES	
Les Îles Britanniques, des Celtes à nos jours	Acquérir le réflexe d'utiliser un vocabulaire riche et varié à l'écrit et à l'oral	Chanson : *Flower of Scotland*	TEST 1
L'école, une conquête, des problèmes, des solutions	Enrichissement du vocabulaire : préfixes et suffixes	Acrostiche : *Respect* Poème : *At school, be cool* Chanson : *The Logical Song*	TEST 2
La science-fiction, reflet de notre histoire scientifique et politique, miroir de nos peurs…	Compréhension de l'oral : anticiper, repérer, inférer, compenser	Lecture : *The Thing*	TEST 3
Les Indiens d'Amérique au-delà des clichés : une écologie en danger		Narration : *The Trail of Tears* Lecture : *Tokalulata Remembers* Chanson : *Indian Reservation*	TEST 4
Les grandes causes défendues en musique, des années 60 à nos jours	Compréhension de l'écrit : les phrases complexes	Rap : *It's Like That* Lecture : *A New Beginning*	TEST 5
La publicité et ses techniques les plus récentes pour cibler les jeunes consommateurs	Production écrite : rédiger un texte argumentatif	Lettre : protesting against an offensive ad Lecture : *On Advertisements*	TEST 6
Panorama du Commonwealth, de sa formation à nos jours	Enrichissement du vocabulaire : les adjectifs composés	Nouvelle : *A Long Walk to Forever*	TEST 7

• Lexique anglais-français et français-anglais (pages 172-203)

New Live 3e

Sept dossiers thématiques.
Dans chaque dossier :

deux leçons

1 Listen and learn *ou* Read and learn

Une première étape conçue pour inciter tous les élèves à participer, quel que soit leur niveau.
Audio ou écrit, ce document court est proche du niveau de production des élèves.

2 Practise speaking *ou* Practise writing

Parler ou écrire en classe pour fixer ce que l'on vient d'apprendre.
Activités variées et très guidées pour que tous les élèves s'impliquent activement.

3 Go forward

S'entraîner à comprendre et à rendre compte de ce que l'on a compris ; approfondir le travail linguistique.
Un document audio ou écrit plus proche de l'authentique.

Think

Réfléchir sur la langue.
Pour chaque objectif (nouveauté ou révision), une tâche simple et accessible.

Rhythm'n sounds

Améliorer prononciation et intonation.
Des exercices basés sur le vocabulaire et les phrases de la leçon.

Memo

Mémoriser les phrases-clés de la leçon et soigner la prononciation.
Pour que les élèves s'approprient ce "Memo", il est placé dans le *Workbook* suivi d'un espace "notes persos". Il est enregistré pour fixer prononciation et intonation en classe ou à la maison.

En fin de manuel :
- les scripts
- un précis grammatical
- une liste de verbes irréguliers
- un lexique bilingue

Dans le guide pédagogique :
- les fiches de visionnement vidéo
- un test et son corrigé par dossier

un *guided tour* culturel

pour une découverte active de la civilisation liée à chaque thème.

Quelques tâches qui guideront les élèves tout au long de leur visite et les inciteront à découvrir activement ces documents.

Quiz enregistré pour parcourir à nouveau ces pages, en s'amusant à tester ses connaissances.

Project work facultatif pour travailler autrement, en autonomie, en groupe, en liaison avec les professeurs d'art et d'histoire-géographie…

Document vidéo authentique une manière vivante et stimulante de compléter cette visite guidée.

Des textes courts et accessibles, des documents authentiques pour ouvrir de belles fenêtres sur le monde anglo-saxon.

fun page

Quelques grands classiques de la chanson des années 60 à nos jours !

creative writing

Écrire pour raconter, exprimer sentiments ou opinions, écrire pour être lu.

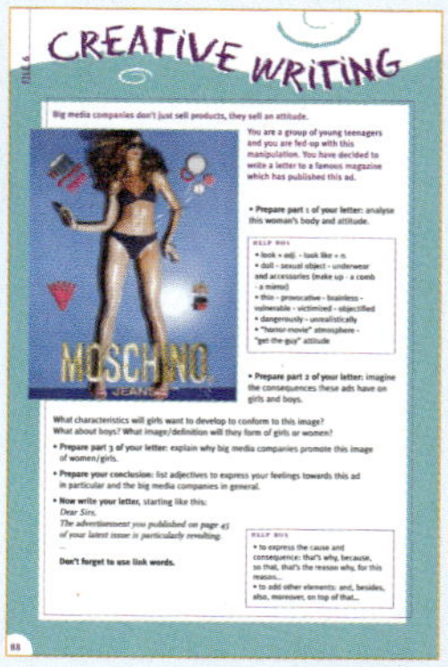

strategies

Un travail méthodologique axé sur le vocabulaire, la compréhension écrite et orale et la production écrite.

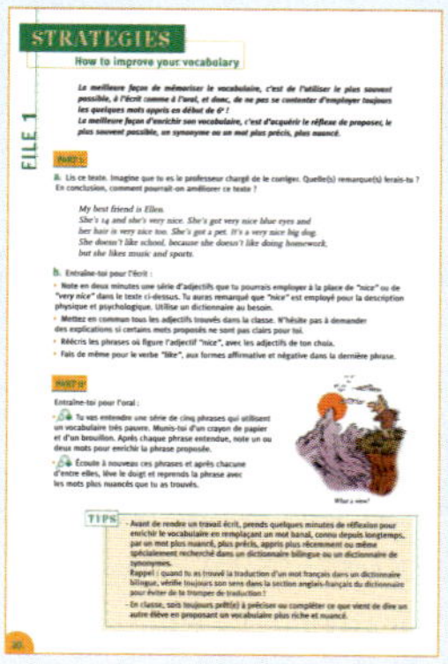

exercises

Des exercices de grammaire, de production écrite et d'expression orale.

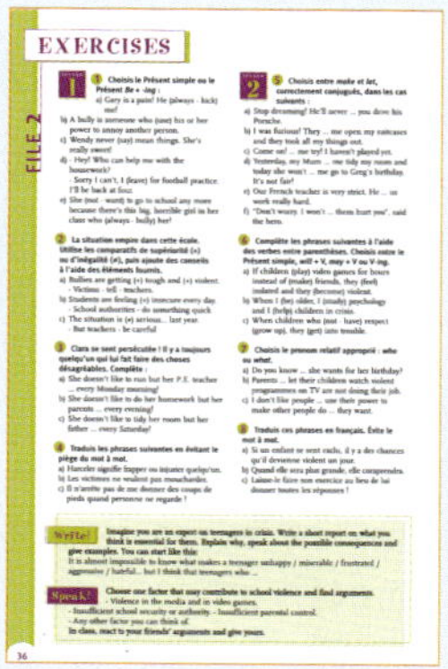

extra reading

Un beau texte, une démarche guidée pour préparer les élèves à la lecture autonome.

Workbook

At School

Toutes les activités proposées pour le travail en classe : exploitation des dialogues et textes, entraînement oral, réflexion sur la langue et phonologie.

Ce logo [W : 1] p. 3 signale qu'il faut se reporter à la *worksheet* 1, p. 3 du *Workbook*.
Les *worksheets* sont photocopiables.

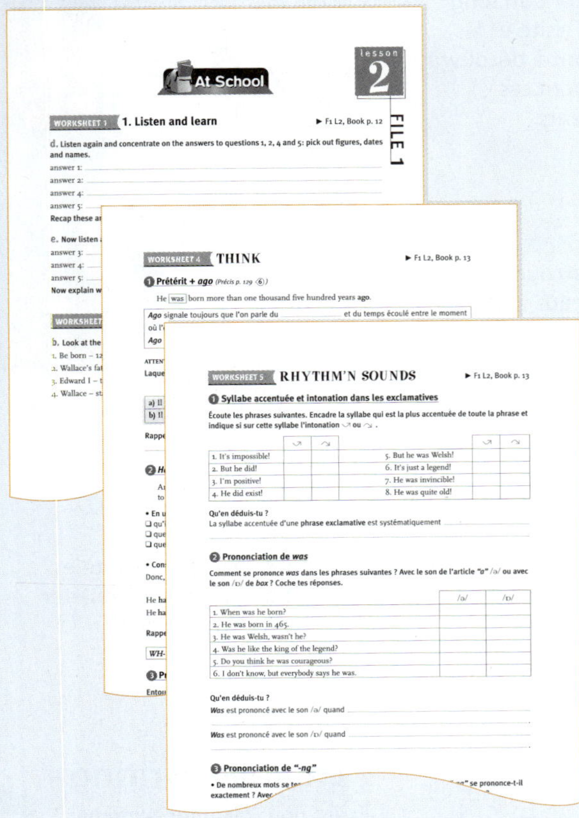

At Home

Au début de chaque leçon, un tableau indique :
- sur quelle partie de la leçon porte chacun des exercices proposés,
- de quel type d'exercice il s'agit.

At Home — File 1 - Lesson 2

Les exercices	portent sur ...	et servent à ...
1	*Listen and learn* (livre p. 12 et p. 119)	Apprendre le vocabulaire.
2	*"A Celtic hero"* (livre p. 119)	Revoir le texte.
3	*Listen and learn* (livre p. 12 et p. 119) *Practise speaking* (livre p. 12) *Think* (WB pp. 17-18)	S'entraîner, avec des conseils pour relire et vérifier.
4 - 5 - 6	*Go forward* (livre p. 13)	Apprendre le vocabulaire.
7 - 8	*"A well-known legend"* (livre p. 13)	Revoir le texte.
9 - 10 - 11 12 - 13	Toute la leçon (livre pp. 12-13, p. 119) *Think* (WB pp. 17-18)	S'entraîner, avec des conseils pour relire et vérifier.

Sont proposés systématiquement pour chaque dialogue ou texte étudié :

- un ou plusieurs exercices destinés à **l'apprentissage** et à la **mémorisation** du vocabulaire.
- un exercice pour **relire activement** le **texte** (script du document oral ou document écrit) et se préparer à en rendre compte.
- Plusieurs exercices d'entraînement assortis de **conseils spécifiques** (analyse d'un exemple, rappel d'une construction, etc.).

L'élève apprend à se relire et à vérifier ses réponses. Il s'agit d'accompagner l'élève dans son travail au moment où il en a le plus besoin : à la maison.

Pour chaque ***Guided Tour*** du manuel, deux exercices sont proposés dans le *Workbook* :
- un exercice pour apprendre le vocabulaire
- un exercice pour redécouvrir activement textes et illustrations.

FILE 1

Celtic connections

Lessons 1 and 2 .... p. 10
- présenter quelqu'un, le décrire
- parler de sa personnalité, de ses habitudes
- raconter des événements du passé
- évoquer des contraintes

Guided Tour .... p. 14

Strategies .... p. 20
- enrichir son vocabulaire

Fun Page .... p. 21

Exercises .... p. 22

Test 1

1. Listen and learn
Celtic creatures

script p. 119

Supernatural creatures
in Celtic regions and countries

a. **Look at the map, spot the Celtic countries or regions.**
You: Scotland is north of ...

b. **Look at the Celtic creatures, listen and repeat their names. Use the help box to speak about them.**
You: Spriggans are ...
They look ...

c. **Do the tasks on worksheet 1 (p. 3 of your workbook).**

HELP BOX
- Scottish - Irish - Welsh - Cornish
- friendly - helpful
- mean ≃ cruel ≠ gentle
- serious ≠ playful

2. Practise speaking

Guessing game.
Team A has information about a supernatural creature. Go to page 118.
Team B has information about another supernatural creature. Go to page 116.
Ask questions to the other team about their creature, then recap all the information and give the creature's name, if you can!

3. Go forward

A Leprechaun watcher

script p. 119

- Look at the map and say everything you can about this part of the British Isles.
- Have a look at this illustration from a website. What is it about? Why do you think people visit it? Imagine what they can do on this site.
- Read the text below and spot on the map the places mentioned. Explain why people visit this site. How do you react? Why?
- Listen to an interview, and do the tasks on worksheet 2 (p. 4).

IRELANDSEYE

http://www.irelandseye.com

www.irelandseye.com
presents

the Leprechaun watch

We are here in the Glen[1] of Cloongallon, near the town of Thurles, in a picturesque part of Tipperary. In the middle of the glen there is a magnificent oak tree which is over 600 years old. The tree has a magical reputation: people think that Leprechauns often come here to find acorns[2] to make their pipes.

Today this tree also serves as a hide: in its trunk, there is a webcam.

This webcam sends pictures 24 hours a day to a website called The Leprechaun Watch. Every day, dozens of people from all over the world visit the site in the hope of spotting a Leprechaun.

1. glen: *vallée* - 2. acorn: *gland*

THINK

1. Adverbes de fréquence.
2. *Wh- questions (what, why, how often, how long)* au Présent simple.
3. *See / hear + V-ing.*

Exercices : W 3 p. 4

RHYTHM'N SOUNDS

1. Intonation des questions.
2. *Are.*

Exercices : W 4 p. 7

MEMO

In your **WB** p. 8

1. Listen and learn
A Celtic hero

script p. 119

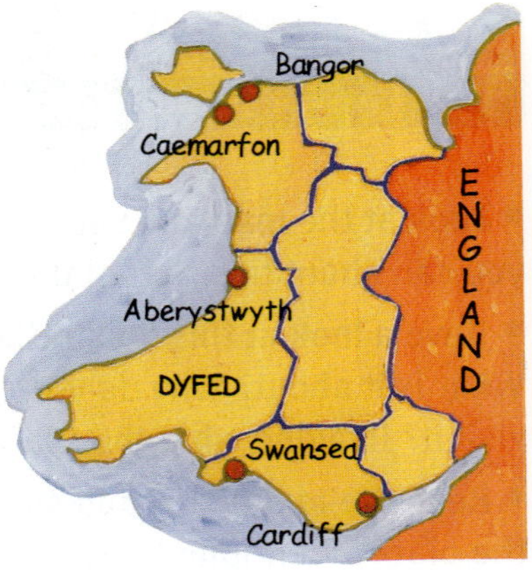

a. Read the title, look at the map, and listen to part 1 of a conversation. Who? Where? What is the problem?

b. Listen to part 2. Is Suzie right?

c. Imagine the questions Douglas and Suzie are going to ask their teacher. Then listen to part 3: correct or complete your list of questions.

d. Do the tasks on worksheet 1 (p. 14).

2. Practise speaking

a. Look at this famous historical character. Do you know him? What can you say about him?

b. Tell Wallace's story with the help of the comic strip on worksheet 2, (p. 14).

c. Team work. Prepare a quiz about William Wallace. Use: when, where, why, how long, how often, who, what. Write down 7 questions like this:

> **1. WHEN DID WALLACE DIE?**
> a) 1271
> b) 1272
> c) 1278
> d) 1305

d. Team A ask questions to team B, then change parts. Don't forget to count points!

Team A: When did Wallace die? In 1271, in 1272, in 1278 or in 1305?
Team B: Wallace died in 1305.
Team A: Are you absolutely certain?
Team B: Yes, we are!
Team A: Is this your last word?
Team B: Yes, it is!

3. Go forward

- **Look at the picture and read the title. Who is the legend about? Tell the class what you know about this legend or list words or names you expect to find in the text. Ask for the vocabulary you need.**
- **Do the tasks on worksheet 3 (p. 16).**

More than five hundred years ago, a man called Sir Thomas Malory wrote *Le Morte Darthur* (1485), the standard legend of Arthur. Today, the legend of King Arthur is still one of the best-known in the world.

A well-known legend

In England, in the fifth century, there was a king called Uther. Uther had no heir so when he died, England was left without a king.

To choose the King of England, Merlin the Wizard placed a sword named Excalibur in a stone. Many men tried to draw the sword out, but they all failed. Arthur, Uther's unknown son, succeeded: he became the King.

When he married Guinevere he received the Round Table as a dowry[1]. This is where he sat with his knights - the most famous being Lancelot, Percival and Galahad. They were men of courage, honour and dignity. Thanks to their help, Arthur won many battles against the Romans and expanded his empire.

After the Romans' defeat, Arthur, Percival and Galahad undertook the Quest for the Holy Grail[2] and they had to stay away from the kingdom for several years.

On their return, Arthur learnt that his wife did not love him any more. She was in love with Lancelot and she fled to France with him.

Arthur was devastated by the treachery of his beloved wife and his favourite knight. He put his cousin Mordred in charge of his kingdom and left for France. Arthur was fighting Lancelot in France when Mordred rebelled. Arthur had to return to England immediately. He fought Mordred and killed him, but he died too.

1. dowry: *dot* - 2. The cup Christ used before his death.

THINK

1. Prétérit + *ago*.
2. *Had* + *to* + V.
3. Prétérit + *for*.
4. Prétérit simple / Prétérit *Be* + *-ing*.
5. *Whereas* / *both*.

✎ **Exercices :** W 4 p. 17

RHYTHM'N SOUNDS

1. Les exclamatives.
2. *Was*.
3. Prononciation de *-ng*.

✎ **Exercices :** W 5 p. 19

MEMO

In your WB p. 20

Celtic connections

... A GUIDED TOUR

1 Do you think "English" is the same as "British"? Look at the map page 205. Then say all you know about England, Wales, Scotland, Ireland and Northern Ireland (capitals, symbols, music, etc.). Now look at pages 15 to 19 to find other elements.

2 Look at pages 15 to 19 again.

a) Pick out all the "Celtic connections" and say how Celtic culture survives in the United Kingdom and Ireland today.

b) Find the different stages in the constitution of the U.K.
Spot the emblems and the patron saints of the different nations in the British Isles.
What is the largest population group in the U.K. today?

c) The Westminster Parliament, in London, lost some of its powers in 1999. Why?

d) Read page 19.
- Explain the presence of army tanks and police vehicles in the Orange March.
- Look at the U.V.F. mural and describe it. Why these flags?
- Look at the Republican mural: according to it, what or who keeps Northern Ireland prisoner?

e) Are there any Celtic connections in France? Give examples.

3 Quiz Now find out how much you know about Celtic connections.

PROJECT WORK

Find out what kind of people the Celts were: where they came from, their conquests, their customs, the influence they still have today, etc. You can work alone or in groups. Look for information in the school library or on the Net, and ask your history teacher for advice. Then give a short presentation to the class, using a chronology, photographs and illustrations.

VIDEO

An invitation to Great Britain.

The Union Flag, or Union Jack, is the flag for the "United Kingdom of Great Britain and Northern Ireland" (U.K.). It incorporates the crosses of St George, St Patrick and St Andrew. But somebody's flag is missing...

Around 5,000 years ago, the Prehistoric inhabitants of England built huge[1] stone structures, like the sacred stone circles at Stonehenge. Today still, at every summer solstice, people come to Stonehenge to worship[2] the sun.

1. huge: *énorme*
2. worship: *vénérer*

ENGLAND

By the 3rd century before Christ (B.C.), the Celts were a very powerful people. Their conquests included parts of Austria, France, Italy, Spain, Asia Minor and England. Their skill* in metalwork is visible in their weapons and jewellery.

*skill: *savoir-faire*

The Romans defeated the Celts and invaded England in 43 A.D. (after Christ). They built roads, viaducts, aqueducts and public baths.

After many invasions and battles, the English Kingdom was unified in the 10th century. St George symbolizes the victory of the Christian faith* over evil (the dragon). He was chosen as the patron saint of England and his cross was adopted as the English flag. The rose is the national emblem of England.

*faith: *foi*

1284: the English annex Wales.

1536: the Act of Union joins England and Wales.

Today, the Welsh represent 1.9% of the U.K. population (the English, 81.5%).
A Celtic language, Welsh is still spoken by about 26% of the population and is taught in some schools.

The English built Conwy Castle (1283) as a defense against Welsh rebellion

WALES

The red dragon is an old symbol of Welsh identity and independence. It is often flown* on St David's Day to celebrate the patron saint of Wales. Prince Charles, the Prince of Wales, is holding a bunch of daffodils, another Welsh emblem.

*be flown: *flotter*

Rich in copper[1], slate[2] and iron, Wales contributed to the Industrial Revolution in the 18th and 19th centuries. Today most mines are closed, but they have left their mark on the landscape.

1. copper: *cuivre*
2. slate: *ardoise*

Evening Post
SWANSEA
REES JONES
ROYAL ROUTES
Preview of the big visit... page 14
JOBS!
WORKPOST
Her Majesty opens first Welsh parliament in 600 years
NATION UNITES FOR GREAT DAY

With the opening of the Welsh Assembly (or Parliament) in 1999, many decisions concerning Wales are made in Cardiff now, not London.

Celtic cross

The Celtic heritage survives in Scottish music, literature and sport. Every year, the Highland Games include traditional Celtic festivities and sports. In the caber competition, the athletes have to throw a wooden pole as far as they can.

St Andrew, the patron saint of Scotland, was crucified on an X-shaped[1] cross. This cross inspired Scotland's flag. The thistle[2] is the Scottish emblem.

1. X-shaped: *en forme de X*
2. thistle: *chardon*

Eilean Donan was built in the 13th century as a defense against Viking raids.

SCOTLAND

1707: Act of Union. Scotland joins England (plus Wales) to form "Great Britain".

1999: opening of the Scottish Parliament in Edinburgh. The Queen remains head of state, and the Westminster Parliament in London is still responsible for important matters like foreign policy and defense.

Today, the Scots represent 9.6% of the British population. Only 60,000 people still speak Scots, a Celtic language.

Fishing village

The Celts invaded Ireland in the 4th century B.C. and dominated the island for nearly 1000 years. There are traces of this Celtic past in Irish architecture, language and folk music.

EIRE

In the 5th century A.D. Saint Patrick brought Christianity to Ireland. Every year, big celebrations honour the patron saint. Today, 94% of the population are Catholics, and less than 4% are Protestants.

The Irish flag symbolizes peace (white) between Catholics (green) and Protestants (orange).

County Clare, West of Ireland

16th century: English Protestants expropriate Irish Catholics and settle on their land.

1800-1801: the Irish Parliament is abolished. An Act of Union forms the "United Kingdom of Great Britain and Ireland". The English influence gets stronger. The Celtic language and traditions start declining.

1921: Anglo-Irish Treaty. After many Irish revolts, Ireland (Eire) becomes an independent state but Northern Ireland (Ulster) remains part of the U.K.

1973: the Republic of Ireland joins the European Community.

2002: unlike the U.K., Ireland joins the Euro Zone. The Celtic harp on Euro coins evokes the country's Celtic heritage.o

July 1690: battle of the Boyne, near Belfast. William of Orange defeated the Catholics. Every year, to celebrate this Protestant victory, Orangemen march through the streets, often causing clashes with Catholics.

Loyalist mural with the Ulster flag and the Union Jack

NORTHERN IRELAND

The population of Northern Ireland (1.8% of the U.K. population) is divided:
- on one side, the *Loyalists* (or Unionists): Protestants who want to remain part of the U.K.
- on the other side, the *Nationalists* (or Republicans): Catholics who want Ulster to be united with the Republic of Ireland.

1999: as in Wales and Scotland, a new Assembly (Parliament) opens in Belfast.

Republican mural in Belfast

Terrorist attacks and ceasefires*, demonstrations and treaties: peace in Northern Ireland is always fragile.

*ceasefire: *cessez-le-feu*

STRATEGIES

How to improve your vocabulary

La meilleure façon de mémoriser le vocabulaire, c'est de l'utiliser le plus souvent possible, à l'écrit comme à l'oral, et donc, de ne pas se contenter d'employer toujours les quelques mots appris en début de 6e !
La meilleure façon d'enrichir son vocabulaire, c'est d'acquérir le réflexe de proposer, le plus souvent possible, un synonyme ou un mot plus précis, plus nuancé.

PART I

a. Lis ce texte. Imagine que tu es le professeur chargé de le corriger. Quelle(s) remarque(s) ferais-tu ? En conclusion, comment pourrait-on améliorer ce texte ?

My best friend is Ellen.
She's 14 and she's very nice. She's got very nice blue eyes and her hair is very nice too. She's got a pet. It's a very nice big dog. She doesn't like school, because she doesn't like doing homework, but she likes music and sports.

b. Entraîne-toi pour l'écrit :

- Note en deux minutes une série d'adjectifs que tu pourrais employer à la place de *"nice"* ou de *"very nice"* dans le texte ci-dessus. Tu auras remarqué que *"nice"* est employé pour la description physique et psychologique. Utilise un dictionnaire au besoin.
- Mettez en commun tous les adjectifs trouvés dans la classe. N'hésite pas à demander des explications si certains mots proposés ne sont pas clairs pour toi.
- Réécris les phrases où figure l'adjectif *"nice"*, avec les adjectifs de ton choix.
- Fais de même pour le verbe *"like"*, aux formes affirmative et négative dans la dernière phrase.

PART II

Entraîne-toi pour l'oral :

- Tu vas entendre une série de cinq phrases qui utilisent un vocabulaire très pauvre. Munis-toi d'un crayon de papier et d'un brouillon. Après chaque phrase entendue, note un ou deux mots pour enrichir la phrase proposée.
- Écoute à nouveau ces phrases et après chacune d'entre elles, lève le doigt et reprends la phrase avec les mots plus nuancés que tu as trouvés.

What a view!

TIPS

- Avant de rendre un travail écrit, prends quelques minutes de réflexion pour enrichir le vocabulaire en remplaçant un mot banal, connu depuis longtemps, par un mot plus nuancé, plus précis, appris plus récemment ou même spécialement recherché dans un dictionnaire bilingue ou un dictionnaire de synonymes.
  Rappel : quand tu as trouvé la traduction d'un mot français dans un dictionnaire bilingue, vérifie toujours son sens dans la section anglais-français du dictionnaire pour éviter de te tromper de traduction !
- En classe, sois toujours prêt(e) à préciser ou compléter ce que vient de dire un autre élève en proposant un vocabulaire plus riche et nuancé.

Fun Page

Flower of Scotland

Oh Flower of Scotland
When will we see yer like again,
That fought and died for
Yer wee bit Hill and Glen
And stood against him
Proud Edward's Army,
And sent him homeward
Tae think again.

The Hills are bare now
And Autumn leaves lie thick and still
O'er land that is lost now
Which those so dearly held
That stood against him
Proud Edward's Army
And sent him homeward
Tae think again.

Those days are passed now
And in the past they must remain
But we can still rise now
And be the nation again
That stood against him
Proud Edward's Army
And sent him homeward,
Tae think again.

R. MB Williamson / The Corries (Music) Ltd

EXERCISES

lesson 1

1 Complète les phrases comme dans l'exemple, à l'aide de la carte des Îles Britanniques, p. 205.

Ex. : London is ... England.
London is in the South of England.

a) Inverness ... Scotland
b) Cardiff ... Wales
c) Belfast ... Northern Ireland
d) Dublin ... Ireland
e) Cornwall ... England

2 Réponds en parlant de toi.

a) What are you like / what do you look like?
b) How often do you phone your friends?
c) How long do you usually stay on the phone with your friends?
d) What sort of clothes do you wear most of the time?

3 Prépare un questionnaire destiné à des adolescents. Inspire-toi des questions de l'exercice 2 en utilisant les idées suivantes :

- watch TV
- surf the Internet
- stay online
- hang out with your friends (places?)
- sort of music - listen to

4 Traduis les phrases suivantes :

a) Les Spriggans sont souvent méchants.
b) Je navigue sur le web trois fois par semaine. Je reste en ligne à peu près une heure d'habitude.
c) Oh non, j'entends quelque chose bouger !

Speak! Speak about yourself for 2 to 3 minutes. Say everything you like about:

- your family - your friends
- your school life - your hobbies
- your favourite sport, music, stars...

lesson 2

5 Mets les verbes entre parenthèses au Temps qui convient : Présent simple ou Prétérit simple.

- I (go) to the cinema last night.
- What (you - see)?
- I (see) *Lord Of The Rings.*
- Really? (you - like) it?
- It (be) really fantastic, I (think) you should go and see it.
- You know, I never (go) to the cinema, I (prefer) to read the book.
- I (enjoy) both things: I (read) the book when I (be) 13, you know ...

6 Rédige des phrases en suivant l'exemple fourni :

Ex. : Arthur - fight - Lancelot - Mordred - rebel
Arthur was fighting Lancelot when Mordred rebelled.

a) Wallace - work - some English soldiers - attack - his wife
b) Wallace - wait for his wife - the English lord - kill her
c) Robert the Bruce - watch - the English - behead - Wallace
d) The English - fight - Robert the Bruce - Edward I - die

7 Trouve les questions correspondant aux éléments soulignés.

a) Karen lost her bag <u>when she was in Japan</u>.
b) Many people <u>fled from Europe</u> during the Second World War.
c) Sean emigrated to America <u>5 years ago</u>.
d) People ate <u>a lot of bread</u> in the Middle Ages.

8 Traduis les phrases suivantes :

a) Le prince Charles est né en 1948, il y a ... ans.
b) Ils ont dû se battre pour protéger leur famille et leurs terres.
c) William Wallace et Robert the Bruce ont tous deux gagné de grandes batailles contre les Anglais.
d) La légende du roi Arthur est très connue tandis que personne ne connaît le vrai roi Arthur.

Write! Write a short paragraph about this famous English king.

- Richard I, the Lionheart: 1157, Oxford/†1199, Aquitaine
- King: 2 September 1189
- Crusade to the Holy Land: 1190
- War against the Sultan of Egypt // Rebellion of Richard's brother: 1191
- Travelling through Austria // Leopold V - capture - the Lionheart: 1192
- Back to England: 1194
- Victory over the French: 1198

FILE 2

Keep the cool in school

Lessons 1 and 2 .... p. 24
- parler de l'influence exercée sur autrui
- donner des conseils
- exprimer la possibilité
- faire des suppositions et des prédictions
- comparer

Guided Tour .... p. 28

Creative Writing .... p. 32

Fun Page .... p. 33

Strategies .... p. 34
- enrichir son vocabulaire

Exercises .... p. 36

Test 2

1. Listen and learn

It hurts!

script p. 120

a. Have a good look at this Calvin cartoon.

- Where do you think the scene takes place?
- Compare the two boys, Calvin and Mo.
- Explain what is going on and imagine why.

b. Look at the girl in the poster and listen to her. What's going on?

- Listen again and write down the key-words. Tell the class the words you picked out, then listen again and spot your friends' words.
- Now read Alison's poem and explain how she feels and why.

You: She feels/is scared because ... is always ...
She feels/is ... because ... makes her ...

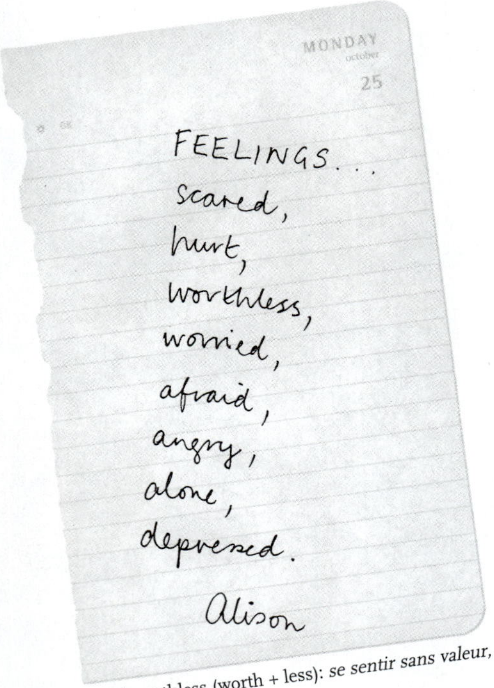

* feel worthless (worth + less): *se sentir sans valeur, nul*

2. Practise speaking

a. What should Alison do? Find some ideas, then tell the class.

You: She should ...
She shouldn't ...

b. Why do you think most victims are unable to stop bullies?

You: Because bullies make them feel ...
Because bullies are ...
Because victims are too ...
Because victims don't want to ...

HELP BOX
- rat = *cafter, moucharder*

3. Go forward

- **Look at the document. Who do you think it is addressed to?**
- **Spot the three questions in the document. Can you answer them? Say everything you can.**

You: A bully is someone who ...
Bullying is ... other people.
Some kids bully because ... / to ...

- **Do the tasks on worksheet 1 (p. 28).**

STOP The Bullies!!

At school, one of the biggest problems is bullying!

WHAT IS A BULLY?

A bully is someone who uses his or her power to hurt, trouble, bother, annoy or oppress another person.

WHAT IS BULLYING?

Bullying can be physical, verbal or psychological.
Physical - it can mean hitting or kicking or pushing or shoving, or making someone do something they don't want to do.
Verbal - it can mean calling someone names, saying or writing mean things, spreading rumors, or threatening someone.
Psychological - it can mean making someone feel unsafe, uncomfortable or scared, leaving them out of activities, ignoring them or making them feel invisible.

WHY DO SOME PEOPLE BULLY?

Some kids bully to make other people afraid of them. They think it will put them in control.
Some kids bully to make themselves look bigger or tougher.
Some kids think that it will make them more popular.
Some kids bully because they feel insecure.
Most bullies want people to look up to them and admire them.
All bullies bully to get attention!
It doesn't matter why someone is a bully -
No one has the right to make someone else feel uncomfortable or unsafe.

Bullying is wrong and should be stopped!

http://www.kidsafe-caps.org/bullies.html

THINK

1. Présent *Be* + *-ing*.
2. Adjectifs et comparatif.
3. *Should*.
4. *Make someone* + V.
5. V-*ing*.
6. *By* + V-*ing*.

✎ **Exercices :** W 2 p. 29

RHYTHM'N SOUNDS

1. /iː/ou /ɪ/?
2. Voyelles accentuées.
3. Lettres non prononcées.

✎ **Exercices :** W 3 p. 31

MEMO

In your WB p. 32

1. Read and learn

Readers' corner:

What makes a child violent?

Wendy writes from Boston, Mass.: Parents are to blame. They let their children watch what they like. They let them play violent video games for hours instead of telling them to go and play with friends. There's no parental control!

Nigel writes from Peyton, Col.: Television and video games are responsible. Action films and cartoons show too much violence: fights and killings are often the main ingredients of the stories, and in most video games, the child plays with deadly weapons.

Terrence writes from Chicago, Ill.: School life is what makes a child violent. If a child is unhappy, if he feels excluded or rejected or if he is repeatedly bullied, he will become violent. School authorities shouldn't let bullies, cliques or gangs frighten and oppress everybody else in the schoolyard.

What is your opinion? Send your answers to Readers' corner, Teens Today, 162 Eagle Nest Circle. Chicago, Illinois 32167 or e-mail us at: teenstoday-readers@chi.us.com

a. Have a good look at the two cartoons and say what you can: describe, explain or comment.

b. Give your own answers to the question in the title. Ask for the vocabulary you need.

c. Scan the letters. Spot the three answers. Are they different from yours?

d. Read and guess the meaning of new words.

e. Recap, giving your opinion.
You: I agree with Wendy. Parents shouldn't let ... / They should ... instead of ...

2. Practise writing

a. Picture yourself in 2030: you've got an 11-year-old kid. Jot down on a piece of paper:
- all the things you will or won't make him/her do,
- all the things you will or won't let him/her do.

Think of: housework, parties, friends, bedtime, hair, clothes... Ask for the vocabulary you need.
E.g.: I'll make her do her homework every day, but I'll let her play video games because they're fun! I won't let him watch horror films, they're too scary and they give you nightmares.

b. Work in pairs: swap papers. Read your friend's paper, then tell the class about it.
You: Laura is cool because she'll let her kid go out every Saturday night!

3. Go forward

The six core strengths

script p. 120

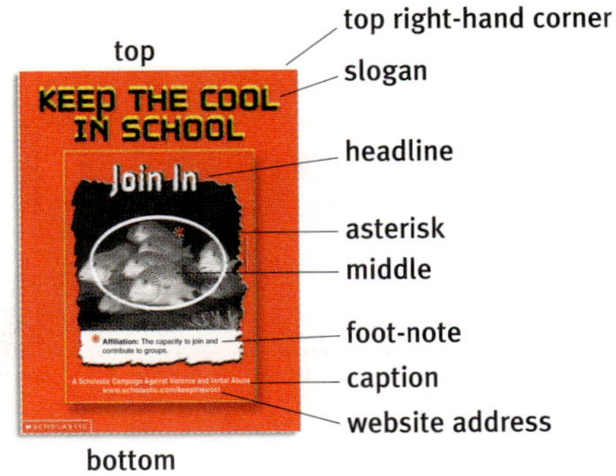

- Have a good look at the six posters below. Say what they are about and justify your answers using the vocabulary given.
- You're going to listen to extracts of "The six core strengths", a presentation by Bruce D. Perry, a leading American expert on children in crisis. Do the tasks on worksheet 1 (p. 37).

①

②

③

④

⑤

⑥

THINK

1. *Let someone* + V.
2. *Instead of* + V-ing.
3. [*When* / *If* + Présent], [*will* +V].
4. *May*.
5. *Who* / *what* (relatifs).

Exercices : W 2 p. 38

RHYTHM'N SOUNDS

1. Lire à voix haute.
2. Opérateurs et négation.
3. Syllabes accentuées.

Exercices : W 3 p. 40

MEMO

In your WB p. 41

Keep the cool in school

... A GUIDED TOUR

1 When you hear the expression "child labour", what centuries or what countries do you think of?
Today, schools are confronted with many problems. Can you name one or two?
Look at pages 29 to 31 and compare with your answers.

2 a) Look at page 29 and say what it is about.
Choose one document and read the corresponding texts. Then describe the document (who, when, where, what for...) and give your reactions to it.

b) Read page 30.
- Explain what truancy is.
- What are the British government and the police doing to prevent truancy?
- What is the link between school results and truancy? Between truancy and youth crime?
- Explain the play on words in the "Rat on a Rat" campaign. Why do you think the police chose rats to represent drug dealers?

c) Read page 31.
- Which document or fact do you find most surprising or shocking? Explain why.
- What responses to gun violence are presented on this page?

d) In many countries, kids don't have access to education. In France, school is a legal right. But it's also an obligation. According to you, what are the pros and cons of this legal obligation?

3 Quiz Now find out how much you know about education issues.

PROJECT WORK

Pick one of the problems presented in this Guided Tour and make a poster about it. You can work alone or in groups. Then organize an exhibition of all the posters in the school library.

VIDEO

Liberty Foundation, South Africa.

USA 1911-1940: from mine to school.

During the Industrial Revolution, boys and girls from poor families played their part in Britain's prosperity: they worked in terrible conditions for very little money.

In the early 20th century, conditions were still hard for teenage miners.

1833. Mills and Factories Act:
- in Britain, working day limited to 12 hours for children over 9.
- younger children are no longer allowed to work. They receive elementary education until age 9.

1891. Factory and Workshop Act: minimum working age raised to 11.

Over 50 years ago, education was declared a fundamental human right. But today, 125 million children in the world still don't go to school, and many have to work.

"NOON HOUR IN THE COAL BREAKER. MANY OF THE YOUNGER BOYS ARE NOT IN THE PHOTOGRAPH." LEWIS HINE PHOTOGRAPHER 1911. COURTESY OF THE RUSSELL SAGE FOUNDATION AND THE PHOTO LEAGUE. © E.H.

Child labour is a problem in western countries too. Some children, especially illegal immigrants or refugees, have no legal protection and are exploited.

Playing truant

Every day in England, 50,000 pupils skip school. So the government has decided to crack down on[1] truancy and to reinforce parental responsibility: if a pupil plays truant too often, the parents can now be fined[2] or even be sent to prison.

1. crack down on: *s'attaquer à*
2. be fined: *avoir une amende*

Charities like VRH (Volunteer Reading Help) enable children to enjoy learning and to become more confident. Kids who do well at school will be less tempted to play truant when they grow up.

Readability
creating 'can do' confidence in children

VRH and TimeBank

A high proportion of offences committed by youths aged 10 to 16 happen during times when they should be at school. To reduce truancy and crime, police officers use surveillance cameras or they patrol the streets.

In the U.S. and in Britain, police officers go into schools to give talks on drugs. In this British campaign, drug dealers are compared to vermin: the police want the public to give information to help stop those rats.

- In the U.S., nearly 30,000 people are killed by gunfire each year.
- Guns are used in 80% of the murders committed by kids under the age of 17.
- 32% of young victims of homicides were murdered by another youth.
- Child poverty has nearly doubled since the 1970s.

More than 40% of students aged 11 to 18 say there are weapons in their school. However, only 1% of young victims are injured at school.

DRAWING THE LINE ON GUN VIOLENCE: Co/Motion Student Poster Contest

In the U.S., easy access to handguns is a major problem. A poster competition organized by teenagers gets high school students to think about the impact of gun violence on their communities.

After a shooting in California, June 2001

There are more safety regulations for teddy bears and toy guns than for real guns! Kidz Voice-L.A. is a teenagers' organization based in Los Angeles. They lobby for gun control legislation and they organize peace marches.

CREATIVE WRITING

1. Here is an example of what students wrote about respect. Observe how it is written.

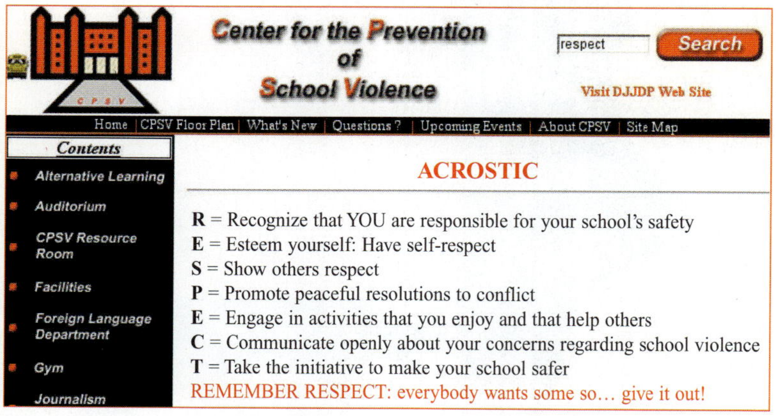
Center for the Prevention of School Violence

respect Search

Visit DJJDP Web Site

Home | CPSV Floor Plan | What's New | Questions ? | Upcoming Events | About CPSV | Site Map

Contents
- Alternative Learning
- Auditorium
- CPSV Resource Room
- Facilities
- Foreign Language Department
- Gym
- Journalism

ACROSTIC

R = Recognize that YOU are responsible for your school's safety
E = Esteem yourself: Have self-respect
S = Show others respect
P = Promote peaceful resolutions to conflict
E = Engage in activities that you enjoy and that help others
C = Communicate openly about your concerns regarding school violence
T = Take the initiative to make your school safer
REMEMBER RESPECT: everybody wants some so… give it out!

- **In groups of four,** choose "respect", or any other word.
- **Brainstorming session:** find as many verbs as possible starting with the letters in the word you selected.
- **Work individually for a few minutes:** use the verbs to find ideas and start writing.
- **Swap papers.** Read and correct your friends' papers, then choose the best ideas and rewrite the acrostic all together.
- **Pass your acrostic on to the next group.** Read another group's acrostic. Suggest changes using a different coloured pen. Pass it on to the next group. Etc.
- **When you get your acrostic back,** read the changes suggested by the other groups. Accept them or reject them. Then write your acrostic on a large piece of paper and stick it on the wall.

2. Look at the poster and read the poem. Observe how it is written.

- **In pairs or in groups,** find a slogan for a campaign against violence at school or any other topic that is important to you.
- **Draw and compose your poster.**
- **Using your slogan as a starting point,** write a short poem: first of all, find as many words as possible about your topic, then write two or three lines, read them to your friends, correct or modify them, etc.
- **Stick your poster and your poem on the wall.**

At school, be cool
Let me be happy
Let me learn things
Let me work in peace
Let me play with you
Let me be carefree
Let me be happy
Let me be

Fun Page

The logical song

When I was young, it seemed
that life was so wonderful,
a miracle, oh it was beautiful, magical.
And all the birds in the trees,
well they'd be singing so happily,
joyfully, playfully watching me.
But then they sent me away
to teach me how to be sensible,
logical, responsible, practical.
And they showed me a world
where I could be so dependable,
clinical, intellectual, cynical.
There are times when all
the world's asleep,
The questions run too deep
for such a simple man
Won't you please,
please tell me what we've learned
I know it sounds absurd
but please tell me who I am
Now watch what you say
or they'll be calling you a radical,
liberal, fanatical, criminal.
Won't you sign up your name,
we'd like to feel you're
acceptable, respectable,
presentable, a vegetable!
At night, when all the world's asleep,
The questions run so deep
for such a simple man
Won't you please,
please tell me what we've learned
I know it sounds absurd
but please tell me who I am.

Supertramp / R. Davies - R. Hodgson

STRATEGIES

How to improve your vocabulary

MOTS DÉRIVÉS. La dérivation est l'ajout, à un mot ou un radical, d'un préfixe (élément qui se place avant) ou d'un suffixe (élément qui se place après) pour former un mot nouveau.

PART I : les préfixes

Le préfixe ne change pas la catégorie grammaticale du mot : un verbe reste un verbe, un adjectif reste un adjectif, mais il en modifie le sens.
Exemple : les préfixes in-, im-, un-, dis-.

uncomfortable

a. Comment modifient-ils le sens du mot auquel ils sont ajoutés ?
Comment le sais-tu ?
Complète : La plupart des préfixes utilisés en anglais sont également utilisés en ... car ils sont d'origine latine ou grecque.

b. Écoute les exemples fournis dans ton *workbook*, page 47, une première fois, puis écoute-les à nouveau et encadre les syllabes accentuées. Enfin, répète-les.

c. Trouve d'autres exemples avec l'aide de tes camarades et de ton professeur. À ton avis, y-a-t-il une ou des règles pour choisir entre *in-*, *im-*, *un-* et *dis-* ? Quelle conclusion en tirer ?

TIPS

- Lorsque tu rencontres un mot nouveau, demande-toi s'il est composé d'un mot entier dont tu connais le sens, et d'un préfixe :
  sens du mot + sens du préfixe = sens du mot nouveau.
- Souviens-toi que les préfixes ne sont pas toujours accentués donc il faut savoir qu'ils existent pour les repérer à l'écoute.
- Pour chaque mot nouveau, vérifie s'il existe son contraire formé grâce à un préfixe. Si oui, mémorise-les ensemble.

PART II : les suffixes

Le suffixe change la catégorie grammaticale du mot : à partir d' un radical ou d' un mot, on peut former soit un verbe, soit un adverbe, soit un adjectif, soit un nom, selon le suffixe ajouté.

A • Les suffixes *-er (-or / -ess), -ly, -ed, -ing, -al, -ful, -less*

a. Tu connais déjà de nombreux mots comportant ces suffixes. Cites-en quelques-uns. À quoi servent ces suffixes ?
Exemples : *teach / teacher* : *-er* permet de former des ... à partir de ...
happy / happily : *-ly* permet de former des ... à partir d'...

b. Écoute les exemples fournis dans ton *workbook*, page 47, une première fois, puis écoute-les à nouveau et encadre les syllabes accentuées. Enfin, répète-les. Que constates-tu ?

c. Associe les trois colonnes ci-dessous :

*interest**ed***	qui est sans ...	... couleurs
*interest**ing***	qui ressent ...	... la nature
*natur**al***	qui est plein de ...	... de l'intérêt
*colour**ful***	qui se rapporte à ...	... utilité
*use**less***	qui crée, qui déclenche ...	

d. Connaître le sens de ces suffixes t'aidera à deviner le sens de mots dérivés, mais en trouver la traduction exacte n'est pas toujours facile !
En voici la preuve dans ces deux exemples :

1. *He's very helpful.* = Il est très ...

Le français ne se sert pas du mot "aide" pour former un adjectif. Il faut penser à l'idée de "rendre des services". Mais on changera de traduction si cet adjectif est appliqué à un livre, un conseil, un outil... : *This tool is very helpful.* = Cet outil est très ...

2. *"I'm bored."* = ...

Existe-t-il un adjectif en français pour traduire *"bored"* ? Comment vas-tu traduire cette phrase alors ?
Choisis d'autres exemples, utilise-les dans une phrase puis tente de les traduire.

B • Suffixes pour former des noms : *-ness, -dom, -hood, -ship*

a. Écoute et répète ces mots. Les suffixes sont-ils accentués ?

adjectifs → noms	noms → noms
happy → happiness *mad → madness* *wise → wisdom* *free → freedom*	*bore → boredom* *king → kingdom* *child → childhood* *man → manhood* *friend → friendship* *king → kingship*

madness

b. Peux-tu deviner facilement le sens de ces noms si tu connais le sens des adjectifs et noms de départ ? Peux-tu trouver facilement leur traduction ? Quels mots risquent de te poser un problème ? Pourquoi ?

c. Que signifient : *politeness, womanhood, relationship* ?

TIPS

- Quand tu rencontres un mot inconnu, repère s'il est formé d'un mot ou d'un radical que tu connais et d'un préfixe ou/et d'un suffixe. Cela doit devenir un réflexe.
- Pour enrichir ton vocabulaire, apprends le sens de base des préfixes et des suffixes que tu rencontres. Tu peux constituer des fiches avec des exemples.
- Regroupe les mots nouveaux que tu apprends par famille :
  Exemple : *nature - natural - unnatural - naturally - unnaturally.*
- Souviens-toi que l'on peut très bien comprendre un mot anglais et ne pas être bloqué dans une lecture par exemple, sans nécessairement savoir le traduire... Ce sont deux exercices "mentaux" différents !

EXERCISES

lesson 1

1 Choisis le Présent simple ou le Présent *Be + -ing* :

a) Gary is a pain! He (always - kick) me!
b) A bully is someone who (use) his or her power to annoy another person.
c) Wendy never (say) mean things. She's really sweet!
d) - Hey! Who can help me with the housework?
- Sorry I can't, I (leave) for football practice. I'll be back at four.
e) She (not - want) to go to school any more because there's this big, horrible girl in her class who (always - bully) her!

2 La situation empire dans cette école. Utilise les comparatifs de supériorité (+) ou d'inégalité (≠), puis ajoute des conseils à l'aide des éléments fournis.

a) Bullies are getting (+) tough and (+) violent.
- Victims - tell - teachers.
b) Students are feeling (+) insecure every day.
- School authorities - do something quick
c) The situation is (≠) serious... last year.
- But teachers - be careful

3 Clara se sent persécutée ! Il y a toujours quelqu'un qui lui fait faire des choses désagréables. Complète :

a) She doesn't like to run but her P.E. teacher ... every Monday morning!
b) She doesn't like to do her homework but her parents ... every evening!
c) She doesn't like to tidy her room but her father ... every Saturday!

4 Traduis les phrases suivantes en évitant le piège du mot à mot.

a) Harceler signifie frapper ou injurier quelqu'un.
b) Les victimes ne veulent pas moucharder.
c) Il n'arrête pas de me donner des coups de pieds quand personne ne regarde !

lesson 2

5 Choisis entre *make* et *let*, correctement conjugués, dans les cas suivants :

a) Stop dreaming! He'll never ... you drive his Porsche.
b) I was furious! They ... me open my suitcases and they took all my things out.
c) Come on! ... me try! I haven't played yet.
d) Yesterday, my Mum ... me tidy my room and today she won't ... me go to Greg's birthday. It's not fair!
e) Our French teacher is very strict. He ... us work really hard.
f) "Don't worry. I won't ... them hurt you", said the hero.

6 Complète les phrases suivantes à l'aide des verbes entre parenthèses. Choisis entre le Présent simple, *will* + V, *may* + V ou V-*ing*.

a) If children (play) video games for hours instead of (make) friends, they (feel) isolated and they (become) violent.
b) When I (be) older, I (study) psychology and I (help) children in crisis.
c) When children who (not - have) respect (grow up), they (get) into trouble.

7 Choisis le pronom relatif approprié : *who* ou *what*.

a) Do you know ... she wants for her birthday?
b) Parents ... let their children watch violent programmes on TV are not doing their job.
c) I don't like people ... use their power to make other people do ... they want.

8 Traduis ces phrases en français. Évite le mot à mot.

a) Si un enfant se sent exclu, il y a des chances qu'il devienne violent un jour.
b) Quand elle sera plus grande, elle comprendra.
c) Laisse-le faire son exercice au lieu de lui donner toutes les réponses !

Write! **Imagine you are an expert on teenagers in crisis. Write a short report on what you think is essential for them. Explain why, speak about the possible consequences and give examples. You can start like this:**
It is almost impossible to know what makes a teenager unhappy / miserable / frustrated / aggressive / hateful... but I think that teenagers who ...

Speak! **Choose one factor that may contribute to school violence and find arguments.**
- Violence in the media and in video games.
- Insufficient school security or authority. - Insufficient parental control.
- Any other factor you can think of.
In class, react to your friends' arguments and give yours.

FILE 3

Science or fiction?

Lessons 1 and 2 .... p. 38
- parler de ses expériences
- faire un bilan maintenant d'événements passés
- rapporter des propos
- exprimer la possibilité

Guided Tour .... p. 42

Strategies .... p. 46
- comprendre un texte oral

Extra Reading .... p. 48

Exercises .... p. 50

Test 3

lesson 1

FILE 3

1. Listen and learn
An unusual poll

script p. 120

① Aliens abducting an earthling.

② A UFO (Unidentified Flying Object) sighting.

a. **Have a good look at the pictures and speak about them.**
Have you ever seen a UFO?
Do you think there is life somewhere in the universe?

An OBE

b. **You're going to hear seven questions from a poll. Listen twice and write down one key-word for each question, then rephrase the questions.**
You: In question one, people are asked if they have ever seen a ghost.

c. **Listen again and answer the questions yourself.**
You: Yes, I have, once/twice/three times ... / No, never.

d. **Conduct the poll in the class.**
Pupil 1: Who has ever seen a ghost? Hands up!
Pupil 2: No one has ever seen a ghost. / Two pupils out of 28 say they have seen a ghost.
Pupil 3: Who has ever ...

e. **What do you think the aim of this poll is? Then listen to the conclusion and react.**
You: I think the aim of this poll is to determine if people ...

2. Practise speaking

Group work: "A crazy poll"

a. **You want to determine if aliens have visited us... so you're going to imagine a poll. Write down five questions working in groups.**
E.g.: 1. Have you ever met a man with pointed ears?

b. **Present your questions to the class and select the ten best questions.**
Group A: In our first question, people are asked if they have ever met a man with pointed ears.

c. **Conduct the poll in the class.**
You: Who has ever seen a child who looks like E.T.?

3. Go forward

- Before reading, can you say what sort of document this is and what it is about? What do the pictures evoke?
- Do the tasks on worksheet 1 (p. 48).

U.S. HIDING KNOWLEDGE OF ALIENS

(CNN) - A CNN/Time poll shows that 80 percent of Americans think the government is hiding knowledge of the existence of extraterrestrial life forms.

While nearly three-quarters of the 1,024 adults questioned for the poll say they have never seen or met anyone who has seen a UFO, 54 percent believe intelligent life exists outside Earth.
Sixty-four percent of the respondents say that aliens have contacted humans, half say they have abducted humans, and 37 percent say they have contacted the U.S. government.
As for the Roswell incident, nearly two-thirds of the respondents to the poll believe that a UFO crash-landed in a field outside the New Mexico town about 50 years ago.

What happened in Roswell?
In one of the most famous UFO "sightings" in U.S. history, Roswell residents in 1947 saw lights in the night sky, followed by a loud explosion. A rancher found the "crash site" and removed a large piece of debris and stored it in his shed.
A few days later, Air Force officials from nearby Roswell Air Force Base inspected the site and the debris, and announced the recovery of a "flying disc". The Air Force quickly retracted that statement, and claimed the debris was from a weather balloon. But several "witnesses" claimed they saw bodies of dead aliens whisked away by the military.

Friend or foe?
Forty-four percent of the respondents say that if they ever meet E.T.s from a galaxy far, far away, they will be friends, while 26 percent think they will be enemies.
Thirty-nine percent don't think they will look very humanoid, while 35 percent think they will probably look "somewhat" human.

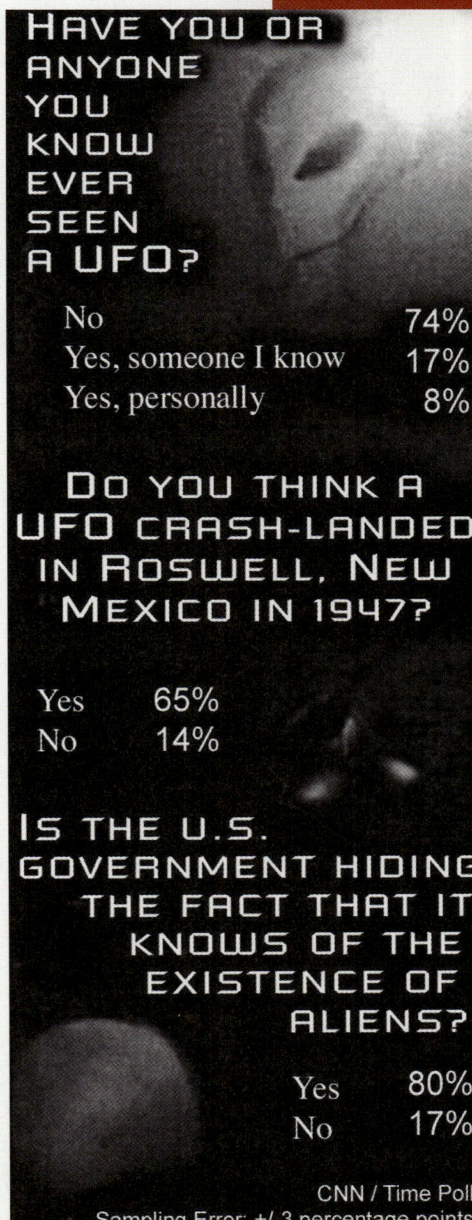

THINK

Révisions :
1. *Present perfect + ever, never.*
2. Les questions avec *Who* comme sujet.
3. Discours indirect avec verbes introducteurs au Présent.

✎ **Exercices :** W 2 p. 49

RHYTHM'N SOUNDS
1. *Have.*
2. Chiffres, etc.
3. Le son /əʊ/.

✎ **Exercices :** W 3 p. 51

MEMO

In your WB p. 52

1. Listen and learn
Are we alone?

script p. 120

Arecibo telescope. The world's largest radio telescope.

SETI RADIO NETWORK
Are We Alone?
The Weekly Radio Show of the SETI Institute

a. Look at the documents then listen. What's the link?

b. Listen again. What sort of program is announced?
Find questions you would like to ask or make a list of words you expect to hear.

c. Listen to this radio show. Concentrate on the three questions and report them.
You: The first caller asks how ...

d. Can you answer the questions? Have a try! Then listen to each answer and say what you've understood.

e. Do the tasks on worksheet 1 (p. 56).

SETI INSTITUTE
Search for Extra-Terrestrial Intelligence

2. Practise speaking

Group-work. Team B: Go to page 116 of your book.

a. Team A: You are aliens. You've abducted earthlings (Team B) and you're questioning them about the technological developments on Earth.
Use the information on the right to ask your questions.
Alien: Have you ... ... yet? (invent / discover / find)
Earthling: Yes, we have.
Alien: How long have you had it?
Earthling: We've had it since ...
Alien: You mean you've had it for ... years.
Earthling: Yes, that's right.
Alien: Have you already ... ...? (invent / discover / find)
Earthling: No, we haven't. /No, not yet!

b. Now, use the information on the right to answer the earthlings' questions.

Team A: ALIENS' QUESTIONS
1. the supersonic plane
2. the pill for eternal youth
3. the satellite
4. teleportation
5. the nuclear bomb

Team A: ALIENS' ANSWERS (given in Earth years)
1. no
2. yes - 1250
3. yes - 1870
4. no
5. yes - 1980

3. Go forward

- Read the title and look at the photo, then say everything you know about the search for intelligent life.
- Read the introduction and explain "We've come a long way since 1600".
- Do the tasks on worksheet 2 (p. 56).

WILL WE MEET E.T.?

In 1600 Giordano Bruno[1] was burnt at the stake because he believed there might be other worlds and other life-forms beyond Earth. We've come a long way since 1600... Now, it's almost heretical *not* to believe in extra-terrestrial life!

Since the creation of SETI, in 1960, astronomers have spent many thousands of hours scanning the skies, searching for a signal coming from a technologically-advanced society. In the past four decades, they have spent more than $100 million and they haven't detected a beep! However, Drake, who founded SETI, remains optimistic. He has calculated that there might be as many as 10,000 high-tech worlds among the Milky Way's 100 billion or more stars!

If there are so many extra-terrestrials out there, why haven't we heard from them yet?

Some scientists say that in most places beyond Earth, radiation and heat levels are so high, life-friendly planets so rare and cosmic bombardments so severe that the only life-forms that might exist would be little green bacteria. They feel we may well be alone in the universe…

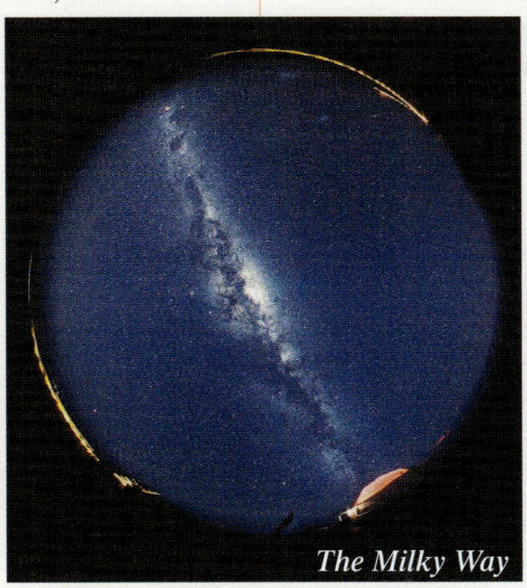

The Milky Way

We have dreamed of meeting intelligent E.T.s for so long. Should we stop looking for "little green men"?

The answer is "no". It is important to continue the quest, not just for microbes on Mars or Europa, but also for signals from some remote[2] world – even if no signal ever comes… if only to remind earthlings of the importance of life and of the importance of protecting what is perhaps its one and only example in the whole universe.

16

1. a defrocked priest from Naples. - 2. *lointain.*

THINK

1. *Present perfect + for / since.*
2. *Present perfect + already / yet / not ... yet.*
3. *Might* et *could.*

✎ **Exercices :** W3 p. 57

RHYTHM'N SOUNDS

1. Questions au *Present perfect.*
2. Syllabes accentuées.

✎ **Exercices :** W4 p. 59

MEMO

In your WB p. 60

Science or fiction?

... A GUIDED TOUR

1 **What science fiction books and films have you read or seen? Were the aliens friendly or unfriendly to humans?**
Now look at pages 43 to 45. Which of these sci-fi stories do you know?

2 **a) Read pages 43 to 45 and choose a title for each page:**
- Sci-fi: an expression of man's fears
- Four types of sci-fi stories
- Making fun of conventions

b) Read page 43.
- Say what you know about the different kinds of aliens represented on this page.
- What are the usual ingredients in a sci-fi story? In what ways is *E.T.* different?

c) Read the texts and chronology page 44.
What films or TV series were inspired by:
- Hiroshima
- the Cold War
- the witch-hunt

In what ways does *The X-Files* differ from science fiction in the 1950s?

d) Read page 45. How do the examples on this page make fun of the sci-fi genre?

e) Do you like science fiction? Why? Speak about your favourite sci-fi hero (human being or alien), and let your classmates guess who it is.

3 **Quiz** **Now find out how much you know about science fiction.**

PROJECT WORK

Choose a science fiction book or movie, and prepare a 5-minute talk on it. You can work alone or in pairs. Talk about the author, the characters and the story. Look for information in the school library or on the Net. Illustrate your talk with photos, comics, book covers, posters, etc.

VIDEO

Fear of the Red Planet.

Long before Armstrong walked on the moon (1969), writers and film-makers dreamt of space travel. In 1902, French director G. Méliès made *Le Voyage dans la Lune*.

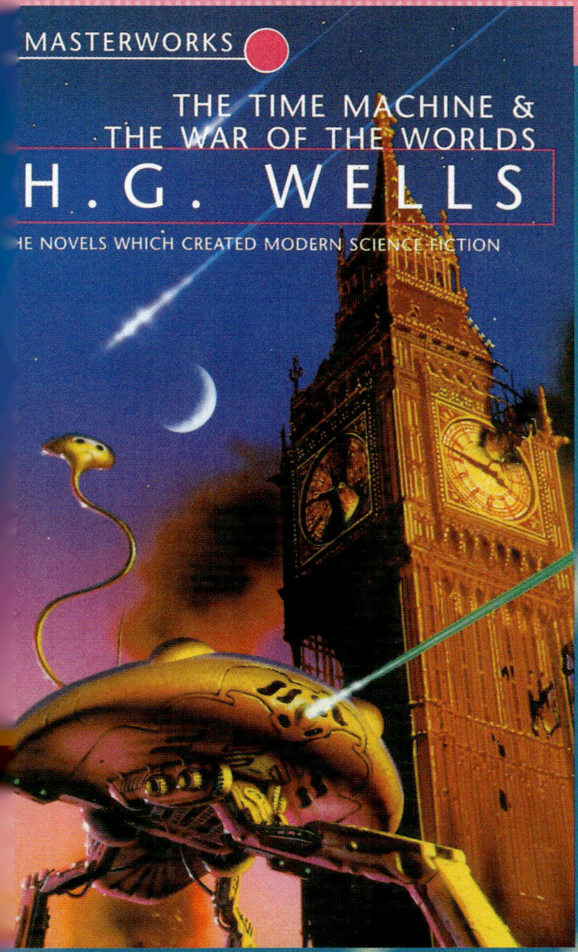

In *The War of the Worlds* (1898), H.G. Wells imagined a Martian invasion. The Red Planet has always fascinated men. For the Romans, it was associated with Mars, the god of war. Maybe that's why Martians are usually seen as aggressive creatures.

In the 1960s, *Star Trek* became a very popular TV series. The Starship Enterprise was equipped with futuristic accessories: a teleportation machine, ray-guns and high-tech electronic gadgets. In their 23rd century space travels, Captain Kirk and his crew* met all kinds of aliens. Half-human, half-Vulcan, Mr Spock had special alien powers.

*crew: *équipage*

Science fiction meets horror: an alien egg grows inside a crew member, and the hideous beast then bursts out of his stomach.
Sci-fi heroes are usually men but in *Alien* (1979), Lt Ellen Ripley faces the murderous monster on her own.

In *E.T.* (1982), a harmless* little alien is adopted by a lonely boy who teaches it how to talk, dress up in women's clothes... and drink beer. The Walt Disney Studio missed a great opportunity: they refused to make the film because they thought the story was not exciting enough.

*harmless: *inoffensif*

In this 1951 film an alien comes to warn humans that their use of nuclear weapons will lead to total annihilation.

1945: the USA drop atomic bombs on Hiroshima and Nagasaki (Japan).

1950s: the Cold War begins. Capitalism (the USA and other western countries) against Communism (the USSR, China, etc.). Fear of a nuclear conflict.
The witch-hunt*: in the USA, the government interrogates hundreds of people suspected of Communist sympathies and anti-American activities.

1980s: end of the Cold War.

*witch-hunt: *chasse aux sorcières*

In 1938, an adaptation of Wells's novel was broadcast* on the radio. It was so realistic that many people really thought that the Martians were invading the Earth!
In 1953, an American film relocated the story from London to Los Angeles.

*broadcast: *diffusée*

Flash Gordon was originally a comics character, created in 1936. In the 1950s TV series, Flash is a member of the Interplanetary Bureau of Investigation (a kind of intergalactic FBI). He has to prevent Ming the Merciless* from conquering the Earth.

*merciless: *sans pitié*

It's 1956, and they're among us! Some aliens have landed in a little American town. They have transformed into duplicates of the townspeople and are gradually taking their place to infiltrate American society.

Unexplained mysteries, supernatural phenomena, cover-ups* and conspiracy theories: the paranoia continues in the 1990s, but this time, the government is the enemy.

*cover-ups: *affaires étouffées*

In the 1970s, Adams's BBC Radio series and novels take all the clichés and conventions of intergalactic travel, and exaggerate them so much that they become absurd and hilarious.

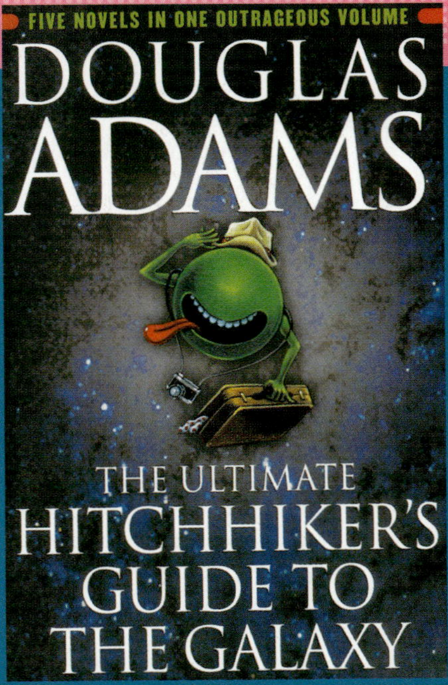

1962 bubble gum card

Tim Burton's *Mars Attacks* (1996) is a parody of classic sci-fi movies. The nasty little green men land on Earth and pretend* they have come in peace. The American president believes they really are friendly (maybe he's watched *E.T.* too many times...). But of course, the Martians soon start ray-gunning everybody. And of course, the good old Yankees win in the end.

*pretend: *faire semblant*

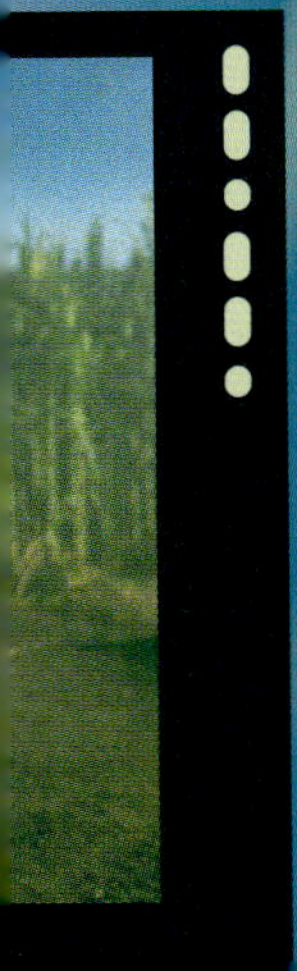

Men in Black (1997, 2002) is a comedy that parodies different film genres. The two detectives are caricatures of action heroes. The aliens come in all shapes and sizes, from cute creatures to slimy weirdoes or horrid insects. But they live on Earth and often behave like humans. So they ridicule us as well as sci-fi stereotypes.

STRATEGIES

How to understand a recorded document

PART I : anticiper

a. Dans la vie, quand on choisit d'écouter une émission de radio par exemple, c'est que l'on a déjà une idée en tête sur le sujet, et on comprend donc mieux ce qu'on entend !
Entraîne-toi à te préparer avant une écoute.

En faisant une recherche sur Internet concernant le "SETI* Institute", tu trouves le document suivant :

Avant de cliquer pour écouter le document audio qui l'accompagne, comment vas-tu te préparer à l'écoute ?

SETI RADIO NETWORK

Are We Alone?
The Weekly Radio Show of the SETI Institute

* Search for Extra-Terrestrial Intelligence

TIPS

Avant de te lancer dans une écoute, prépare-toi à l'aide de tout ce dont tu disposes (titre, annonce du thème, photo, illustration, etc.) et note tes idées :
- devine de quel type de document il s'agit, fais plusieurs propositions ;
- dis tout ce que tu sais ou ce que tu voudrais savoir sur le sujet ou le document ;
- pose-toi des questions ;
- mobilise tout le vocabulaire que tu as en mémoire sur ce sujet ou le vocabulaire que tu penses entendre dans ce type de document.

b. Dans un document enregistré, il n'y a pas que les mots qui sont importants !
Entraîne-toi à te servir de ce qui n'est pas "la langue".

- À quoi vas-tu prêter attention lors de la première écoute ?
- Quels indices, quelles informations, cette première écoute t'a-t-elle apportés ? Complète tes notes.

TIPS

À la première écoute, tire le maximum d'indices de ce qui est non-linguistique :
- la musique, les bruitages et bruits de fond sont le "décor" : ils mettent dans l'ambiance et donnent des indices sur le thème ;
- les voix et surtout le ton employé permettent de déterminer le type de document (interview, reportage, publicité, récit, etc.), l'humeur et/ou les sentiments des interlocuteurs.

c. L'anticipation ne sert que si l'on s'en sert !
Entraîne-toi à te servir de ton travail d'anticipation pour "débroussailler" le terrain !

- Comment vas-tu utiliser les notes prises lors de l'anticipation pour mieux écouter et comprendre le document ?
- Qu'as-tu compris ? Est-ce suffisant ou as-tu besoin de réécouter ? Si oui, dans quel but ?

TIPS

- Lors de l'écoute, garde sous les yeux les notes prises pendant l'anticipation : entoure, barre, mets des points d'interrogation...
- Après l'écoute du document :
  - récapitule ce que tu as compris ;
  - fais le point sur ce qui te reste à vérifier ou à trouver pour orienter ta prochaine écoute.

PART II : repérer - inférer - compenser

a. Que de mots ! On n'a pas le temps de tous les noter !
Entraîne-toi à te servir des répétitions pour aller à l'essentiel.

- Le mot *"life"* est répété cinq fois. Écoute et lève le doigt chaque fois que tu l'entends.
Fais de même pour : *"aliens"* (3 fois), *"Earth"* (2 fois). Quels autres mots sont répétés deux fois ?
- En quoi ces mots sont-ils essentiels au message ?

> **TIPS**
> Parmi les mots accentués, ceux qui sont répétés plusieurs fois sont au cœur du message ou du thème. Ils te seront très utiles pour aller à l'essentiel.

b. Il y a beaucoup de choses que tu peux prévoir !
Entraîne-toi à prendre de l'avance.

Écoute le début de quelques phrases. Peux-tu deviner ce que pourrait être la suite de ces phrases ? Fais des propositions puis vérifie.

> **TIPS**
> Quand tu écoutes, prends de l'avance !
> Sois toujours prêt à faire des micro-prédictions sur les mots ou les idées qui peuvent logiquement venir après ce que tu viens d'entendre.
> Ainsi, tu libéreras ton attention pour mieux comprendre la suite.

c. Quels mots vont avec quels mots ?
Entraîne-toi à repérer les pauses dans un flot de paroles.

- Écoute un extrait et lève le doigt à toutes les fins de phrases. Qu'est-ce qui te permet de les repérer ?
- Lis cette phrase dans ta tête, puis à haute voix. Où reprends-tu ton souffle ? Pourquoi ? Écoute et repère les pauses que le présentateur a choisi de faire.

  But if you'd like to know if there's life beyond Earth or, at least, learn a bit about the search for extra-terrestrial life, listen to our new show Are We Alone?
- Pourquoi est-ce important de repérer ces pauses lors d'une écoute ?

> **TIPS**
> Comme en français, en anglais :
> - une phrase se termine par une intonation descendante suivie d'une pause marquée ;
> - dans une phrase, on reprend son souffle entre groupes de sens.
>
> Sers-toi de cette "ponctuation orale" pour segmenter ce que tu entends en unités de sens plus courtes.

d. À l'écoute, il est utile de savoir comment les phrases se construisent en anglais !
Entraîne-toi à mobiliser tes connaissances grammaticales.

- Peux-tu compléter les blancs dans les phrases ci-dessous ? Réfléchis, repère les groupes nominaux, les verbes, les adjectifs, etc. et note tes propositions puis écoute et vérifie.
  - Are We Alone? *is your chance ... call and ask questions of the men and women who conduct the world's largest ... most comprehensive search ... life beyond Earth.*
  - *if they're just as curious about life ... in the universe ... you are.*
- Entraîne-toi sur une autre phrase : commence par noter les mots accentués, repère les groupes de sens en les marquant d'une barre, puis réfléchis aux mots qui manquent, que tu n'a pas entendus ou qui sont presque inaudibles : sers-toi de tes connaissances grammaticales, puis écoute et vérifie.

> **TIP**
> Souvent, on entend à peine les mot-outils : ils sont très courts et généralement inaccentués.
> Mais si on sait lequel on peut s'attendre à entendre, on le reconnaît !

EXTRA READING

The thing

A terrible catastrophe has happened: nearly all the people on Earth have gone blind[1]. The narrator remembers the appearance of a new plant, the triffid... not long before the trouble began.

My introduction to a triffid came early. It so happened that we had one growing in our own garden. The plant was quite well developed before any of us noticed[2] it, for it had taken root behind the bit of hedge that screened the rubbish heap. It wasn't doing any harm[3] there, and it wasn't in anyone's way.

Nowadays when everyone knows only too well what a triffid looks like, it is difficult to recall how odd[4] and somehow foreign the first ones appeared to us. Nobody, as far as I know, felt any misgivings[5] or alarm about them then.

I have a picture in my memory of my father examining ours and puzzling[6] over it. He leant over it, peering[7] at it through his glasses and blowing gently through his moustache. He inspected the straight stem, and the woody bole from which it sprang. He gave curious, if not very penetrative attention to the three small, bare sticks which grew straight up beside the stem. He smoothed[8] the green leaves between his finger and thumb as if their texture might tell him something. Then he peered into the curious, funnel-like formation at the top of the stem. I remember the first time he lifted me up to look into that conical cup.

a. Have a good look at the illustration, read the first sentence of the text, the first sentence of paragraph 3, lines 15-17, and complete:
This plant is a ... The narrator is the ... and the man holding him is his ...

b. Read the introduction to the text.
• Recap: The narrator is a man now. The events in the text took place ... the "catastrophe" happened, when the narrator was a ... ...
• What caused this "catastrophe"? Imagine how. Find one or two ideas.

c. Read paragraph one.
• Where was the triffid exactly? Answer with the help of the illustration.
• Find the two reasons why nobody uprooted* it. Quote from the text.

* uproot: *déraciner, arracher*

d. Read paragraph two.
Nowadays: in the present (of the text)
Then: in the past, when the first triffids appeared.
Recap: Nowadays, everybody ... the triffids ..., whereas then, the triffids seemed ... : nobody knew them and nobody suspected they were ...

e. Read paragraph 3 with the help of the illustration.
• Why did the narrator's father examine the triffid? Quote from the text.
At the time, did the triffid look dangerous ❐?, inoffensive/harmless ❐?
• Did he discover what it was? Yes ❐, No ❐
• Did he make lots of efforts to crack the mystery? Yes ❐, No ❐
Quote from paragraph 2, to explain why.
• What about you, the reader? You know this plant is dangerous. Read its description again. Is there anything scary about it? Can you find any clues?

f. Read paragraph 4. It is similar to paragraph 1. Match each extract from § 1 with an extract from § 4.

§ 1:
- Quite well developed
- Not doing any harm / Not in anyone's way
- Behind the hedge, next to the rubbish heap

§ 4:
- in neglected spots
- four feet high
- quietly, inoffensively, peacefully

But the suspense grows! Complete:
Paragraph one is about one triffid in a garden. In paragraph four, we learn there were ... of triffids all over the ....

g. Read the last sentence. It comes as a complete surprise and as a shock. What is possible to guess? Can you explain why not?

I did not touch it, but I knew it must be sticky because there were flies and other small insects struggling in it. More than once my father ruminated that it was pretty queer[9], and observed that one of these days he really must try to find out what it was. I don't think he ever made the effort.

The thing would be about four feet high then. There must have been plenty of them about, growing up quietly and inoffensively, with nobody taking any particular notice of them. And so the one in our garden continued its growth[10] peacefully, as did thousands like it in neglected spots[11] all over the world.

It was some little time later that the first one picked up its roots, and walked.

From The Day of the Triffids, *1951, by John Wyndham*

NOTES

1. **blind:** aveugle.
2. **notice:** remarquer.
3. **harm:** mal.
4. **odd:** *strange.*
5. **misgivings:** craintes.
6. **puzzle:** s'interroger.
7. **peering:** *looking attentively.*
8. **smooth /smu:ð/:** lisser, caresser.
9. **pretty queer:** *quite strange.*
10. **growth:** croissance.
11. **neglected spots:** coins laissés à l'abandon.

EXERCISES

lesson 1

1 Réponds à ces questions par une réponse brève. Repère bien le premier mot de chaque question : l'opérateur.

a) Have they ever visited Scotland? - Yes, ...
b) Do you like him a lot? - Yes, ...
c) Has she ever had bad dreams? - No, ...
d) Did you meet her at school? - No, ...
e) Have you seen the new telescope? - Yes, ...

2 Retrouve les questions qui ont provoqué les réponses suivantes :

a) Hugh (has experienced an O.B.E.).
b) Look! I've bought pizza and cakes for tonight's party. Is that OK?
c) The maths teacher (is missing).
d) No! I've never seen a UFO!
e) No one (has ever seen a UFO).

3 Rédige les questions de cette enquête :

In this very unusual poll, people are asked if they believe in spirits, if they have ever heard strange, unknown voices, if they have ever communicated with dead people, if they have ever experienced a feeling of "déjà-vu" and if they are ready to try hypnosis.

4 Traduis. Attention au mot à mot !

a) Est-ce que tu as déjà rencontré un homme qui ressemble à un extra-terrestre ?
b) Qui est déjà allé en Chine ?
c) La moitié des personnes sondées pensent que des extra-terrestres ont enlevé des humains.
d) Dans ce sondage, on demande aux gens s'ils croient aux fantômes.

lesson 2

5 Réponds aux questions suivantes selon les indications fournies.

a) Have scientists found a pill for happiness yet? - (No)
b) How long have Americans had the nuclear bomb?
- (1945 - about 60 years)
c) Has NASA already sent people to Mars?
- (No)
d) How long have authors written about Martians?
- (more than a century - the publication of *The War of the Worlds* in 1898)

6 Remets de l'ordre dans ces questions et ajoute les majuscules.

a) found / you / the pill / youth / for / yet / eternal / have / ?
b) have / SETI / worked / how long / for / you / ?
c) already / have / bought / a telescope / they / ?
d) invent / you / teleportation / did / when / ?
e) every day / scan / how long / the sky / you / do / ?
f) did / how long ago / begin / the NASA program / ?
g) people / how many / in / believe / E.T.s / ?

7 Traduis. Évite les pièges !

a) Depuis plus de quarante ans, les astronomes du SETI cherchent un signal venant d'une société technologiquement avancée.
b) Je m'appelle Laura. Je lis des livres de science-fiction depuis que j'ai 13 ans.
c) Nous envoyons des signaux depuis l'invention de la radio... et s'il y a des créatures intelligentes dans l'univers, elles ont sûrement inventé la radio aussi.

Write! **Read the documents in lessons 1 and 2 again and express yourself! Write five to ten sentences starting like this:**

- I believe there is ...
- I don't believe there is ...
- I don't believe people who say they have ...
- I agree with scientists who think / say / believe ...
- I find it ridiculous / stupid / ludicrous to think that ...

Speak! **Role-play: pick one of the following roles and get ready to defend your position. You'll have to speak for at least one minute in front of the class. Find arguments in the texts or do some personal research.**

- *The believer*: you are certain E.T.s have already tried to contact us. Give your arguments.
- *The non-believer*: you don't believe in E.T.s, you don't think there could be intelligent life out there. Justify your opinion.
- *The SETI astronomer:* you've been an astronomer at SETI for ten years and you haven't detected a beep yet! But you remain optimistic. Explain why.

FILE 4

Cowboys and Indians revisited

Lessons 1 and 2 .... p. 52
- utiliser la voix passive
- rapporter des ordres
- rendre compte d'évolutions
- exprimer la quantité

Guided Tour .... p. 56

Creative Writing .... p. 60

Fun Page .... p. 61

Extra Reading .... p. 62

Exercises .... p. 64

Test 4

1. Read and learn

Native Americans hunting buffaloes on the prairies.

LIFE ON THE PRAIRIES

In the winter, Native Americans lived in the safety of their village homes but in the summer, they chased buffalo herds across the prairies of the Great Plains of North America.

They were very respectful of the environment: buffaloes were hunted not only for their meat, but also for their hides or skins, for their hair, their horns, etc. Some historians estimate that over 70 different items* were made from the buffalo.

* *items: things.*

23

a. Describe the painting (who? where? when? what? why?) and say all you know about these people and animals.

b. Read the caption and the text. What have you learnt? Recap.

c. Now explain in what way Native Americans were "very respectful of the environment".
You: In the buffalo, everything was ... / nothing ...

HELP BOX
- waste: *gaspiller* - throw away: *jeter*

2. Practise speaking

a. Look at the picture and repeat the words.

b. **Guessing-game.** Team A go to worksheet 1 (p. 67). Team B go to worksheet 1' (p. 69).

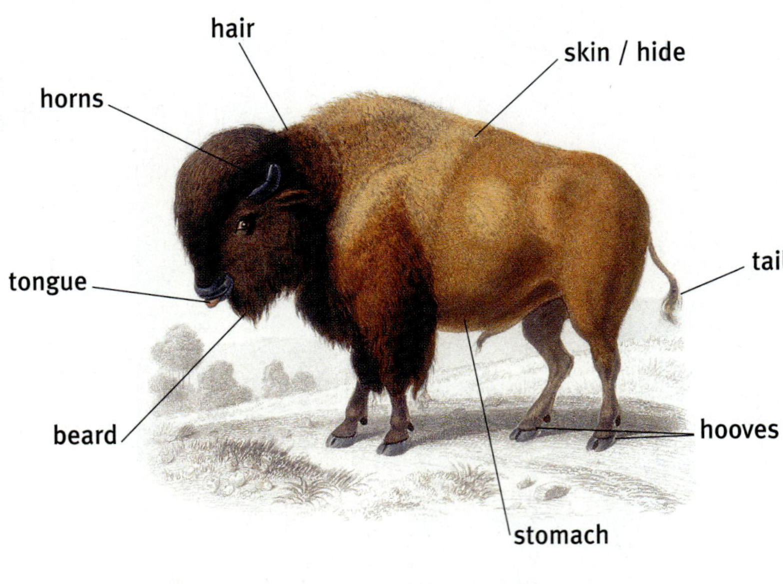

3. Go forward

- Look at the photo, read the title and react. Read the caption and say all you know about this period of history. What do you think the article is going to be about?
- Do the tasks on worksheet 2 (p. 68).

A heap of 40,000 buffalo hides waiting to be loaded onto railway wagons in Dodge City, Kansas, in 1874.

THE BIG MASSACRE

Until the early 1800s, there were about 60 million buffaloes roaming[1] the vast Great Plains area of North America: they were the lords of the prairies. The inhabitants of the great plains depended on the buffaloes for everything but they seldom[2] killed more buffaloes than they needed to survive and they used every part of the buffaloes they killed.

By 1885, there were only 500 buffaloes left! It was the arrival of large numbers of white settlers that nearly caused their extinction. At first the buffaloes were killed for their meat and hides. But afterwards they were shot down "for fun". Later still, the buffaloes were slaughtered to get rid of the Indians. The government believed that if all the buffaloes were killed then all the Indians would die because they would have nothing to eat, and so the massacre continued.

Today the numbers have increased to about 300,000 and the buffaloes are no longer in danger of becoming extinct.

24

1. roam: *parcourir* - 2. seldom: *rarement.*

THINK

1. Énoncés à la voix passive.
2. *By* + date.

✎ Exercices : W 3 p. 70

RHYTHM'N SOUNDS

1. *Was / were.*
2. Lire à voix haute.

✎ Exercices : W 4 p. 71

MEMO

In your WB p. 72

1. Listen and learn

A promise

script p. 121

a. What Indian tribes do you know? Make a list. Look at the map and check. Are there any tribes on your list that you can't find on the map?

b. Listen and repeat the names of the Indian tribes.

c. Listen to a conversation. Where does it take place? What Indian tribe is it about?

d. Do the tasks on worksheet 1 (p. 76).

2. Practise speaking

Look at the picture and read the caption. Use the help box and speak about Native American children during detribalization.

Native American children in a boarding school during detribalization.

You: Children were sent to boarding-schools. They were forbidden to ...

HELP BOX

- send - teach - give - tell (to + V) - ask (to + V) - forbid (to + V)
- boarding-schools - a strict Christian education - American-style haircuts - the official version of Native-U.S. history - English language - wear American-style clothes - wear their tribal clothes - speak English - speak their native languages.

3. Go forward

- Do the tasks on worksheet 2 (p. 76).

A tipi encampment on the Great Plains in 1834.

THE LAKOTAS

The Lakota nation was one of the greatest Indian nations. Their story is a sad example of what happened to all native Americans in the course of the 19th century.

From vast plains to sterile reservations

Originally, the Lakotas lived and hunted buffalo herds across the vast plains of Minnesota, Dakota, Montana and Nebraska, but over the years, their territory became smaller and smaller.

In the 1868 Treaty of Fort Laramie, they were offered a territory that stretched from the Missouri River to the sacred Black Hills but in the 1880s, the Lakota nation was split. The people were parked in smaller reservations where there was little land to farm, no game to hunt, and nothing to do.

② People queuing for food on a reservation in 1899.

Sacred places spoiled

The Black Hills, the Lakotas' most sacred place on Earth, were shown no respect. Although the Hills were granted to the Lakotas in 1868, they have been constantly exploited by non-Indians.

In the 1870s gold was discovered there, and the Hills were invaded by hordes of gold diggers.

In the 1930s the faces of four American presidents were carved into the side of one of the hills: the Lakotas were outraged but helpless to stop this.

Since World War II, the Black Hills have been exploited as a tourist resort. To top it all, uranium has been extracted from the Hills for about fifty years and many rivers on the reservations have been polluted.

Mount Rushmore in the Black Hills.

Today more and more Lakotas want the Black Hills back. Pressure groups are becoming more and more insistent: they want the Fort Laramie treaty to be respected and they hope the Black Hills will be given back to them soon.

65

THINK

1. Énoncés passifs avec *give, offer, grant...*
2. Style indirect avec *ask, forbid, tell* + *to* + V.
3. *Although.*
4. Accroissement progressif.
5. Quantifieurs.

✎ **Exercices :** W 3 p. 77

RHYTHM'N SOUNDS

1. Voix passive.
2. Syllabes accentuées.

✎ **Exercices :** W 4 p. 81

MEMO

In your WB p. 82

Cowboys and Indians revisited

... A GUIDED TOUR

1 **Say all you know about Native Americans, in the past or in the present.**

2 **a) Read page 57.**

- Pick out the two usual clichés about Indians.
- Explain how and why Indians have become a symbol for Environmentalists.
- Look at the Cherokee Indian on the right and describe him. Read the text. What was this picture used for?

b) Read page 58.

- Why are tribes often tempted to accept polluting industries?
- Make a list of the various consequences of these industries on Indian peoples.
- Imagine the consequences of gambling on Indian communities.

c) Read page 59.

- Explain what environmental discrimination is. Name the victims.
- Find two ways of fighting for environmental justice.
- Indians take action to protect their natural resources. Give an example.

d) Think of other environmental problems, in your country or elsewhere in the world. Discuss them in class.

3 **Quiz** **Now find out how much you know about Indians and the environment.**

PROJECT WORK

Each student, or group of students, should choose one Cowboy movie. Watch your movie and prepare a short report on it: say who it was directed by, name the actors and tell the story. Then discuss with your friends how Indians are represented in the different films.

VIDEO

Pollution: it's a crying shame.

Disney's female version of the Noble Savage, Pocahontas (1995) is wild and beautiful. She falls in love with a paleface, but she cannot leave her Eden* to follow him because she could never survive in his corrupt world.

*Eden: *paradis*

To the first European settlers, Indians were the enemy and were represented as bloodthirsty savages on galloping horses, attacking convoys and murdering palefaces. That cliché reappeared later in Cowboy movies.

In the past, Indians respected Mother Earth, lived in harmony with nature and rarely wasted natural resources. So in the 1960s, when people started worrying about the environment, they turned to Indians as an ecological model. A 1970s anti-pollution campaign showed a Cherokee crying for the lost purity of his Native land.

The cliché of the "Noble Savage" was used in Hollywood movies too. In *Dances with Wolves* (1990) Kevin Costner had a clear message: the white man is bad and should learn from Indian wisdom and traditions.

Bloody savages or noble ecologists?
Exaggerations and clichés only tell part of the story...

A lot of polluting industries choose to settle on Indian reservations because environmental laws are less strict there.

The Peabody Coal Company exploits coal mines on Hopi and Navajo land in Arizona. In exchange, it provides jobs and pays the tribes $9 million a year. But the Indians worry: their region is very arid, and yet P.C.C. wastes huge quantities of water. On top of that, it generates gases that pollute the Grand Canyon and the sacred Four Corners region.

Radioactive pollution may be the most serious long-term threat to Native peoples. Health problems related to radiation exposure have increased dramatically in the Navajo population near uranium mines. And yet, the U.S. Department of Energy encourages (and pays) tribes to store even more toxic waste*. So Indians often face a dilemma: poverty or pollution.

*waste: *déchets*

Since the discovery of oil on Navajo reservations in Utah (1956), oil companies have drilled 577 wells there, contaminating the area's springs* and ground water.

*springs: *sources*

Only 11 U.S. states allow gambling. But Indians can have casinos on their land, and this attracts many tourists. A lot of Indians have started gambling too...

Earth First!
the radical environmental journal

Polluting industries are a threat to Indians, but also to other minorities: 60% of Afro-Americans or Hispanic Americans, and many poor white people, live in communities with uncontrolled toxic waste sites. This is called "environmental discrimination". Civil rights activists and ecologists have joined Indian campaigners to fight for environmental justice.

Indians camped for months to protest against nuclear waste sites in the Mojave Tribe desert, California. The flag is flown upside-down as a distress signal.

Diné CARE

http://dinecare.indigenousnative.org

Native environmentalists want to get rid of polluting industries, even if they know that their own people will probably lose their jobs as a result.

Native groups have developed initiatives to protect their natural resources. Some use modern technology to monitor their wildlife, others take part in planting projects to reintroduce native species.

CREATIVE WRITING

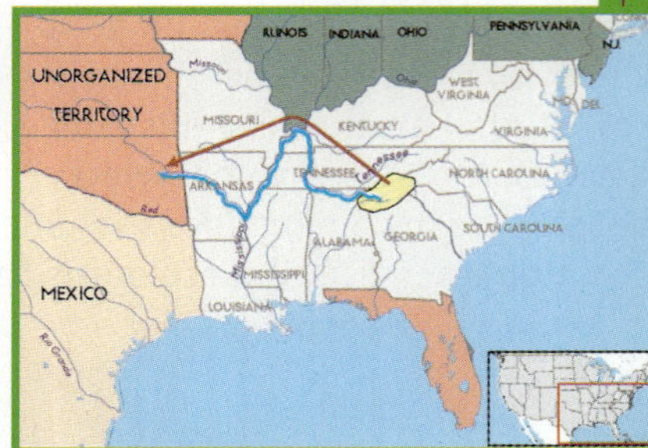

Cherokee lands
water road
land road

THE TRAIL OF TEARS

Originally, the Cherokee Indians lived in Georgia.
In 1835 the treaty of New Echota was signed and ratified by the United States Senate. President Andrew Jackson was given the right to remove the Cherokees from Georgia. On May 17th, 1838 General Winfield arrived at New Echota with 7,000 men. In the summer the Cherokee nation was invaded: men, women and children had to leave their homes and walk a thousand miles to Oklahoma. They had little food. 4,000 Cherokee died. The route became known as the Trail of Tears.*

** faire partir*

- **Read the story of "The Trail of Tears".** Imagine you are:
  1. a Cherokee who survived the removal,
  2. a historian writing a book to denounce the massacre of the Indians.
- **Re-write the text,** expressing the point of view you have chosen.
  Here are **some tips** to help you write an interesting and moving text:

1

- Write your text as a **first person narrative:** *My name is ..., I was ...*
- Give as many details as you can about yourself: name, age, family ...
- Use verbs like "remember", "forget"... and adjectives to describe your feelings.
- Say what you were doing; how you, or others around you, reacted: when the soldiers arrived, during the removal, at your arrival in Oklahoma.

2

- Write your text as a **third person narrative:** *President Jackson ..., the authorities ..., the soldiers ...*
- Give facts to inform and explain: names, dates, numbers.
- Use adjectives and adverbs to make your reader sympathise.

- **Work with a friend to improve on your first writing:** look up words in a dictionary, avoid repetitions, check the tenses (use the past) and the forms (active or passive?), think of the punctuation and capital letters.

Fun Page

Indian reservation

They took the whole Cherokee nation
Put us on this reservation
Took away our ways of life
The tomahawk and the bow and knife
Took away our native tongue
And taught their English to our young
And all the beads we made by hand
Are nowadays made in Japan

Cherokee people, Cherokee tribe
So proud to live, so proud to die

They took the whole Indian nation
Locked us on this reservation
Though I wear a shirt and tie
I'm still part redman deep inside

Cherokee people, Cherokee tribe
So proud to live, so proud to die

But maybe someday when they learn
Cherokee nation will return, will return,
will return, will return, will return

Paul Revere and The Raiders / J. D. Loudermilk

EXTRA READING

Tokalulata remembers

My name is Tokalulata or, in your language, Red Fox. I was a young brave when my uncle defeated General Custer in a great battle[1] to protect our sacred places.

Almost everything I knew then passed away, leaving the world empty. The blood of 20 million buffaloes has been spilled[2] on to the plains. The wild[3] horse has been enslaved; the vast forests have been cut down; the eagle[4] has been shot from the sky; the rivers, lakes and streams have been polluted and the atmosphere poisoned, and the Indian is a prisoner of the civilization that has overwhelmed[5] him.

I have found peace by accepting the fate[6] of my people. I have acted in the movies and Wild West shows, yet I have never forgotten my happy, free childhood when I lived in a tepee and heard the coyotes calling under the stars... when the night winds, the sun and everything in our world reflected the wisdom[7] of the Great Spirit.

I remember seeing my mother bending over an open fire roasting buffalo meat and my father returning at night with an antelope on his shoulder. I shall never forget when my grandfather taught me to make a bow[8] and arrow[9], and a fish hook[10] from the rib[11] of a field mouse.

At bedtime, my mother would tell me stories about her childhood, when the tribes still hunted the buffalo on foot and the few white men who came among them were welcomed as friends.

No people had a deeper love of family than the Sioux. They never punished their children by beating them. I once heard an old Indian say, "We love our children, and beat our horses; the white man loves his horses and beats his children." That's a big difference!

a. Read from line 1 to 5.
Who speaks to whom?
Who won the battle?

b. Read from line 6 to 15. How many changes are listed here? What was affected by the changes?
• air • water • earth
• humans • animals • trees and plants
What is the final consequence to the changes?
What is important in this paragraph?
• the people who caused the changes
• the victims of the changes
How do you know?

c. Read from line 16 to 30. Choose the correct sentence.
• Tokalulata has rebelled against the whites.
• He is integrated in the white society and he has forgotten his past.
• He is integrated in the white society, but he is nostalgic about his past.
Pick out the two verbs which convey nostalgia (one of them is repeated twice).

d. Read from line 24 to the end and pick out all the elements referring to the Indian way of life and religion:
• where they lived
• what they lived by
• what they lived on
• family relationship
• how they communicated
• their god

e. Contrast the whites' and the Indians' attitude to life. Concentrate on the verbs in paragraphs 2 (lines 6-15), 5 and 6 (lines 31-42) for the whites and in paragraphs 4, 5 and 6 (lines 24-42) for the Indians.

f. Do you think this vision of Indian life is realistic or idealized?
The text is moving. Why? Pick out three reasons.
• he gives personal examples
• his memories are very vivid
• he uses a lot of adjectives
• it's a first person narrative

From my mother I learned the folklore of ancient times. She told me about the birds and animals that lived on the plains and in the forests. We were told that the Great Spirit looked after everything in nature. We never knelt[12] in prayer, but were taught to look up to the sky, and we used to dance and sing in praise[13] of the buffalo and the eagle. The sun was the smile of the Great Spirit. Without that smile, the Indian knew no one could exist, for the sun is the power of all things.

We do not have a written language, so old people had to pass on all knowledge to the next generation. They taught the chants and rituals of the dances and ceremonies and also the sign language, through which the many tribes with different spoken languages could communicate. In the same way, our bright face paint that you call war paint says many things: it can show happiness, sorrow[14], peace, which tribe you belong to, where you live.

From Key Stage 3, English - Letts Educational *by John Barder*

NOTES

1. in 1876
2. spill: répandre.
3. wild: sauvage.
4. eagle: aigle.
5. overwhelmed: englouti.
6. fate: sort, destin.
7. wisdom (adj. wise): sagesse.
8. bow /bəʊ/: arc.
9. arrow: flèche.
10. fish hook: hameçon.
11. rib: côte(s).
12. kneel, knelt, knelt: s'agenouiller.
13. sing in praise of: chanter les louanges.
14. sorrow ≠ happiness.

EXERCISES

lesson 1

1 Lis le paragraphe suivant. Certains mots sont nouveaux mais ils ressemblent au français. Vérifie leur sens dans ton lexique après avoir essayé de deviner. Puis recopie ce paragraphe en conjuguant les verbes au Prétérit et en choisissant entre la voix active et la voix passive.

In Native American traditions, elderly people (show) a lot of respect. Old men and women (value) for their experience and skills and they (teach) younger members of their families. But, sometimes, they (sacrifice). When they could no longer follow the group or when the group (endanger) by one of the elders, the old man or old woman (leave) behind to die.

2 Lis le texte suivant. Puis réécris-le en mettant en avant le livre et le film.

First, Michael Blake wrote a book called *Dances with Wolves*. It was in 1988. In 1990 Kevin Costner, the famous American actor, turned *Dances with Wolves* into a huge cinema hit. Kevin Costner produced and directed the film. The Academy of Motion Pictures nominated the film for 12 Oscars and finally awarded the film 7 Oscars.

3 Complète avec les éléments suivants : *on, for, later still, by, at first, until, afterwards, as*. Puis propose une traduction de ces phrases.

a) Don't worry, I'll be back ... 11 o'clock.
b) ... the early 20th century, lots of boys worked in mines.
c) Our next meeting is ... Tuesday.
d) Buffalo stomachs were used ... cooking pots.
e) ..., buffaloes were hunted ... their meat, but ... they were killed for fun. ..., they were slaughtered to get rid of the Indians.

lesson 2

4 Choisis entre la voix passive et la voix active et complète ce texte au Prétérit.

Geronimo, or Goyathlay, was born in 1829. He was an Apache. He (know) for his incredible invulnerability and he (give) the name of Geronimo. When Geronimo and his people (remove) from their lands, he (rebel).
He (make) the promise that his people would return to their lands, but the promise (never keep).
Geronimo was the leader of the last American Indian fighting force. Because he (fight) with extraordinary courage, he (become) the most famous Apache of all. He (die) in 1909.

5 Exprime les changements qui se produisent dans les réserves indiennes aujourd'hui comme dans l'exemple.

Ex. : There are ↗ casinos on the reservations.
There are more and more casinos on the reservations.

a) People have got ↗ money to live on.
b) Some people are getting ↗ rich, but ↗ people are gambling.
c) The reservations are getting ↗ comfortable.
d) There are ↗ Native Americans fighting for equal opportunities.

6 Traduis. Attention au français !

a) Les Lakotas se virent offrir un territoire.
b) On leur a accordé les "Black Hills" en 1868.
c) Il y avait peu de nourriture, peu de terre à cultiver et pas de gibier à chasser.
d) Les "Black Hills" sont exploitées par les Américains depuis des années bien que ce soit l'endroit le plus sacré de la terre pour les Lakotas.
e) Peu de gens savent ce qui est vraiment arrivé aux Indiens au 19e siècle.

Write! **Write a short paragraph about one of these two topics:**
- Buffaloes and their importance in the life of Native Americans.
- What happened to Native Americans and buffaloes with the arrival of the Europeans.

Use the texts in the lessons or find more information in encyclopedias or on the Internet.

Speak! • **Prepare five to ten questions about Native Americans, buffaloes, white settlers, etc. Re-read the texts of your lessons to find ideas.**
• **Make sure you can answer your own questions, and revise your texts to get ready to answer your friends' questions.**
• **In class, play in teams: ask and answer questions.** If you make a mistake, in a question or in an answer, another member of your team can help you correct it. You score one point for each correct question or correct answer.

FILE 5

Young and rebellious

Lessons 1 and 2 .... p. 66
- raconter des événements du passé, avec des points de repère passés
- rapporter des propos

Guided Tour .... p. 70

Creative Writing .... p. 74

Strategies .... p. 75
- comprendre un texte écrit

Extra Reading .... p. 76

Exercises .... p. 78

Test 5

lesson 1

FILE 5

1. Read and learn

THE BOONDOCKS

IS THE MOST TALKED-ABOUT COMIC STRIP IN THE U.S. TODAY.

Meet Aaron McGruder, creator of *The Boondocks*.

A few years ago, Aaron McGruder, then a young college* student, decided to create a comic strip inspired by his love of hip-hop culture. The result was *The Boondocks*, the story of a group of African-American city kids.

The Boondocks was first published in 1997 in the independent student newspaper of the university of Maryland, but before that, it had appeared on the Internet. When McGruder finished his studies, in 1998, *The Source* (one of the country's largest urban music magazines) had already begun publishing the strip.

By the time McGruder turned 29, in 2003, the Boondocks had already appeared in over 250 newspapers and they had become the heroes of a very popular TV series.

* university

a. Look at the picture. Imagine who these people are and describe them (age, ethnic origin, style).

b. Read paragraph one of the text and complete your answers.

c. Do the tasks on worksheet 1 (p. 89).

HELP BOX

• dark-skinned - good-looking - black-haired - a hairband - dreadlocks - an Afro - trainers - hat

2. Practise writing

- Look at the photograph. Do you know who this hip-hop artist is? Say everything you know about her.
- Go to worksheet 2 (p. 89).

3. Go forward

Raptime

script p. 121

- Look at the photos, read the title. What is this article about? Do the tasks on worksheet 3 (p. 90).
- Listen to the recording. What sort of document is it? Who is it for? What is it about?
- Say everything you know and everything you have understood about this band.
- Now do the tasks on worksheet 4 (p. 91).

HIP • HOP CULTURE

The term hip-hop is used to describe a cultural movement which includes specialised styles of dance, graffiti art and music.

It all began during the mid-1970s with pioneers like DJ Kool Herc, Grandmaster Flash and Afrika Bambaataa.

From the mid 1980s to the 1990s, with bands like Run DMC or Public Enemy, hip-hop entered its golden era. Rap became more popular than it had ever been before.

Introduced by NWA, Ice-T and Ice Cube, gangsta rap was the most successful rap form in the 1990s. Rap became more violent than it had ever been before.

In the 1990s, thanks to Bobby Brown and Puff Daddy, New Jack Swing, another sub-genre of hip-hop appeared…

THINK

1. *Pluperfect.*
2. *Pluperfect + when, already, before that, ever.*

✎ **Exercices :** W 5 p. 92

RHYTHM'N SOUNDS

1. *Pluperfect : had.*
2. /ʌ/ ou /æ/ ?

✎ **Exercices :** W 6 p. 93

MEMO

In your WB p. 94

lesson 2

FILE 5

1. Read and learn

a. Look at the headline and the photograph. What happened?

b. Do the tasks on worksheet 1 (p. 98).

Monday, March 10th

Vandals breach airport defences

mobile gantry

GRAFFITI vandals attacked a Cathay Pacific jumbo jet at Brisbane Airport yesterday between 2 and 3am. They wrote a large graffiti tag name (VAS&AIKE) and caused damage estimated at thousands of dollars.

At a press conference, the airport authorities explained that the vandals had cut the fence with a pair of pliers* and that they had used a mobile gantry to reach the wing of the aircraft.

Reporters asked if the security patrols had heard or seen anything unusual. The airport authorities admitted no security patrols had done rounds that night.Worse still, when the reporters asked why a mobile gantry had been left near the aircraft, the airport authorities said they couldn't give any explanations, but added they were going to investigate. They announced that security at the airport would be considerably reinforced.

* *tenailles*

2. Practise speaking

The police press conference

script p. 122

- Listen to the police press conference about the attack on the jet at Brisbane airport.
- Then listen again and report what the police and the reporters said or asked, using the following verbs: say, ask, want to know, answer, add, explain, admit.

3. Go forward

- Before reading, say what you know or ask questions about graffiti and graffiti artists.
- Do the tasks on worksheet 2 (p. 99).

art or vandalism?

Depending on how you define graffiti, it has been around for hundreds, if not thousands, of years, although it has taken many forms and delivered just as many messages—the political, the obscene, the territorial, the artistic. The current wave of graffiti was inspired by and is an integral part of hip-hop culture, which was born in the late '70s.

Much of modern graffiti manipulates letter form and type to the point that letters and words become unrecognizable. Most of the words are merely[1] the artist's name, or his crew[2]'s name, or a short message. The letters take on three-dimensional shapes, and some artists add textures, shadows and flourishes. The average mural can be created in 30 to 45 minutes. Most artists start by rolling over old tags, and then go to work with their cans.

"There are 150 spray paint colors available[3] in the U.S., but artists create more colors by mixing paint from half-empty cans" says one artist who signs himself Music.

"Three years ago", Music tells us, "I travelled all around the country by hopping trains and I painted along the way. I wrote my pseudonym, Music, and my area code to identify my home region. Lots of artists do this, that's why a lot of graffiti is in train yards." " But today", Music says, "I'm more interested in the art and I'm more concerned with the respect of other painters than with writing my pseudo all around the country!".

Music doesn't defend the vandalism aspect of graffiti art, but he says there should be more public art space—especially in a world where corporate logos and imagery are omnipresent. "Look everywhere and you'll see logos and advertisements, but none of it is personal. Graffiti art is a response to commercial saturation."

1. merely: simply - 2. crew: *bande, équipe* - 3. available: *disponible*

THINK

1. Style indirect avec verbes introducteurs au Prétérit.
2. *Million, thousand, hundred, dozen.*

✎ **Exercices :** W 3 p. 100

RHYTHM'N SOUNDS

1. Formes faibles.
2. Lettres non prononcées.
3. Mots de plusieurs syllabes.

✎ **Exercices :** W 4 p. 101

MEMO

In your WB p. 103

Young and rebellious

... A GUIDED TOUR

1 Can you name bands or singers whose music has a social or political content? Now look at pages 71 to 73 to find more examples.

2 a) Look at pages 71 to 73 again. What causes have mobilised young people since the 1960s?

b) Read page 71 and find a title for it.
Then look at the Woodstock poster on the left: how are peace and music symbolized in the drawing?

c) Read page 72.
- Explain what the Civil Rights movement is: where, what for, different tendencies...
- Look at the album cover and describe it. Why two planets?

d) Read page 73:
- Describe the Sex Pistols album cover. What did the Punk movement rebel against?
- Look at the Live Aid photograph. On either side of the stage, there is a poster. What continent is represented? Describe the poster and explain what it is trying to say.
- Music celebrities can have a social and political role, and inspire young people. Find examples on this page.

e) In your opinion, what is the most important cause represented in this Guided Tour? Why?

3 Quiz Now find out how much you know about youth protest.

PROJECT WORK

Find out about the May 1968 youth protest in France. Find people (friends, relatives, teachers) who were there or who know about it. Interview them about what happened. Then present the results of your interviews to the class, and compare with what you have learned about the same period in the USA and in Britain.

VIDEO

Rebellious!

At the Isle of Wight Rock Festival, 1970

1962: Fear of a nuclear conflict. The U.S.S.R. plans to install nuclear missiles in Cuba, threaten the USA.

1963-1975: U.S. war against Vietnam.

1966: American TV and newspapers show destruction caused in Vietnam by U.S. bombs. Growing opposition to the war.

By the 1960s, 70 million children from the U.S. post-war baby boom had become teenagers. A new youth culture emerged, and many youngsters rejected the conservative values of their parents' generation. They asked for peace, love and freedom, gathering* at huge rock events like the 1969 Woodstock Festival.

*gather: *se rassembler*

Singers Jimi Hendrix, John Lennon, Joan Baez or Bob Dylan gave voice to youth revolt and ideals. In *Times They Are A-Changin'*, Dylan told politicians and parents to change their way of thinking.

In Britain too, young protesters met at music events like the Isle of Wight Festival or at anti-nuclear marches.

The Civil Rights movement fights for an end to racial segregation and discrimination.
Reverend Martin Luther King mobilised students and ordinary citizens. He organized many strikes*, marches, and rallies to defend the rights of black Americans. Blues and Gospel singers like Josh White or Aretha Franklin often sang at these rallies. M.L.King was awarded the Nobel Peace Prize in 1964. He was shot on April 4th, 1968.

*strike: *grève*

M.L.King believed in Christian values and non-violence. On the contrary, Malcolm X, a charismatic leader of the Nation of Islam party, demanded equality "by any means necessary", including violence. His ideas influenced the Black Panther party, formed in California in 1966: they created schools and medical centres in ghettos. They also recruited angry youths ready to take up arms against the white oppressor.

Malcolm X

Unlike European rap, American rap is largely a black phenomenon and often deals with* identity issues. Precursors like The Last Poets were close to the Black Panthers. Some other rappers followed the Nation of Islam call: revolution, not integration.

*deal with: *traiter de*

In the 1970s, the Sex Pistols and other Punk bands rejected both the Establishment and the 1960s' idealism. The Punk movement believed the world was rotten* anyway, and that there was no point in trying to make it a better place.

*rotten: *pourri*

Since the 1970s, mass youth protest has declined, but some showbiz stars use their celebrity for good causes. In 1985, pop singer Bob Geldof organized Live Aid, an international music event that raised funds to relieve* famine in Africa.

*relieve: *soulager*

Rock Star Bono, of the band U2, campaigns for the reduction of the Third World debt and for development aid: he uses the media to lobby world leaders and to influence public opinion.

In big U.S. cities 48% of the black teenagers who die, die through homicide; and most of them are victims of "Black on Black Crime". Rap pioneer Afrika Bambaataa founded the Zulu Nation movement to promote peace, love and unity. He uses hip-hop to turn kids away from violence.

*turn s.o. away from: *détourner quelqu'un de*

After the murder of Jam Master Jay of Run DMC in 2002, Public Enemy rapper Chuck D launched* the Hip-Hop for Peace Project.

*launch: *lancer*

CREATIVE WRITING

Rap is poetry spoken to music. It obeys some fairly strict rules:
- It has to rhyme.
- It has to have a beat: in general 4 or 8 beats per line. The beats are usually on the stressed syllables of the words.

Rap doesn't have to be violent. It can be about anything you want. It can deliver a strong message, tell something that happened to you or be just for fun!

a. Read and listen to this "poem". Repeat it twice.

Earth Day Rap

The sky is high and the ocean is deep
But we can't treat the planet like a garbage heap.
Don't wreck it, protect it. Keep parts of it wild,
So there can be a future for your great grandchild.
Boycott, petition, let the big business know,
That if we mess it up here, there's nowhere else to go.
Only one person can do it and that person is you.

- **Listen to some rap music,** reading the poem in your head at the same time.
- **Rap along** with the music when you feel ready!

b. Now write a short rap in groups. Decide if you want to:
- speak about peace, love, friendship, war, racism, violence, pollution, money...
- speak about yourself, your family or friends, your future... or any other topic.

- **Brainstorming session:** find as many words as possible about your topic, find words that rhyme, then organize your ideas.
- **Start writing**, keeping the beat in mind. Here are some examples of introductory lines to get you started:

They pick on me, cos' I love to dream
Cos' I'm not like them, I won't play in a team...

The world's crazy and people are fools
Believe me, guys, I won't follow your rules...

I'm in my car, looking at the stars
But you, my brothers, are stuck behind bars...

STRATEGIES

How to understand long sentences

Pour devenir un bon lecteur, il faut apprendre à comprendre les phrases complexes (composées de plusieurs propositions), sans se laisser décourager.

a. Lis la phrase suivante :

Depending on how you define graffiti, it has been around for hundreds, if not thousands, of years, although it has taken many forms and delivered just as many messages -the political, the obscene, the territorial, the artistic.

Le lexique pose-t-il des problèmes de compréhension dans cette phrase ?
Justifie ta réponse.
Qu'est-ce qui rend cette phrase difficile à comprendre ?

b. Recopie la phrase sur ton cahier et :

- relie le pronom *"it"* au nom auquel il se réfère ;
- souligne les verbes conjugués : combien y-a-t-il de propositions ?
- encadre les mots de liaison, puis mets entre crochets les différentes propositions ;
- connais-tu le sens et/ou la fonction des mots que tu viens d'encadrer ? Ceci est essentiel pour comprendre les liens qu'ils établissent dans la phrase.
- repère quels mots ne sont pas répétés pour alléger la phrase.

c. Une phrase complexe est toujours plus nuancée qu'une série de phrases simples car elle établit des liens divers entre les faits ou opinions présentés.

Dans la phrase ci-dessus, le journaliste a mis en relation trois faits :

- *Graffiti has been around for hundreds of years.*
- *Graffiti has taken many forms.*
- *Graffiti has delivered just as many messages -the political, the obscene, the territorial, the artistic.*

Explique en français ce que la phrase complexe ajoute comme nuances et en quoi celles-ci sont importantes.

d. Entraîne-toi à comprendre la phrase suivante en suivant les étapes proposées ci-dessus.

Although graffiti that grew out of hip-hop is created for artistic and egotistical reasons, it has often been associated with vandalism because most of it is done without permission and because gangs use it to mark territory and to identify themselves.

TIPS

Pour comprendre une phrase complexe :

- relie chaque pronom (personnel ou relatif) au nom auquel il se réfère ;
- soulige les verbes conjugués pour repérer les différentes propositions ;
- encadre les mots de liaison et assure-toi que tu en connais le sens et/ou la fonction ;
- retrouve les faits ou opinions présentés et les liens établis entre eux dans la phrase complexe.

A new beginning

by Aaron McGruder

① ② ③

④

⑤ ⑥ ⑦ ⑧

a. Write down what you know about this comic strip, the author and the characters.

b. Have a good look at the pictures. How old do you think these two boys are? Where are they?

- in a city
- in the country
- in a small town
- in a suburb[1]

How do they look?

- relaxed
- bored
- carefree[2]
- ill-at-ease[3]
- happy
- angry

1. suburb: *banlieue* - 2. carefree: *insouciant* - 3. ill-at-ease: *mal à l'aise.*

c. Read frame 1 and write down in your copy book:

- the time of year
- their names
- where they come from
- where they live now

NOTES

1. **upscale neighborhood:** quartier huppé (riche et chic).
2. **look forward:** se réjouir d'avance.
3. **nestled in the warm embrace of suburbia:** nichés dans la chaleur d'une banlieue chic.
4. **jack:** piquer, voler (Lexus: voiture japonaise de luxe).
5. **stuck:** coincé.
6. **subway stop:** station de métro.
7. **ball court:** terrain de basket.
8. **Chinese carry-out place:** restaurant chinois avec plats à emporter.
9. **rib shack:** baraque à frites.
10. **pilgrims in an unholy land:** pèlerins en terre profane.
11. **well-off:** aisés, riches.
12. **run amok:** se déchaîner.

d. Read frame 2. Who speaks in the square bubble?
Read frames 3 and 4. Do the boys really "look forward" to a new life?
Justify your answer:
They'd like to ... to Chicago because they think there's ... in this suburb.

e. Read frames 5 and 6 and complete with these adjectives: dangerous, rich, safe, poor.
The people in Woodcrest are ... and the streets are ... .
In the South side of Chicago, the people are ... and the streets are ... .

f. Read frames 7 and 8. What is Huey trying to say to his little brother?

- You can do what you like here, nobody will stop you.
- You can relax and have a normal life now, nobody will mug* you.

Does his little brother understand?

*mug: *agresser*

g. What is the comic strip for?

- to inform
- to make people think
- to make people laugh

h. What is funny?

- The discrepancy[1] between what the author says and how the characters feel. *Frame(s) n°* ...
- The way the characters compare their new neighborhood to Chicago. *Frame(s) n°* ...
- The discrepancy between the way the boys look and the way they speak. *Frame(s) n°* ...
- The fact that Riley doesn't know at all how to behave[2] in this new place. *Frame(s) n°* ...

1. discrepancy: *écart, décalage* - 2. behave: *se comporter.*

EXERCISES

FILE 5

lesson 1

1 Relie les phrases suivantes comme dans l'exemple. Sois logique !
Ex. : Sandra left. Peter arrived. (when)
When Peter arrived, Sandra had left.

a) The owners forgot to lock the back door before going on holidays. The gangsters managed to get in easily. (because)
b) My father forgot an important file. He went back home at lunch time. (because)
c) Peter finished reading Sandra's letter. He gave her a call. (when)
d) Rockefeller became the richest man in the world. He died. (when)

2 Complète le paragraphe suivant avec : ***by the time, when, already, before, ever.***
My grandfather was an extraordinary character. He was the youngest of 5 children. ... he was 13, his father died. He was very courageous: he worked really hard, and ... he was 15, he had ... finished high school. He went to university because he wanted to become a sports teacher. Nobody in the family had ... been to university .... Unfortunately, ... he was 22 he was the victim of a car accident and he became handicapped. So he went back to evening school and he worked harder than ever. ... he was 30, he was married, he and his wife had ... had 3 children and he had become a well-respected engineer.

3 Traduis.

a) Quand je suis arrivé, la fête avait déjà commencé.
b) Le temps que j'ouvre la porte, le voleur s'était déjà enfui.
c) Elvis Presley a changé la face du Rock'n'Roll. Personne n'avait jamais chanté comme lui auparavant.
d) À l'âge de 7 ans Mozart avait déjà composé ses premières sonates.

lesson 2

4 Mets les phrases suivantes au style direct :

a) He said he had bought a new bike the month before.
b) The two friends told the teacher they had worked together the day before.
c) He asked his girlfriend if she had already visited London.
d) The girl answered that she had never been to England.
e) The police asked the suspect where he had been the night before.

5 Mets la conversation suivante au discours indirect.

- "Did you buy that book about Australia, Greg?", Mary asked.
- "Yes, I did." Greg answered.
- "Have you started reading it?" Mary asked.
- "I've looked at the pictures!" Greg replied.

6 Complète les phrases suivantes de façon logique. Choisis *dozen* ou *dozens*, *hundred* ou *hundreds*, *million* ou *millions*.

a) The dinosaurs disappeared several ... years ago.
b) ... of people were killed during the Second World War.
c) Napoleon died nearly two ... years ago.
d) Agatha Christie wrote ... of books.
e) Go and get me three ... eggs, please.

7 Traduis le paragraphe suivant :
Hier j'ai rencontré Stanley, un vieil ami. Je ne l'avais pas vu depuis une douzaine d'années car il était parti aux États-Unis. Il m'a dit qu'il avait gagné des millions de dollars aux États-Unis. Il a ajouté qu'il avait acheté une maison dans notre village. Je lui ai dit que j'étais ravie.

Write! **Write a paragraph about the life of a member of your family (or create an imaginary character if you prefer). Insist on what was extraordinary in his/her life. Use:** when, by the time, already, before, ever... before.

Speak! **Work in groups of 5. Your teacher will give you an opinion poll sheet. Use it to find out what the pupils in your group think about graffiti.**

- **Each member of the group chooses one of the five questions in the poll, asks it to the other members of the group and writes down the answers.**
- **Each member reports his/her result back to the class.**

You: When asked if they thought graffiti was art or vandalism, 4 pupils out of 5 in our group said they thought graffiti was vandalism.

- **Each member writes down the other groups' results then gives the final percentage.**

You: When asked ..., ... % of the people in our class said ...

FILE 6

Being or buying?

Lessons 1 and 2 .... p. 80
- comparer une situation présente à ses expériences passées
- imaginer une réalité différente
- émettre des jugements sur le passé
- comparer des quantités

Guided Tour .... p. 84

Creative Writing .... p. 88

Strategies .... p. 89
- rédiger un texte argumentatif

Extra Reading .... p. 92

Exercises .... p. 94

Test 6

1. Listen and learn

Cool hunting

script p. 122

Cool hunting

"Cool" has become a multi-billion-dollar business!
Teenagers desperately want to look cool and be cool... and it's the first time in the history of mankind that they have represented so much money, so much power– a market targeted by big companies...
But... what's cool? What music is cool? What clothes are cool? Ask the cool hunters... It's their job to find out: they go cool hunting... Who do they hunt? You, the teenager!

a. Read the title of the article and have a close look at the photo. Who? What? Where? Imagine what "cool hunting" may mean...

b. Read the article. Say everything you've understood. So, what is a cool hunter?

c. Read the article again and explain why big companies use cool hunters.

d. Listen to cool hunters and do the tasks on worksheet 1 (p. 110).

2. Practise speaking

Pair-work. Play cool hunting.

a. Pupil B: You are a teenager. A cool hunter is visiting you at home. Go to page 117.
Pupil A: You're a cool hunter. You are very friendly and very polite. Use the information below.
Pupil A: You look ...! / You sound ...!
Pupil B: Yeah, well, I've been ...
Pupil A: Really! Do you mind if I ...? / May I ...? / Can I ask you what ...?

- look dead tired
- have a look at your CDs

- sound excited
- have a turn

- sound exhausted
- your favourite brand of sports shoes

b. Change roles.
Pupil B: You're a cool hunter. Go to page 117.
Pupil A: You are a teenager. A cool hunter is visiting you at home. Use the information below.

- use a new shampoo

- shop all day

- go out a lot lately

3. Go forward

Radio forum

script p. 122

- **Have a look at the pictures. Say all you can about these people, characters, sports, etc.**
- **What is the text about?**

You: The text gives definitions of ...

- **Read and suggest explanations for the words you don't know, using what you said about the people or characters in the pictures. Explain what a "submissive consumer" is.**

You: It is someone who ...

- **React. Do you think these stereotypes reflect what teenagers are? Are you shocked, angry, amazed, amused? Why?**
- **Listen to some teenagers' reactions and do the task on worksheet 2 (p. 111).**

the merchants of COOL

Meet the mook and the midriff, the stereotypes for youth... created by the giant media corporations in order to turn young people into submissive consumers.

Boys 15-24 are the mook. The mook is loud, crude, infantile and brainless. He is a mix between a South Park character and a WWF *(World Wrestling Federation)* fan.

Girls 11-16 are the midriff. The midriff is image-obsessed. Her body is her only concern and her only asset. She is a sexual object and proud to be so. She is a Diaper Diva*, Britney Spears-style.

Does the media version of teenagers represent you?
Join our forum and let's hear what you have to say to the merchants of cool!

Our radio forum: "Have your say", every Tuesday from 7 to 8 pm 2129790644

* *bébé diva*

THINK

1. *It's the first time* + *Present perfect.*
2. Superlatif + *Present perfect.*
3. *Present perfect Be* + *-ing.*
4. *Would rather* + V.

✎ **Exercices :** W 3 p. 112

RHYTHM'N SOUNDS

1. Have been V-ing.
2. <th>.

✎ **Exercices :** W 4 p. 114

MEMO

In your WB p. 115

lesson 2

FILE 6

1. Listen and learn
A world that could die

script p. 122

a. Have a good look at the documents. Describe them, comment on them, then establish a link with the title "A world that could die".

b. Listen (or watch the video). What type of document is it? What is it about?

c. Listen again and pick out the nationalities, countries and the comparisons, then recap.

d. Listen to the beginning of a second document on the same topic. Make suggestions to finish the sentence.

e. Listen to the whole document and explain why the BND idea was launched.

2. Practise speaking

a. Choose a topic and think of some of the problems related to it (causes, consequences...). You can work in groups and look for the information and the vocabulary you need.

TOPICS	PROBLEMS
Pollution	people consume too much - produce too much waste
Violence	too many guns - too easy to get / buy

b. Imagine things were different.

E.g.: If people consumed less, they'd produce less waste.
If there weren't so many guns/If people didn't buy so many guns, there wouldn't be so much violence.

c. Think of a special day or event (such as BND) and prepare a radio advertisement about it.

3. Go forward

- Have a look at the photos and posters.
Say everything you know about BND.
Then say what people do on a BND.
- Internet forum: do the tasks on worksheet 1 (p. 120).

BUY NOTHING _ Enough is enough!

Back Forward Stop Refresh Home AutoFill Print Mail

Adress : http://www.buynothingday.co.uk

Wanadoo Google Download

Favorites History Search Scrapbook Page Holder

BND: HAVE YOUR SAY ON OUR INTERNET FORUM

1. Demonstration at the mall. Big sign: CONSUMER CULTURE DESTROYS ECOSYSTEMS. CELEBRATE BUY NOTHING DAY. Then we had a BND party all afternoon. We had a potlatch, i.e., everybody brought nice things to give away to each other. Music, food, good company. Looking forward to our second annual potlatch and party next year.
Matt, Wisconsin, USA

2. Good for you, Matt! *I* didn't do it... but I admit it's a good idea... I should have thought about it more, and I should have talked about it with friends... maybe next year I'll get involved, I suppose it's worth trying , and it looks like it's good fun too...
Jessica, Calgary, Alberta, Canada

3. Logos dominate our landscape. People seem to think the only way to be happy is to buy what the ads say. By having their "brands" on our bodies we are saying, "You own us." Let's have a day for ourselves. BND is all about freedom and SELF RESPECT.
Tom, Pittsburgh

4. My first BND away from home. I celebrated by bringing my friends at school home-made sandwiches, cookies, coffee, and juice and so they didn't have to buy lunch. I might not have affected millions of people but I feel it was worth it: we got to talking about consumerism, the environment, the global economy... My best BND so far!
Lola, Berlin, Germany

5. Wow, I'm impressed, it must have been terribly unnerving NOT to go to the shops for ONE whole day!! RIDICULOUS! When I think about it... I've been celebrating BND at least four days a week for years now... Do I get a medal, or what? Big deal!
Meg, Glasgow, Scotland

6. I did not celebrate buy nothing day... however I have calmly NOT been buying BIG BRAND NAMES for several years. And my friends have been laughing at me ever since! They say it's no use boycotting... I know I don't make much difference on my own, but what if ALL YOU guys did the same?
Rod, Cleveland

Internet zone

THINK

1. *If* + Prétérit, *would* + V.
2. *You'd better* + V.
3. Emploi nominal des adjectifs de nationalité.
4. Quantifieurs au comparatif.
5. Modal + *Have* + participe passé.
6. *Present perfect Be* + *-ing* avec *for* et *since*.
7. *Worth* + V-*ing* / *No use* + V-*ing*.

✎ **Exercices :** W 2 p. 120

RHYTHM'N SOUNDS

1. Accent de phrase.
2. Modal + *have* + participe passé.

✎ **Exercices :** W 3 p. 124

MEMO

In your WB p. 125

Being or buying?

... A GUIDED TOUR

1 Where and when can you see advertisements? Give examples of adverts that target teenagers. Look at pages 85 to 87 and find more examples.

2 **a) Read page 85.**
- Spot two ways advertisers use to get to know their potential customers.
- What do you think of Pantene's advertising strategy?

b) Look at the adverts on pages 86 and 87, and spot the use of these techniques:
- identifying with a celebrity
- identifying with people your age
- humour
- repetition (name, image or colour of the product)
- suggesting the product instead of showing it
- shock strategies

Some ads are made to sell, some aren't commercial. Find examples of both.
Now choose one advert and describe it. Do you think it's effective? Why or why not?

c) Look at page 87.
- How do advertisers penetrate schools?
- Why is it so important for advertisers to enter the classroom?

d) Do you think you are influenced by advertising? Would you be influenced by celebrity endorsement? Why or why not?

3 **Quiz** Now find out how much you know about advertising.

PROJECT WORK

You've decided to organize a "No Logo Day" at school, when labels and brands are forbidden. Discuss in groups the importance of logos in teenage culture. Choose a slogan and make a poster announcing the NLD. Put up your posters around the school, and see if your campaign works! Then discuss the impact of your experiment in class.

VIDEO

Celebrity sells.

Advertising is everywhere: letterboxes, buses, taxis, magazines, the radio, television...
Teenagers have a lot of buying power from pocket money or part-time jobs. In the U.S. they spend over $175 billion a year. That's why advertisers target them, using questionnaires, cool hunters or Internet surveys to know what their preferences and interests are.

Posters in the streets of London

The first banner ads, or "spamming", appeared on the Internet in 1994. 97% of visitors to a website never click on the ads, so some ads promise gifts or money to attract your attention. Mobile phone spamming is also developing: advertisers send you an SMS and you can win a prize if you reply.

You're a girl aged 14-24? You're a singer-songwriter? Pantene gives you a chance to become a star. If you win the Pantene music competition, you'll give a concert in Central Park and get a recording contract!

Make a girl famous, and everybody will talk about your brand on TV, on the radio and on the Net...

Become *fun*, trendy, popular. Just do it! Just buy it!

Teenagers love Buffy the Vampire Slayer: she's famous, cool, funny, and she's got that "natural look". Use Maybelline and you too can cheat, and pretend that nature made you perfect. Because you're worth it...

Shock advertising can be used to make you aware* of social problems: compose a clever close-up, focus on the foreground, address the spectator directly, and the message is stronger.

*aware: *conscient*

You want to be successful, hip and strong like the world's number one tennis players? Drink milk! It's on everybody's lips, white, white and white on black.

Most schools welcome ads for charities or for anti-smoking campaigns, but they refuse commercial advertising. So advertisers have to find other ways of entering the classroom.

Companies like Coca-Cola or Pepsi offer schools millions of dollars. The catch: guess what the schools' vending machines have to sell?

In Canada and the U.S., media companies give schools TV sets and satellite TV. The catch: all the students have to watch a twelve-minute programme every day in class, including two minutes of commercials for teenage products. Other companies give schools computers, software and online access. The catch: the students are submitted to non-stop spamming. Some schools and students boycott this brainwashing[1] and prefer to do without[2] the equipment.

1. brainwashing: *lavage de cerveau* - 2. do without: *se passer de*

Planet Gruv provides, for free, high-tech sound and light equipment for big school parties. The catch: the event is sponsored by advertisers. Hundreds of schools usually opposed to on-campus promotion are now opening their doors.

CREATIVE WRITING

Big media companies don't just sell products, they sell an attitude.

You are a group of young teenagers and you are fed-up with this manipulation. You have decided to write a letter to a famous magazine which has published this ad.

- **Prepare part 1 of your letter:** analyse this woman's body and attitude.

> HELP BOX
> - look + *adj.* - look like + *n.*
> - doll - sexual object - underwear and accessories (make up - a comb - a mirror)
> - thin - provocative - brainless - vulnerable - victimized - objectified
> - dangerously - unrealistically
> - "horror-movie" atmosphere - "get-the-guy" attitude

- **Prepare part 2 of your letter:** imagine the consequences these ads have on girls and boys.

What characteristics will girls want to develop to conform to this image?
What about boys? What image/definition will they form of girls or women?

- **Prepare part 3 of your letter:** explain why big media companies promote this image of women/girls.
- **Prepare your conclusion:** list adjectives to express your feelings towards this ad in particular and the big media companies in general.
- **Now write your letter,** starting like this:

Dear Sirs,
The advertisement you published on page 45 of your latest issue is particularly revolting.
...

Don't forget to use link words.

> HELP BOX
> - to express cause and consequence: that's why, because, so that, that's the reason why, for this reason...
> - to add other elements: and, besides, also, moreover, on top of that...

STRATEGIES

Learning how to write

Tu as appris à rédiger des textes argumentatifs en classe de français. Tu vas constater que les techniques sont les mêmes en anglais.

PART I : la préparation

Voici un exemple de sujet argumentatif, c'est-à-dire un sujet qui te demande de débattre :
Ce qui est dit te semble-t-il vrai ou non ? es-tu d'accord ou non ? et pourquoi ?

Advertisements have a lot of influence on what teenagers are.
Do you agree with this statement? Why or why not?

a. Bien comprendre le sujet.

Commence toujours par réfléchir calmement au sujet : note ce à quoi chaque mot te fait penser.

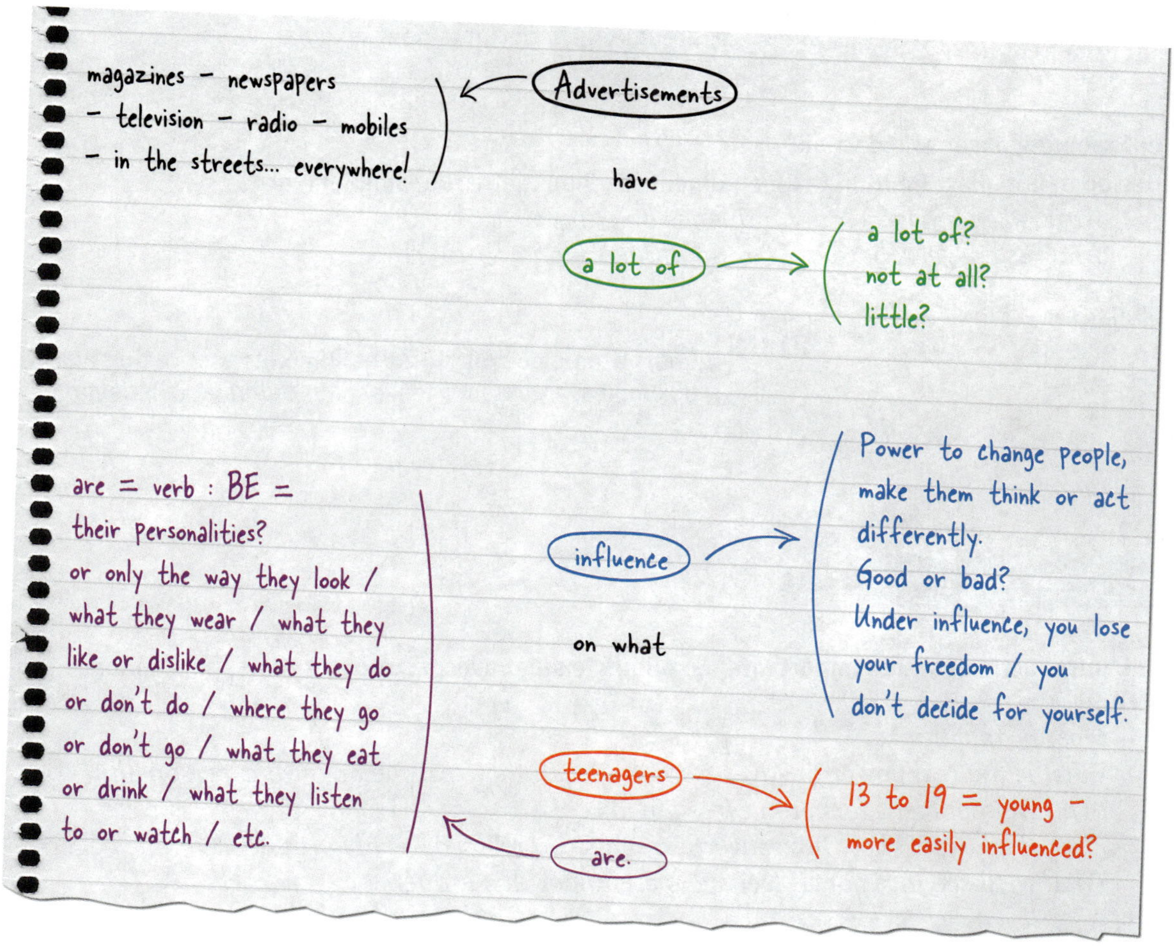

TIPS

Avant de commencer à rédiger, passe quelques minutes à réfléchir sur les mots mêmes du sujet, le stylo à la main :
- va chercher la définition des mots-clés du sujet dans un dictionnaire unilingue ;
- recherche des synonymes et des contraires ;
- écris en anglais tout ce qui te vient à l'esprit sans essayer d'organiser tes pensées à ce stade.

b. Trouver des idées.

Une fois que tu as bien compris le sujet, cherche des exemples concrets. Ceci te donnera des arguments pour débattre. Tu trouveras des exemples :

- dans ton expérience personnelle,
  Ex. : *I know adverts in music magazines or video clips on TV have a lot of influence on what I listen to ..., but I'm not interested in clothes or cosmetics and adverts won't change me!*
- auprès de tes amis, que tu pourras interroger,
  Ex. : *Some of my friends say adverts don't have an influence on what they wear, but others admit that adverts in magazines have a lot of influence on what they buy: Nike, Gap....*
- dans les documents dont tu disposes ou que tu peux rechercher sur ce thème,
  Ex. : *Lots of teenagers buy products advertised by celebrities. / Teenagers watch a lot of television so they see a lot of commercials. / For teenagers, it is very important to be cool ...*

TIPS

- Note en vrac tous les exemples, toutes les expériences qui pourront illustrer ton propos.
- Sers-toi de ton analyse du sujet (a) pour tirer de ces exemples (b) les idées et arguments importants pour le débat.

c. Savoir organiser sa rédaction.

Décide de ton plan. Pour un texte argumentatif, il peut être tout simplement :

part 1: Adverts have a lot of influence on ... because ...
part 2: But adverts have little or no influence on ... because ...

TIPS

Choisis ton plan puis classe et numérote tout ce que tu as écrit (exemples, arguments, idées) pour ordonner ta rédaction.

PART II : la rédaction

a. L'introduction est très importante : explique le sujet avec tes propres mots, puis annonce ton plan.

- *Most people think...*
- *What is the real power of advertisements? Can they really change your personality?*
- *Is it true that teenagers aren't free any more?...*
- *First of all, we'll show how advertisements can really have a big influence on teenagers... Then we'll see that not all teenagers are under this influence...*

b. Le développement doit être clair et logique. Utilise des mots de liaison.

- pour ajouter : *and, besides, on top of that, moreover, also, too...*
- pour contredire : *but, however, and yet...*
- pour opposer deux idées : *on the one hand ..., on the other hand ...*
- pour exprimer la cause et la conséquence : *that's why, because, so ... that, for this reason...*

c. Conclue en donnant ton opinion.

Personally I think ... / In my opinion ... / I'd say that ...

d. Améliore ton premier jet.

- Vérifie les liens logiques dans ton texte : à quels mots les pronoms se réfèrent-ils ? les mots de liaison sont-ils bien choisis ?
- Enrichis ton vocabulaire : y a-t-il des répétitions ? des mots trop banals ?
- Vérifie l'ordre des mots dans tes phrases (comme la place des adjectifs) ainsi que la ponctuation et les majuscules.

TIPS

- Rédige au crayon de papier et en sautant des lignes.
- Dans l'introduction, prouve que tu as compris le sujet en le reformulant, puis annonce ton plan.
- Respecte ton plan, en illustrant tes arguments par les exemples que tu as trouvés.
- Dans la conclusion, donne ton opinion personnelle.
- Retravaille toujours ton premier jet : soigne la logique de ton argumentation, la construction de tes phrases, la richesse de ton vocabulaire et la présentation générale de ton travail.

PART III : entraîne-toi

Voici ce qu'a écrit un élève de 3e, sans aucune aide et sans suivre les techniques décrites ci-dessus. Comment pourrais-tu améliorer ce premier jet ?

Mennechet
Frédéric
3e 5

Have advertisements a lot of influence on what teenagers are ?

First of all, the adverts show them all the new styles of clothes and as teenagers want to be " in ", they naturally buy them. For example, if they see Michael Jordan wearing shoes, they will want to wear the same.

Also, all the adverts for music give them a preview of it so they help them to decide what to buy. It's the same thing for drinks. Teenagers will buy Coca-Cola and not a simple cola or soda because they have seen an advert which said that Coca-Cola is the best soda in the world so they want to drink this one and not another.

In my opinion, ads have a lot of influence on what teenagers are because all that they buy give them a personality and an image.

EXTRA READING

On advertisements

All advertisements, particularly television advertisements, are totally and hopelessly un-English. They are too direct, too definite, too boastful[1]. Why not imagine a national British style in television advertising instead of imitating the American style of breathless superlatives with all their silly implications *(buy our shampoo and you'll get a husband; buy our perfume and you are sure to be attacked by hungry males in Bond Street[2]; smoke our pipe tobacco and you will become a suntanned Adonis[3])*. I feel sure that the effect of these advertisements could be vastly improved if they were made more English.

Some ads, for example could suggest gambling[4]:

Grapirex: it may relieve[5] your headache or of course it may not. Who can tell? Try it, you may be lucky. The odds against you are only 3 to 1.[6]

Or:

Try your luck on Bumpex Fruit Juice. Most people detest it. You may be an exception.

Or appeal to[7] the Englishman's sense of fair play. A beautiful half nude girl (you cannot do without them in any advertisements, British, American or anything else) might call to the public:

S.O.S., we are doing badly. Business is rotten[8]. Buy Edgeless Razor Blades and give us a sporting chance. Honestly, they are not worse than other makes[9].

Or appeal to the Englishman's inborn honesty: *Use BUBU Washing Powder. By the way, have you ever tried the whiteness test? Here is Mrs Spooner from Framlingham. Now, Mrs Spooner, which would you say is the whiter of these two pairs of knickers?*

Mrs Spooner: This one.

Announcer: You are perfectly right, Mrs Spooner. That is the one washed in PRIDE. So you don't get your five pounds, Mrs Spooner – No fear[10]. Nevertheless ladies and gentlemen, just go on using BUBU. Who likes that blinding[11], vulgar whiteness, in any case. After all, people don't see your knickers. At least they shouldn't. Bubu washes greyest.

Or just moderate your language, be vague and incoherent, in other words natural:

Can you tell the difference between our margarine and our hair tonic? We can't.

Adapted from George Mikes

③

NOTES

1. **boastful:** *pretentious.*
2. **Bond Street:** *famous street in London.*
3. **Adonis/ə'dəʊnɪs/:** *in Greek mythology, a very handsome youth loved by Aphrodite the goddess of love.*
4. **gamble:** parier de l'argent.
5. **relieve:** soulager.
6. **The odds against you are only 3 to 1:** Votre handicap n'est que de 3 contre 1.
7. **appeal to:** faire appel à.
8. **rotten:** *very very bad.*
9. **make(s):** marque(s).
10. **No fear:** *out of the question.*
11. **blinding:** aveuglant.

a. Read paragraph one (line 1 to 16) and write the corresponding summary in your copy book.

- English advertisements are very effective because they imitate the American style.
- Television advertising in Britain would be more effective if it were made more English.
- The English are unable to imagine a British style in advertising, so they imitate the Americans'.

b. Read the three American ads (line 9 to 13) and write down the three stupid implications or consequences in your copy book.

c. Read from line 17 to the end. Match the pictures and lines from the text.

Picture 1: line ... to ...
Picture 2: line ... to ...
Picture 3: line ... to ...
Picture 4: line ... to ...

d. In this text, the language and the techniques used in advertising are ridiculed. Find examples of:

- funny names of makes
- ads telling the whole truth
- words or expressions with a negative meaning
- ironic implications, allusions and exaggerations
- caricatures of tests
- caricatures of American slogans

e. Choose one of the products advertised and imagine a classical slogan for it. Now explain what a parody is.

④

EXERCISES

FILE 6

lesson 1

1 Recompose des phrases complètes à l'aide des éléments fournis. Utilise le *Present perfect*.

a) my cousins / visit / London / . / It's the first time
b) I / finish / . / not ... yet
c) she / hear of / cool hunters / . / never ... before
d) I / watch / a wrestling match / . / It's the first time
e) you / try bungee-jumping / ? / ever

2 Rédige ce que dirait un enfant dans ces trois situations, en utilisant : *"wash the dog"* au Temps et à la forme qui convient :

a) Il montre le chien tout propre à son père. "Look Dad! I ..."
b) Il s'excuse d'être tout sale et mouillé en arrivant à table. "Er, sorry, I ..."
c) Il dit qu'il a lavé le chien il y a deux jours. "I ..."

3 Construis des phrases sur le modèle de l'exemple en utilisant les éléments fournis.

Ex. : It's the most beautiful place I've ever visited.

a) delicious - meal / you - ever - cook
b) pretty - girl / I - ever - see
c) good - book / he - ever - write
d) interesting - people / we - ever - meet
e) sad - movie / she - ever - make

4 Traduis.

a) C'est la première fois dans l'histoire de l'humanité que les entreprises ciblent les adolescents.
b) - Tu as l'air crevé !
- Je suis beaucoup sorti ces derniers temps.
c) C'est l'histoire la plus dégoûtante que j'aie jamais entendue !
d) J'aimerais mieux rentrer à la maison qu'aller au cinéma avec cet idiot !

Speak! What do you have to say to the merchants of cool? Do you think that advertisements "tell" you what a girl or a boy should be? Do they make you conform to a stereotyped image? Re-read lesson 1 then find your own examples and arguments. Discuss in class.

lesson 2

5 Complète les phrases suivantes en utilisant le Prétérit ou *would* + V.

a) What (happen) if the Chinese or the Indians (pollute) as much as the Americans do?
b) If we (use) more public transport, pollution (decrease) rapidly.
c) If the whole world (live) the American way of life, our planet (not - last) more than twenty years.
d) If somebody (ask) you to stop buying big brand names, how (you - react)?

6 Donne ton avis comme dans l'exemple.

Ex. : John lied to her, so she left him. (tell her the truth): He should have told her the truth.

a) Roberts, the centre forward, tackled a player from behind and the referee didn't say anything. (give him a yellow card)
b) Fred was seriously injured in an accident last night. (wear his helmet)
c) When they got to the top of the mountain, Joanna realised Damian had forgotten the camera. (check the bag herself).

7 Imagine ce qui a dû se passer en utilisant *must* :

Last night, a country house was burgled.

a) The dog didn't bark. The burglars (drug him).
b) There was a ladder leaning against the wall. They (climb up onto the roof).
c) No window was broken. They (come down the chimney).
d) The safe wasn't forced. They (crack the secret code).

8 Traduis.

a) Tu ferais mieux de partir maintenant ! Tu vas rater ton train.
b) Je n'ai pas fêté BND parce que cela fait des années que je boycotte les grandes marques !
c) Son anglais est excellent parce qu'il vit en Angleterre depuis 2001.
d) Notre planète est en danger parce que nous consommons trop ! Je dis cela depuis des années et regardez autour de vous ! Rien n'a changé !
e) Mes amis disent que ça ne sert à rien de boycotter les grandes marques mais je pense que ça vaut le coup d'essayer.

Write! Write a short paragraph to explain to a friend what BND is and what it is for. Think of pollution and the problem of "big brand names". Conclude by giving your opinion. Do you think it is useful? effective? Why or why not?

FILE 7

Commonwealth connections

Lessons 1 and 2 .... p. 96
- imaginer un passé différent
- insister sur un fait et en donner la conséquence
- émettre des regrets et des souhaits

Exercises .... p. 100

Strategies .... p. 101
- enrichir son vocabulaire

Guided Tour .... p. 102

Extra Reading .... p. 108

Test 7

1. Read and learn

Sir Alexander Mackenzie

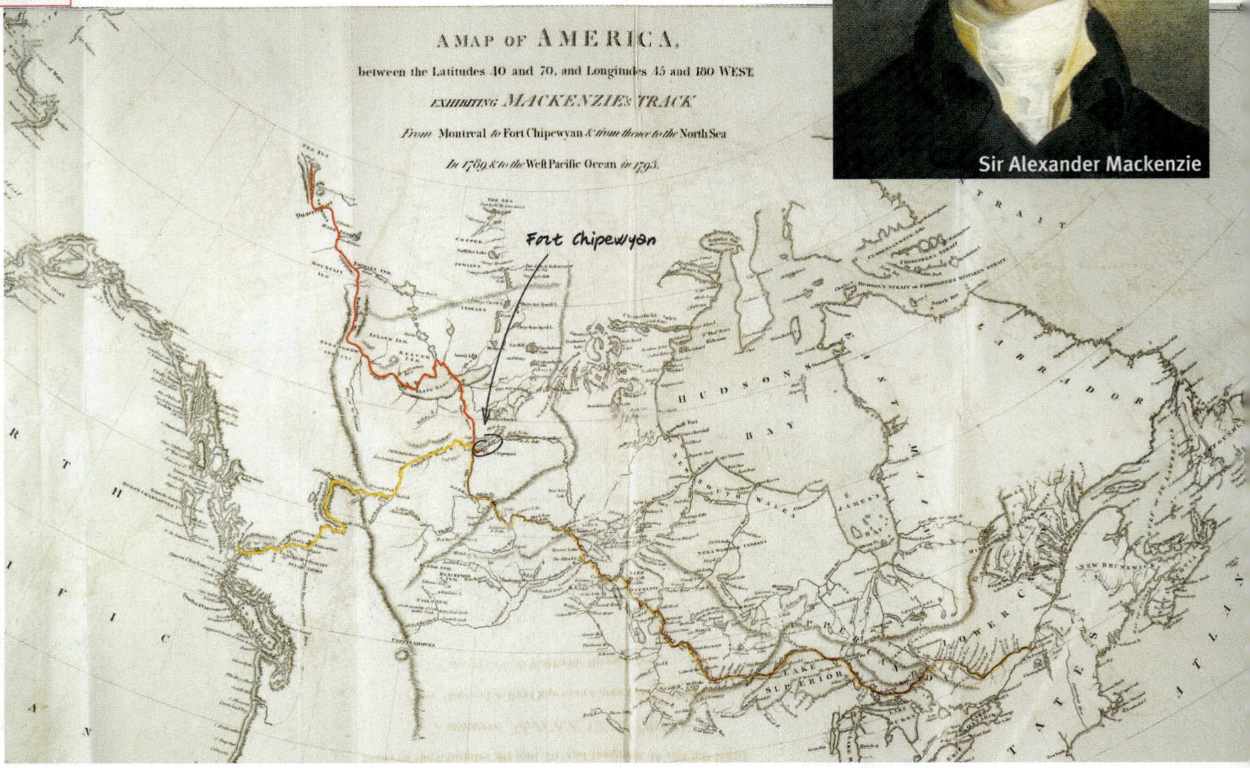

OUTSTANDING EXPLORATIONS

First Voyage (June 3, 1789 - Sep. 12, 1789)

In June 1789, Mackenzie, a fur trader, embarked on his first remarkable journey from Fort Chipewyan in search of a route to the Pacific Ocean. He was accompanied on the canoe expedition by French-Canadian voyageurs and Indian hunters and interpreters. It was a Chipewyan who guided his party.
They travelled the length of the De Cho River (about 1650 km) in an amazing 14 days... but reached the Arctic Ocean. Ending up at the wrong ocean was such a disappointment, that Mackenzie named the river "The River of Disappointment".
It is now called the Mackenzie River, in his honour.

Second Voyage (Oct., 1792 - July, 1793)

Mackenzie set off on his next adventure on October 12, 1792. He still relied almost totally on Native people to provide food and supplies, to paddle his canoe and to show him the way. Experiencing great hardship and suffering, they reached the Pacific Ocean after a gruelling journey over the coastal moutains. Mackenzie left an inscription on what is now known as Mackenzie Rock. People can still read it today.
After his two epic adventures, Mackenzie wrote a book that brought him fame and fortune.
In 1802, King George III knighted him for his outstanding Canadian explorations.
Sir Alexander Mackenzie realized the dream of a Canada stretching from sea to sea.

"In this voyage I was not only without the necessary books and instruments, but also felt myself deficient in the sciences of astronomy and navigation; I did not hesitate therefore, to undertake a winter's voyage to England, in order to procure one and acquire the other."

• **Do the tasks on worksheet 1 (p. 131).**

2. Go forward

Wishes and regrets

script p. 123

- Do the tasks on worksheet 2 (p. 131).

Benjamin Franklin (1706-1790), by Norman Rockwell (1926)

Napoleon (1769-1821) after his abdication, by P.H. Delaroche

Canada, in Algonquian "meeting place", is now an independent state, part of the Commonwealth... but about two hundred years ago, its fate almost took, not one, but two very different turns. [...]*

* one of the Native languages

THINK

Révisions :

1. *If* + *pluperfect*, *would have* + participe passé.
2. *Such* + groupe nominal.
3. *I wish... / If only...*
4. *I regret* + V-*ing*.

✎ **Exercices :** W 3 p. 132

RHYTHM'N SOUNDS

1. *So* et *such*.
2. Mots de plusieurs syllabes.

✎ **Exercices :** W 4 p. 135

MEMO

In your WB p. 136

lesson 2 Meet Canadian Superheroes

• Do the tasks on worksheet 1 (p. 141).

FILE 7

Captain Canada flies past the Peace Tower in downtown Ottawa, after a fierce battle with Super-Mafia's giant robot who wanted to kidnap Queen Elizabeth II during her visit to Canada to promote national unity.

A champion of Bilingualism and Multiculturalism, Angloman wields[1] various deadly Angloweapons, such as his indestructible Bilingual Shield[2] (Stops everything) and his Apostrophe Darts[3] (explosive and non-explosive).

1. wield: manier - 2. shield: bouclier
3. darts: flèchettes.

Great Scott! Canada's Greatest Scottish Superhero. Born with a bagpipe for a set of lungs[1], he is stronger than a cup of Tim Horton[2]'s coffee, smarter than your average hockey player -an upright[3], upstanding[3] citizen!

1. lungs: poumons - 2. Tim Horton: Canada's largest and best-known coffee chain - 3. upright: upstanding: virtuous.

Joe Shuster was born in 1914 in Toronto, Canada.
His family later emigrated to Ohio, U.S.
He drew Superman from 1938 to 1947.

A martial arts expert, she, too, protects Canada from organized crime. She carries a nonlethal weapon* shaped like a French Canadian fleur-de-lys that protects her by producing bright flashes of light.

* nonlethal weapon: arme qui ne tue pas

Super Shamou performs daring* rescues of children in peril, while teaching them some realities of life in the North.
The world's first Inuk superhero!

* audacieux

FACTS ABOUT CANADA

POPULATION: around 30 million inhabitants.

UNITY:

- **Quebec**

  1968: René Lesvesque founds the **separatist** Parti Quebequois.

  1980: Separatists lose the **Independence Referendum.**

  1995: Quebeckers vote against sovereignty: 50.6 % to 49.4 %

- Birth of **a new territory** on April 1, 1999: **Nunavut.**

  Separated from the Northwest Territories.
  It is ruled by **native** self-government because **the Inuit** make up 85 % of the population.

LANGUAGES:

- National or official languages: English (approx. 60% of the population) and French (approx. 24%).
- Non-official or heritage languages: approx. 16 %.

- Two main Native languages: **Inuktitut** and Algonquian.
- The number of languages listed for Canada is 85.

IDENTITY:

Canadians today reflect **a vast diversity of cultural heritages and racial groups.** This **multicultural diversity** is a result of centuries of **immigration.**

1971: policy of **multiculturalism** = Canadian identity based on public acceptance of difference and support of cultural pluralism. Ethnicity is not a threat to **Canadian identity,** it is Canadian identity.

EXERCISES

lesson 1

1 Les catastrophes s'enchaînent ! À chaque étape, les choses auraient pu aller mieux... Imagine !

a) Max's alarm clock didn't ring, so he missed his bus to work.
If his alarm clock ... (ring), he ...
b) He ran to work and lost his wallet with his credit card in it.
c) He didn't realize his wallet was lost so he didn't call the bank.
d) The person who found the wallet wasn't very honest ... Max lost eight hundred pounds!

2 Compose des phrases qui insistent sur un fait puis en donnent la conséquence logique. Utilise *such...* ou *so...* pour insister et introduis la conséquence avec *that*. Utilise les éléments suivants :

a) The Beatles were a very popular band.
The Queen knighted them.
b) Harry Potter's adventures are exciting.
Millions of kids read them.
c) Nobel was sorry he had invented dynamite.
He created the Nobel Peace Prize.
d) Mackenzie was a strong-willed man.
He never gave up on his dream.
e) In the 1812 war, the First Nations fought with remarkable courage. They defeated the British.
f) The Indians were devoted people.
They helped Mackenzie till the end.

3 Traduis :

a) Si seulement j'avais une machine à remonter le temps !
b) J'ai toujours regretté d'avoir quitté l'Angleterre.
c) Je me souviens d'avoir entendu un cri puis plus rien...
d) J'aimerais pouvoir passer quelques semaines au Canada.
e) Si j'avais beaucoup de temps et beaucoup d'argent, j'organiserais une expédition en Antarctique.

Write! Write a short paragraph about Canada, past and present, using the information in both lessons.

Speak! Look for information about another outstanding expedition that took place in the 19th or in the 20th century in an encyclopedia or on the Net and tell the story to the class. Here is a very useful site to get you started: http://www.EnchantedLearning.com/explorers/

STRATEGIES

How to improve your vocabulary

LES ADJECTIFS COMPOSÉS. L'anglais est une langue très créative. On peut en particulier former de nombreux adjectifs composés... à condition de connaître les règles de formation !

a. Observe l'illustration et lis la légende. Repère les trois adjectifs composés. Comment sont-ils formés ? À quoi sert le premier mot de l'adjectif composé ?

This blue-eyed boy has got light-brown hair. He's very good-looking.

b. Écoute les adjectifs suivants. Propose une explication ou traduction pour chacun d'eux avec l'aide de ton professeur. Puis, écoute-les à nouveau, encadre les syllabes accentuées dans ton *workbook*, page 143, et répète-les.

dark-blue	strong-willed
red-haired	blue-eyed
bright-red	funny-looking
hard-working	kind-hearted
dark-skinned	sweet-smelling
absent-minded	old-fashioned
light-brown	good-looking

c. Classe les adjectifs ci-dessus en trois catégories selon la façon dont ils sont composés. Quel modèle suivent-ils ?
1. *blue-eyed*
2. *light-brown*
3. *good-looking*

d. Entraîne-toi. Voici huit mots avec lesquels tu peux former quatre adjectifs composés. Sauras-tu les trouver en utilisant les règles de composition que tu as découvertes ?
adjectifs : *good / left / pale / fast / blue*
noms : *hand / humour*
verbe : *move*

TIPS

Pour créer des adjectifs composés en anglais :
- souviens-toi que le premier mot définit, qualifie, nuance le mot principal ;
- apprends les règles de composition. En voici trois :
  1. adjectif-adjectif
  2. adjectif-nom+*ed*
  3. adjectif-verbe+*ing*

Pense à les utiliser dans tes descriptions, en sachant que ces adjectifs composés n'existent pas toujours en français.
Exemple : un monstre à trois têtes = *a three-headed monster.*

Commonwealth connections

... A GUIDED TOUR

1 Name three countries belonging to the Commonwealth of Nations. Then look at pages 103 to 107 to find more examples. Locate those countries on the map, page 204 of your book.

2 a) Read page 103. Name one difference between a colony and a member of the Commonwealth.

b) Read page 104. The Commonwealth encourages mutual cooperation. Find examples.

c) Read page 105. What is the proportion of young people in the Commonwealth? How does the Commonwealth help young people? Find three examples.

d) Read pages 106 and 107.
- Commonwealth immigrants found things difficult when they arrived in Britain. Find and imagine some reasons why.
- How do Commonwealth immigrants and their descendents contribute to Britain's culture and lifestyle? Find three examples.

3 **Quiz** Now find out how much you know about the Commonwealth.

PROJECT WORK

Commonwealth Quiz! Work in teams. Choose two Commonwealth countries and find information on them in the library or on the Internet (facts and figures, population, capital, location, etc.). Then prepare a list of five questions on each country. Play the quiz in class and see what team wins!

VIDEO

Hindu Festivals.

By the 19th century, Britain was the greatest commercial, industrial and naval power in the world, with colonies on every continent (25% of the world's surface and population): India, Canada, Ireland, Australia, Pacific islands, the West Indies, parts of Africa and Asia, etc. "The sun never set on the British Empire"...

1867-1910: Canada, Australia, New Zealand and South Africa become self-governing "Dominions".

1931: the Dominions become freely-associated members of the "British Commonwealth of Nations".

1949: the word "British" is dropped. The "Commonwealth of Nations" is born.

After WWII: decolonisation accelerates. Many ex-colonies decide to join the Commonwealth. They all recognize the British monarch as the symbolic head of the Commonwealth.

The Dominions and colonies made a great contribution to the two World Wars.

Today 54 independent states (1.7 billion people, or 30% of the world's population) belong to the Commonwealth. From Canada to Papua New Guinea, despite their diversity, they cooperate for social and economic development.

Celebrating Diversity
Commonwealth Day • 11 March

Fishing in the Caribbean

The Commonwealth Fund for Technical Cooperation sends experts to developing countries like Bangladesh or the Fiji Islands. They give advice on agriculture, fishing, commerce, credit management, transport, tourism or ecology.

Bangladeshi women learning how to manage credit

Sharing expertise in the Fiji Islands

The Commonwealth Council can suspend countries that don't respect democracy or human rights.
South Africa was suspended in 1961 because of its racist Apartheid laws. The Commonwealth applied economic and sports boycotts against South Africa and it campaigned for the release* of the black activist Nelson Mandela.
In 1994, South Africa rejoined the Commonwealth after Mandela was elected President.

*release: *libération*

Two-thirds of the Commonwealth population are under 29. The Commonwealth Youth Programme helps young people 15-29 to get an education, to set up a business or to contribute to their community. The Commonwealth also gives grants to enable students to travel or study abroad. English is spoken in most Commonwealth countries, which makes exchanges easier.

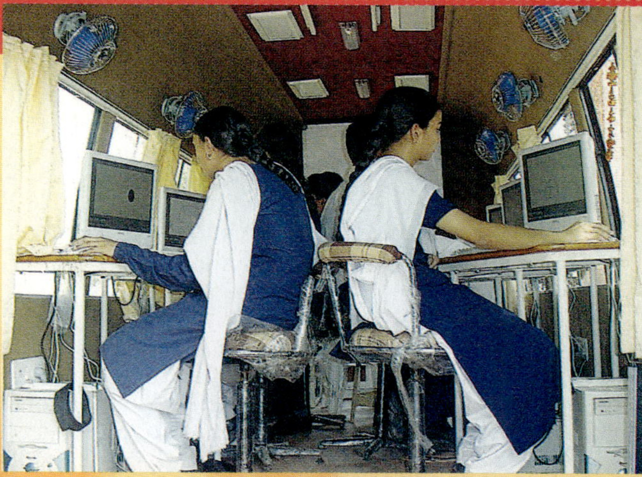

In India, the CYP runs a mobile computer training centre, teaching computer skills to disadvantaged youths all over the country.

The Commonwealth Medical Association sponsors health education programmes on drugs and infectious diseases: 60% of the people infected with HIV live in Commonwealth countries, and there are 28.5 million HIV-positive adults and children in Africa (550,000 in Western Europe).

Like the Olympic Games, the Commonwealth Games take place in a different country every 4 years. The first Commonwealth Youth Games were held in 2000.
The C.G. Federation also works to encourage education through sports activities.

1947: Independence and Partition of India. Creation of the Muslim state of Pakistan. Violence between Hindus and Muslims.

1949: India joins the Commonwealth.

1950s-1960s: Massive Indian and Pakistani immigration causes protests and racism (Commonwealth citizens have free entry into Britain).

Today, over half of Britain's Asian population is British-born, and no longer "immigrant", but racial tensions subsist.

Gandhi in England to negociate Indian independence

INDIANS AND PAKISTANIS IN BRITAIN

Indian and Pakistani traditions are kept alive in Britain through cultural events, festivals and food.

Bollywood films (Bombay's Hollywood) are very popular among Britain's Asian community. Meanwhile, some British films examine the clash of cultures and generations: in *Bend it like Beckham* (2001), an Asian girl wants to become a professional footballer, to her parents'despair.

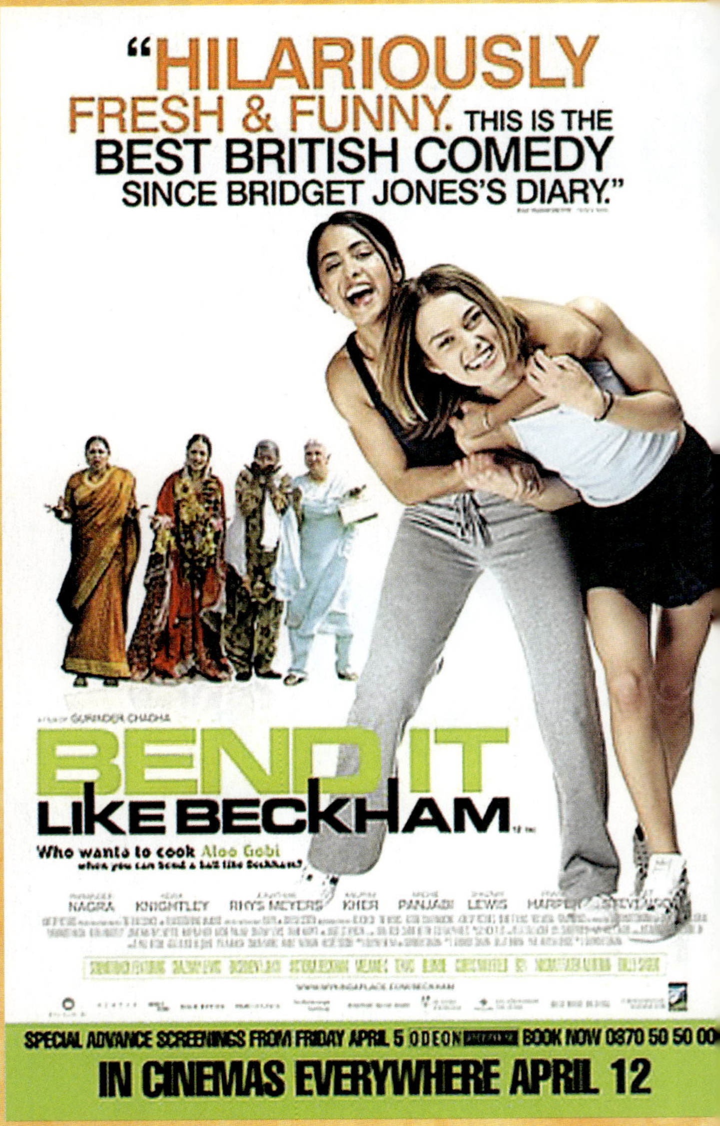

Bollywood video shop in London

Mending a fishing net, St Lucia

The economy of the Caribbean islands (Jamaica, St Lucia, Trinidad, Barbados, etc.) depends on sugar cane, bananas, fishing and tourism.

1950s: 30,000 West Indians a year arrive from the Caribbean.

1961-62: 98,000 West Indian immigrants arrive in Britain. The Commonwealth Immigration Act restricts entry into Britain.

Today, multi-ethnic Britain still goes through violent patches*.

*patches: *épisodes*

WEST INDIANS IN BRITAIN

In London's West Indian quarter

Jamaican Reggae star Jimmy Cliff

The West Indian heritage, like the Asian heritage, influences today's multi-ethnic pop, dub, rap and electronic music.

The Notting Hill Carnival

In 1966, London's Caribbean community decided to organize a carnival procession to celebrate their cultural heritage. Every year now, thousands of people come from all over the world to see the spectacular floats*, costumes and drum bands at the Notting Hill Carnival.

*floats: *chars*

A long walk to forever

They had grown up next door to each other, on the fringe of a city, near fields and woods and orchards[1], within sight of a lovely bell tower that belonged to a school for the blind.

Now they were twenty, had not seen each other for nearly a year. There had always been playful, comfortable warmth between them, but never any talk of love.

His name was Newt. Her name was Catharine. In the early afternoon, Newt knocked on Catharine's front door.

Catharine came to the door. She was carrying a fat, glossy[2] magazine she had been reading. The magazine was devoted entirely to brides[3]. "Newt!" she said. She was surprised to see him.

"Could you come for a walk?" he said. He was a shy person, even with Catharine. He covered his shyness by speaking absently, as though what really concerned him was far away, as though he were a secret agent pausing briefly on a mission between beautiful, distant, and sinister points. This manner of speaking had always been Newt's style, even in matters that concerned him desperately.

"A walk?" said Catharine.

"One foot in front of the other," said Newt, "through leaves, over bridges."

"I had no idea you were in town," she said.

"Just this minute got in," he said.

"Still in the Army, I see", she said.

"Seven more months to go," he said. He was a private first class in the Artillery. His uniform was rumpled[4]. His shoes were dusty. He needed a shave. He held out his hand for the magazine.

"Let's see the pretty book," he said.

She gave it to him. "I'm getting married, Newt," she said.

"I know," he said. "Let's go for a walk."

"I'm awfully busy, Newt", she said. "The wedding is only a week away."

"If you go for a walk," he said, "it will make you rosy. It will make you a rosy bride." He turned the pages of the magazine. "A rosy bride like her, like her, like her," he said, showing her rosy brides.

Catharine turned rosy, thinking about rosy brides.

"That will be my present to Henry Stewart Chasens," said Newt. "By taking you for a walk, I'll be giving him a rosy bride."

"You know his name?" said Catharine.

"Mother wrote," he said. "From Pittsburgh?"

"Yes," she said. "You'd like him."

"Maybe," he said.

"Can you come to the wedding, Newt?" she said.

"That I doubt," he said.

"Your furlough[5] isn't for long enough?" she said.

"Furlough?" said Newt. He was studying a two-page ad for flat silver[6]. "I'm not on furlough," he said.

"Oh?" she said.

"I'm what they call A.W.O.L.[7]," said Newt.

"Oh, Newt! You're not!" she said.

"Sure I am," he said, still looking at the magazine.

"Why, Newt?" she said.

"I had to find out what your silver pattern is," he said. He read names of silver patterns from the magazine.

"Albermarle? Heather?" he said. "Legend? Rambler Rose?" He looked up, smiled. "I plan to give you and your husband a spoon," he said.

"Newt, Newt tell me really," she said.

"I want to go for a walk," he said.

She wrung[8] her hands in sisterly anguish.

"Oh, Newt you're fooling me about being A.W.O.L.," she said.

Newt imitated a police siren softly, raised his eyebrows.

"Where from?" she said.

"Fort Bragg," he said.

"North Carolina?" she said.

"That's right," he said. "Near Fayetteville where Scarlet O'Hara went to school."

"How did you get here, Newt?" she said.

He raised his thumb, jerked it in a hitchhike gesture. "Two days," he said.

"Does your mother know?" she said.

"I didn't come to see my mother," he told her.

"Who did you come to see?" she said.

"You," he said.

"Why me?" she said.

"Because I love you," he said.

"Now can we take a walk?", he said. "One foot in front of the other through leaves, over bridges."

They were taking the walk now, were in a wood with a brown-leaf floor. Catharine was angry and rattled[9], close to tears.

"Newt," she said, "this is absolutely crazy."

"How so?" said Newt.

"What a crazy time to tell me you love me," she said. "You never talked that way before." She stopped walking.

"Let's keep walking," he said.

"No," she said. "So far, no farther. I shouldn't have come out with you at all," she said.

"You did", he said.

"To get you out of the house," she said. "If somebody walked in and heard you talking to me that way, a week before the wedding."

"What would they think?" he said.

"They'd think you were crazy," she said.

"Why?" he said.

Catharine took a deep breath, made a speech. "Let me say that I'm deeply honored by this crazy thing you've done," she said "I can't believe you're really A.W.O.L., but maybe you are. I can't believe you really love me, but maybe you do. But..."

.../...

NOTES

1. **an orchard** /'ɔ:tʃəd/: un verger.
2. **glossy:** en papier glacé.
3. **bride:** mariée.
4. **rumpled:** froissé.
5. **a furlough** /'fɜ:ləʊ/: une permission.
6. **flat silver:** argenterie mate.
7. **A.W.O.L. (absent without leave):** absent sans permission, déserteur.
8. **wring one's hands:** se tordre les mains.
9. **rattled:** ébranlée.

"I do," said Newt.

"Well, I'm deeply honored," said Catharine, "and I'm very fond of you as a friend, Newt, extremely fond, but it's too late." She took a step away from him. "You've never even kissed me," she said, and she protected herself with her hands. "I don't mean you should do it now. I just mean this is all so unexpected. I haven't got the remotest idea[10] of how to respond."

"Just walk some more," he said. "Have a nice time."

They started walking again.

"How did you expect me to react?" she said.

"How would I know what to expect?" he said. "I've never done anything like this before."

"Did you think I would throw myself into your arms?" she said.

"Maybe," he said.

"I'm sorry to disappoint you," she said.

"I'm not disappointed," he said. "I wasn't counting on it. This is very nice, just walking."

Catharine stopped again. "You know what happens next?" she said.

"Nope," he said.

"We shake hands," she said. "We shake hands and part friends," she said. "That's what happens next."

Newt nodded. "All right," he said. "Remember me from time to time. Remember how much I loved you."

Involuntarily, Catharine burst into tears. She turned her back to Newt, looked into the infinite colonade of the woods.

"What does that mean?" said Newt.

"Rage!" said Catharine. She clenched her hands. "You have no right."

"I had to find out," he said.

NOTES

10. **I haven't got the remotest idea:** Je n'ai pas la moindre idée.

11. **in the stockade:** au trou.

"If I'd loved you," she said, "I would have let you know before now."

"You would?" he said.

"Yes," she said. She faced him, looked up at him, her face quite red. "You would have known," she said.

"How?" he said.

"You would have seen it," she said. "Women aren't very clever at hiding it."

Newt looked closely at Catharine's face now. To her consternation, she realized that what she said was true, that a woman couldn't hide love. Newt was seeing love now. And he did what he had to do. He kissed her.

"You're hell to get along with!" she said when Newt let her go.

"I am?" said Newt.

"You shouldn't have done that," she said.

"You didn't like it?" he said.

"What did you expect?" she said. "Wild abandoned passion?"

"I keep telling you," he said, "I never know what's going to happen next."

"We say good-bye," she said.

He frowned slighty. "All right," he said.

She made another speech.

"I'm not sorry we kissed," she said. "That was sweet. We should have kissed. We've been so close. I'll always remember you Newt, and good luck."

"You too," he said. "Thank you, Newt," she said.

"Thirty days," he said.

"What?" she said.

"Thirty days in the stockade[11]," he said, "that's what one kiss will cost me."

"I, I'm sorry," she said, "but I didn't ask you to go A.W.O.L."

"I know," he said.

"You certainly don't deserve any hero's reward for doing something as foolish as that," she said.

"Must be nice to be a hero," said Newt.

"Is Henry Stewart Chasens a hero?"

"He might be, if he got the chance," said Catharine.

She noted uneasily that they had begun to walk again. The farewell had been forgotten.

"You really love him?" he said.

"Certainly I love him!" she said hotly. "I wouldn't marry him if I didn't love him!"

"What's good about him?" said Newt.

"Honestly!" she cried, stopping again. "Do you have any idea how offensive you're being? Many, many things are good about Henry! Yes," she said, "and many, many, many things are probably bad too. But that isn't any of your business. I love Henry, and I don't have to argue his merits with you!"

"Sorry," said Newt.

"Honestly!" said Catharine.

Newt kissed her again. He kissed her again because she wanted him to.

They were now in a large orchard.

"How did we get so far from home, Newt?" said Catharine.

"One foot in front of the other through leaves, over bridges," said Newt.

…/…

"They add up the steps," she said.

Bells rang in the tower of the school for the blind nearby.

"School for the blind," said Newt.

"School for the blind," said Catharine. She shook her head in drowsy wonder. "I've got to go back now," she said.

"Say good-bye," said Newt.

"Every time I do," said Catharine, "I seem to get kissed."

Newt sat down on the close-cropped grass under an apple tree.

"Sit down," he said.

"No," she said.

"I won't touch you," he said.

"I don't believe you," she said.

She sat down under another tree, twenty feet away from him. She closed her eyes.

"Dream of Henry Stewart Chasens," he said.

"What?" she said.

"Dream of your wonderful husband-to-be," he said.

"All right, I will," she said. She closed her eyes tighter, caught glimpses of[12] her husband-to-be. Newt yawned.

The bees were humming in the trees, and Catharine almost fell asleep. When she opened her eyes she saw that Newt really was asleep.

Catharine let Newt sleep for an hour, and while he slept she adored him with all her heart.

The shadows of the apple trees grew to the east. The bells in the tower of the school for the blind rang again. "Chick-a-dee-dee-dee;" went a chick -a-dee-dee-dee[13].

Somewhere far away an automobile started, nagged and failed[14], nagged and failed, failed still. Catharine came out from under her tree, knelt by Newt.

"Newt?" she said.

"H'm?" he said. He opened his eyes.

"Late," she said.

"Hello, Catharine," he said.

"Hello, Newt," she said.

"I love you," he said.

"I know," she said.

"Too late," he said.

"Too late," she said.

He stood, stretched groaningly[15]. "A very nice walk," he said.

"I thought so," she said.

NOTES

12. catch glimpses: apercevoir.

13. chickadee: oiseau de la famille des mésanges.

14. nagged (slang) and failed: démarrer et caler.

15. groaningly /'grəʊnɪŋlɪ/: en grognant.

16. turn oneself in: se rendre, se livrer.

"Part company here?" he said.

"Where will you go?" she said.

"Hitch into town, turn myself in[16]," he said.

"Good luck," she said.

"You, too," he said. "Marry me, Catharine?"

"No," she said.

He smiled, stared at her hard for a moment, then walked away quickly.

Catharine watched him grow smaller in the perspective of shadows and trees, knew that if he stopped and turned now, if he called to her, she would run to him. She would have no choice.

Newt did stop. He did turn. He did call.

"Catharine," he called.

She ran to him, put her arms around him, could not speak.

From Literary Cavalcade by *Kurt Vonnegut, Jr.*, 1960

HOW TO READ A SHORT STORY

Read the title and ask a few questions about this walk:

You: Where ... to? Is "forever" a place?

PART 1: line 1 to line 17

a. Try and find as much information as you can about the characters and the setting.

b. What would you like to know now?

See how you can be an active reader in your workbook (p. 143).

TIPS

The title and the beginning of a short story are very important because they give precious information about the characters and the setting.

PART 2: line 18 to line 104

a. Find the answers to your questions and recap orally what you've learned so far.

b. Read this passage again and concentrate on the characters. Take notes in your workbook (p. 144), then recap.

c. Imagine what's going to happen or answer the following questions about Catharine: Will she go? Does she love him?

TIPS

You must always be active when reading. Look for information about the characters' personalities and the situation they are in. Ask yourself questions, then look for the answers.
Imagine the rest of the story... and every now and then, recap all you know.

PART 3: line 105 to line 175

a. Make up you mind: does Catharine love him or not? If you can't decide or if you can't justify your answer, you'll find some help in your workbook (p. 144).
Now, take your pick:

- She loves him and she wants him to know.
- She is very angry and doesn't love him at all.
- She loves him and is trying hard to fight back her feelings.
- She doesn't love him and is trying hard to make him understand this.

b. What about Newt? What does he believe at this point (line 175)?

- He doesn't know whether she loves him or not.
- He finally understands she doesn't love him.
- He realizes she does love him.

PART 4: line 176 to line 197

a. Decide if you guessed right about how Catharine felt and what Newt believed.

b. Show that Catharine's attitude hasn't changed.

TIPS

When reading a dialogue, don't be fooled by what the characters say: pay attention to the way they act or react, to what they express (their body language), then draw your own conclusions.

PART 5: line 198 to line 210

a. At this point, Newt stops her from going back home.
How does he manage to do that? If you can't answer, you'll find help in your workbook (p. 144).

b. How would you describe Newt?
- He lacks confidence.
- He is clever.
- He is cunning.
- He is hesitant.
- He is determined.
- He is awkward.

TIPS

Read between the lines and pay careful attention to the characters' true intentions when they say or do things.

PART 6: line 211 to line 227

a. Sum up what Catharine says about Henry. Pick out the adverbs and say what the tone is.

b. What happens at the end of the passage? What does it reveal about Catharine's true feelings and about Newt's personality?

TIPS

Study the tone and the role of adverbs. Say what they reveal about the characters' psychology.

PART 7: line 228 to line 272

a. Note the changes in the actions and in the place. What does the orchard symbolize?
• plentifulness • peace and quiet • the garden of Eden
What does the school for the blind symbolize?
• suffering • Catharine's refusal to see her own feelings • Newt's determination

b. Which of these words apply to Catharine or Newt? Justify your answers by quoting from the text.
• revelation of love • jealousy • submission • irony

c. Now complete the sentence:
The long walk is over because… • they have stopped quarrelling • she has stopped fighting back her feelings • Newt has accepted his defeat.

TIPS

Pay attention to the changes in settings and what they mean and to the changes in the characters' attitude or feelings.

PART 8: line 273 to line 296

a. Why do they speak so little? Choose the right answers:
- They are cross.
- Everything has been said.
- They have nothing to say.
- They understand each other without speaking.

b. Pick out the sentence that shows that Catharine has changed and become more mature, aware of her own feelings.

c. Guess the end (remember the title) then read it (lines 297 to 300) and check your predictions.

TIPS

A short story often ends with a final twist (something unexpected but in fact announced in the title and many times throughout the story).
It is always interesting to read the story again and find the clues.

ABOUT the whole short story

a. What is the sentence Newt keeps repeating all along the short story?
What does it reveal about him?
- He likes walking.
- He knows where he is going.
- He has a set goal in life.
- He wants to show her the orchard.
- He wants Catharine to be rosy for her wedding.

b. What does the walk symbolize for Catharine?
• the way to love • the way to the orchard • the way to self-awareness

PAIRWORKS Pupil B (Practise speaking) p. 116

- File 1 lesson 1
- File 3 lesson 2
- File 6 lesson 1

SCRIPTS p. 119

PRÉCIS GRAMMATICAL p. 124

VERBES IRRÉGULIERS p. 168

EXPRESSIONS p. 170

LEXIQUE

ANGLAIS - FRANÇAIS p. 172

FRANÇAIS - ANGLAIS p. 190

CARTES p. 204

- Commonwealth
- Grande Bretagne
- États-Unis et Canada

PUPIL B

Practise speaking file 1 lesson 1

Guessing game. Team B. (Team A: Go to page 118)

a. Have a look at the Spriggan and read the information about it. Team A has exactly the same type of information about their creature.
Get ready by finding the five questions Team A will ask you.
E.g.: Cornwall ➜ Where does your creature come from?

- Cornwall
- ugly, small - long beard - big feet
- old rags* (usually)
- look after castles (most of the time)
- mean - cruel (kidnap babies - often)

* *haillons*

b. Answer Team A's question about the Spriggan. Give all the details. Then listen to their recapitulation and correct them if necessary.

c. Now ask these same five questions to Team A and find out about their creature. Then, recap all the information about Team A's creature. Can you give its name?

Practise speaking file 3 lesson 2

Group-work.

a. Team B: You are earthlings. Aliens (Team A) have abducted you.
Now they're questioning you. Use the information on the right to answer their questions.
Alien: Have you ... ... yet? (invent / discover / find)
Earthling: Yes, we have.
Alien: How long have you had it?
Earthling: We've had it since ...
Alien: You mean you've had it for ... years.
Earthling: Yes, that's right.
Alien: Have you already ... ...? (invent / discover / find)
Earthling: No, we haven't./ No, not yet.

Team B: EARTHLINGS' ANSWERS
1. yes - 1947
2. no
3. yes - 1957
4. no
5. yes - 1945

b. Now, ask questions to Team A, the aliens.
Use the information on the right.

Team B: EARTHLINGS' QUESTIONS
1. time travel
2. the pill for eternal youth
3. telepathy
4. a pill for happiness
5. teleportation

Practise speaking file 6 lesson 1

Pair-work. Play cool hunting.

a. **Pupil B: You are a teenager. A cool hunter is visiting you at home. Use the information below.**

Pupil A: You look ...! / You sound ...!
Pupil B: Yeah, well, I've been ...
Pupil A: Really! Do you mind if I ...? / May I ...? / Can I ask you what ...?

- listen to music all night

- play my new video game (for the first time)

- run (for miles)

b. Change roles.
Pupil B: You're a cool hunter. Use the information below.
Pupil B: Your hair look ... ! / You sound ... !
Pupil A: Yeah, well, I've been ...
Pupil B: Really! Can I ask you what ... ? / Do you mind if I ... ? / May I ... ?

- hair look great
- brand

- sound exhausted
- have a look at your bags

- look dead tired
- your favourite places

Practise speaking file 1 lesson 1

Guessing game. Team A. (Team B: Go to page 116)

a. Have a look at the Brownie and read the information about it. Team B has exactly the same type of information about their creature.
Get ready by finding the five questions Team B will ask you.

E.g.: Scotland ➜ Where does your creature come from?

- Scotland
- small (3 feet tall) - pointed ears - long fingers
- brown clothes (always)
- do the housework (work at night - usually)
- friendly and helpful - most of the time

b. Now ask these five same questions to Team B and find out about their creature. Then, recap all the information about Team B's creature. Can you give its name?

c. Answer Team B's questions about the Brownie. Give all the details. Then listen to their recapitulation and correct them if necessary.

FILE 1 • lesson 1

Listen and learn

Celtic creatures

Tara: Can I have a coke, please?
Waitress: There you go!
Tara: Thanks.
John: Excuse me... Where do you come from?
Tara: Me? I'm from Ireland... Why?
John: I am writing a report about Celtic supernatural creatures. I know the Brownies, from Scotland and the water-fairies from Wales... Are there any supernatural creatures in Ireland?
Tara: Sure... In Ireland we have Leprechauns.
John: Leprechauns... you say. What are they like?
Tara: Leprechauns are small, they are about a foot tall with a beard and a pointed nose. They often wear spectacles.
John: What do they do?
Tara: Well, Leprechauns are fantastic shoe-makers... they make shoes and sell them... that's why they are very rich, but they don't look rich, they usually look poor...
John: How come? What do they wear?
Tara: Leprechauns always wear green clothes, ...green is their favourite colour, you see. But their clothes are usually very old and worn-out because they absolutely hate spending money.
John: And are they good or bad fairies?
Tara: Leprechauns are friendly, most of the time... but they sometimes play practical jokes!!
John: Thanks for your help... Oh, and... um, I'm John... I'm in Year 11.
Tara: I'm Tara... I'm in...

Go forward

A Leprechaun watcher

Interviewer: Hi, what's your name...and how old are you?
Roddy: I'm Roddy O'Neil. and I'm 24 years old.
Interviewer: Where are you from Roddy?
Roddy: I'm based in Duluth, Minnesota.
Interviewer: So tell me Roddy... Are you a regular visitor to The Leprechaun Watch?
Roddy: Yeah, I love it. I'm a real addict.
Interviewer: How often do you visit this site?
Roddy: I visit it once or twice a week.
Interviewer: How long do you stay?
Roddy: Usually for a quarter of an hour, sometimes more, it depends...
Interviewer: And do you often see Leprechauns?
Roddy: Do I often see Leprechauns? Are you kidding? They are very small and they are really excellent at hiding, you know... so they are terribly difficult to spot, but sometimes I see... something unusual.
Interviewer: Oh yeah? like what?
Roddy: Well, I don't know what it is but... er... It's so exciting! Sometimes I see a strange shadow moving around or a tiny spot shining in the moonlight...
Interviewer: Oh! And what do you do then?
Roddy: I do the same thing every other Leprechaun watcher does: I report my sighting on the site so all the Leprechaun watchers around the world can hear about it.
Interviewer: So you really like Leprechaun-spotting, huh?
Roddy: I sure do! It's great fun... Why don't you try it?

FILE 1 • lesson 2

Listen and learn

A Celtic hero

Douglas: What? No way... It's impossible!
Suzie: But he did! I'm positive! He did exist!!
Douglas: No, he didn't! It's just a legend...
Suzie: Okay, well... Let's ask the history teacher... we'll see who's right! Excuse me, Miss...
Miss Nash: Yes, Suzie, what is it?
Suzie: Douglas here, tells me that King Arthur is just a legend, that he didn't really exist! But I don't agree with him. Can you tell us? Did he or didn't he exist?
Miss Nash: Well, everybody knows the King Arthur of the legend... but a King Arthur did exist and some historians say the legend comes from him.
Douglas: Oh really... And... um... When was he born?
Miss Nash: Let me look it up... there... He was born more than one thousand five hundred years ago... um... In 465.
Suzie: Where did he come from?
Miss Nash: He was Welsh. He lived in South Wales, in a province called Dyfed!
Douglas: Was he like the King Arthur of the legend?
Miss Nash: Well, he was very courageous, he fought many battles.
Suzie: Did he win many?
Miss Nash: Oh yes, many! Between 485 and 496 he won 12 great battles... against the Saxons. People thought he was invincible! But, he wasn't... of course!
Douglas: So how did he die? and when?
Miss Nash: He died in a battle... he was quite old, more than 75 years old..., he died in 542...

FILE 2 • lesson 1

Listen and learn
It hurts!

Alison: There's this big girl in my class... She sits next to me because she says she's my best friend, but she's not! She's always bullying me! She's always kicking me or slapping me when no one's looking... It hurts! She says everybody hates me because I'm ugly and stupid and a bore... and that hurts too...

And she makes me do things I don't want to do... cheat or steal things from others... If I don't want to do it, she says it's OK, but I know it's not OK... and I'm scared to death... and then, she follows me on my way back home and she hits me really hard... I don't want to go to school any more...

Here's my poem:

Feelings...
scared,
hurt,
worthless,
worried,
afraid,
angry,
alone,
depressed.
Everyone has feelings, so why bully?

FILE 2 • lesson 2

Go forward
The six core strengths

It's almost impossible to know what makes a child violent. But we do know that children who have these six core strengths won't become violent.

This first core strength is the most important of them all. Children who can't make friends, or who are unable to attach will isolate themselves and they may become frustrated or indifferent.

The capacity to join in activities with others is also very important because we are social animals! Children who are unable to join groups may feel rejected or excluded and they may become aggressive or hateful.

Now, the third core strength, the capacity to self-regulate, is essential. If a child doesn't develop it, he won't be able to control his actions or reactions. For example, he may express anger by kicking or hitting another child, or he may say mean things or hurtful remarks...

This last core strength is crucial because the source of all violence is lack of respect, for oneself and for others. When kids don't have respect, they value nothing, they don't value life, they don't value love, they don't value themselves and so, with no respect, children will become violent, they will say or do hateful things... but what they hate and ridicule in others is often what they hate in themselves.

Now... when children become young adults, they'll meet many many different kinds of people and they'll need to be able to listen, negociate, compromise and cooperate. Having respect is accepting others as they are, and this is crucial to make friends, join in and be a happy young adult!

FILE 3 • lesson 1

Listen and learn
An unusual poll

You're going to hear 7 questions. For each question, say if you've had this experience more than twice, once or twice, or never. Relax, listen to the questions and think... then listen again and write down your answers. Ready?

Question number 1: Have you ever seen a ghost?

Question number 2: Have you ever seen or dreamed about UFOs?

Question number 3: Have you ever woken up at night, paralyzed, with the feeling that a strange person or presence or something else was in the room?

Question number 4: Have you ever had an out-of-body experience, or OBE?

Question number 5: Have you ever experienced missing a period of time, not knowing where you were and what you did during this period of time?

Question number 6: Have you ever seen unusual lights or balls of light in a room?

Question number 7: Have you ever found strange unexplained scars on your body?

If you have answered "Yes" to four or five of questions 3 to 7, there is a strong possibility that aliens have abducted you... even if you can't remember anything.

FILE 3 • lesson 2

Listen and learn
Are we alone?

The aliens are coming...

Yeh! Well... maybe they are and maybe they aren't... *Are We Alone?* is your chance to call and ask questions. You'll get straight answers.

So join us for our weekly talk show *Are We Alone?* Produced by the SETI institute.

Radio show:
Jim: Good morning... thanks for taking my question er... How do you search for extra-terrestrial intelligent life?
Astronomer: At the SETI Institute, astronomers search for radio signals. You see, if there are intelligent aliens out there, they have certainly invented the radio! That's why, at SETI, we have looked for radio signals since the creation of the institute in 1960, that is for more than 40 years.

Brenda: Hi, I'm Brenda. Please, tell me... Why are E.T.s always more intelligent or more advanced than we are... I mean... in books or in movies?
Astronomer: Hello Brenda... Let me explain... the galaxy's been around for 15 billion years and the Earth has been around for 4.6 billion years so the Earth is much younger... that's why we suppose E.T.s are much more advanced... we suppose that they have existed for much longer!

Bruce: Hello, this is Bruce. Here is my question: OK, so there might be life in the universe... some bacteria, some traces of water or whatever... but do you *really* believe there could be *intelligent* life out there?
Astronomer: Well... You see, if one in a million planets with life has come up with intelligent creatures or even... one in ten million... that might be good enough! That's why, at SETI, we're still searching for intelligent life! We might be lucky... some day!

FILE 4 • lesson 2

Listen and learn

A promise

Paiute, Shoshone, Ute, Navajo, Apache, Blackfoot, Crow, Cheyenne, Arapaho, Lakotas or Sioux, Pawnee, Comanche, Shawnee, Cherokee, Choctaw, Seminole.

Teacher: We are now entering the Sioux section of the museum. Does anybody know the real name of the Sioux?
Student 1: The Lakotas?
Teacher: That's right! The Lakotas were the only tribe to defeat the U.S. Army in open battle. Did you know that?
Student 2: You mean... they won a battle against the U.S. Army...
Teacher: That's right... so in 1868, in Fort Laramie, Chief Red Cloud signed a peace treaty with the U.S. Army. In this treaty, the Lakotas were offered 2 things. They were offered a territory, and they were made a promise. They were promised that they would be left in peace... but...
Student 1: But they weren't left in peace...
Teacher: No.
Student 3: Were they attacked by the U.S. Army?
Teacher: Not exactly.
Student 2: So what happened then?
Teacher: As early as the 1880s... only 10 years after the treaty was signed, "detribalization" began...
Student 1: Detribalization?
Teacher: Yes, let's move to the next section and I will tell you about "detribalization"...

FILE 5 • lesson 1

Go forward

Raptime

Thanks for tuning in, you rap-lovers. Tonight "Raptime" is about a very special band – three boys, Joseph Simmons, Darryl MacDaniels and Jason Mizell from the middle-class New York borough of Queens. They had been rap fans for years when Joseph's brother, Russell, encouraged them to form a rap group.
Well, they did it! They formed "Orange Crush"... Now, who knows "Orange Crush"? We all do... because in 1982, the boys left school and changed the name of their group to... Run DMC.
Run DMC was not just another rap group, they revolutionized rap! They changed the face of rap forever!
Their first single "It's like that", in 1983, was a shock! A real breakthrough! Listen to these rock guitar samples. So aggressive! No other rappers had ever done that before. And the lyrics! So powerful! So meaningful! They really had something to say!
Now, in 1984, with their first album, simply called "Run DMC", something incredible happened! For the first time in the history of rap, an album sold more than one million copies... No rap album had ever reached gold record status before.
Their second album "King of Rock" was released in 1985. It was a huge hit too... Run DMC became incredibly popular! No rappers had ever been so popular before.
On top of that, in 1986, with the hit single "Walk this way", they managed to break into the white market... and this is something no other rap group had ever managed to do.
Run DMC released their 3rd album, *Raisin' Hell*, in

1987. It sold over 3 million copies in the USA, becoming the first platinum rap album, the first rap album to go to Number 1 in the R&B charts, and the first rap album to enter the U.S. top 10.
That's all for tonight... Meet me tomorrow night same time. Till then, keep rapping!

FILE 5 • lesson 2

Practise speaking
The police press conference

Police: We think the investigation will be long and difficult.
Reporter: Can you explain why?
Police: Because the two vandals were very careful.
Reporter: Have you found any fingerprints or any clues?
Police: No, we haven't. They worked with gloves.
Reporter: Are there any witnesses you can question?
Police: No, but we are going to question all the graffiti artists in Brisbane.
Reporter: Is it a crime to write graffiti?
Police: No, it isn't, most of the time. But Vas & Aike committed a crime because they broke into the airport and because they caused thousands of dollars of damage.

FILE 6 • lesson 1

Listen and learn
Cool hunting

- Excuse me, what are you drinking? Sprite? OK, thanks...
- Hi there! I see you've been buying stuff... do you mind if I take a look in your bags?
- Wow! I love your tattoo! Can I take a picture? Won't take long...
- Nice smell... you've been using hair conditioner... may I ask you what brand?
- Hi guys, can you tell me what music you' ve been listening to lately?

Go forward
Radio forum

Mediator: OK let's hear your reactions... Lorrie?
Lorrie: I'm Lorrie , I'm 15 , I'm a girl and guys say I'm cool and good-looking and I'm very happy with this, but it doesn't mean I think of myself as a sexual object...
Diana: I'm Diana, I'm 14 and I totally agree with Lorrie... this is revolting! It's the most degrading thing I've ever heard! We have a brain too!
Mediator: Ned?
Ned: That's the point! In both stereotypes, boys and girls are brainless...
Luke: Ned's right... I imagine the mook spends his time watching wrestling on TV and cracking dirty jokes...
Lorrie: ...and the midriff spends hours shopping and doing her hair I suppose...
Mediator: Does this reflect what you do? Diana?
Diana: No! I'd rather read a good detective story or go ice-skating than go shopping!
Mediator: Luke?
Luke: Well, I'd rather *play* sports than *watch* sports on TV! And I find wrestling violent and crude... and I know lots of words, not just four-letter words like, you know, "beep", "beep" and "beep"!
Mediator: OK, so you don't want to turn into a mook or a midriff, but you'd rather buy a product advertised by Britney Spears than a product advertised by an unknown girl...
Lorrie: Maybe so... but trust me, now, I'll think twice about it!
Ned: Me too... because, honestly, we aren't the morons they think we are.

FILE 6 • lesson 2

Listen and learn
A world that could die

The average North American consumes five times more than a Mexican, ten times more than a Chinese person, and thirty times more than a person from India.
(Burp!)
We are the most voracious consumers in the world... a world that could die because of the way we North Americans live.
Give it a rest!
November 29th is Buy Nothing Day.

What would happen if the Chinese consumed as much as we do?
Or if the Indians polluted as much as we do? What would happen if the whole world lived the American way of life? How long would our planet last?
You'd better think about it... Stop shopping, buy nothing, start living!
Participate by not participating!
November 29th is Buy Nothing Day.

FILE 7 • lesson 1

Go forward

Wishes and regrets

Canada, in Algoquian "the meeting place", is now an independent state, part of the Commonwealth... but about two hundred years ago, its fate almost took, not one, but two very different turns.
In 1812, for various reasons, a war broke out between the newly-founded United States of America and their ex-rulers, the British. The Americans had always regretted not incorporating Canada, the 14th colony as they called it, into the USA... so they took this opportunity to try and throw the British out of the northern American continent once and for all. They attacked Canada and that's when Canada's fate could have taken a different turn... but it didn't! The British resisted, thanks to the help of the First Nations. Canada remained British and the Americans promised never to attack and invade it again.
Now, that's not the end of the story... Apparently, around the same time, the French Emperor, Napoleon Bonaparte had a dream... He dreamed of reconquering New France. It is said that Napoleon took a great interest in Mackenzie's book and he supposedly used it to plot an invasion of Canada from the Mississippi River. That's when Canada's fate could have taken a second very different turn... but it didn't! As every serious history book will tell you, Napoleon invaded Russia, not Canada...
So it is that Canada remained British and from then on, it gradually and peacefully evolved into an independent State, part of the Commonwealth.

PRECIS GRAMMATICAL

La grammaire, qu'est-ce que c'est ?

Les quelques milliers de langues parlées dans le monde ont en commun les **deux** principes de fonctionnement suivants :
1. Chacune possède **un ensemble de sons** (voyelles et consonnes) à partir desquels sont fabriqués **les mots** (noms, verbes, adjectifs etc.).
L'anglais en comporte 49 et le français 36, alors que la moyenne se situe autour de trente sons.
2. Pour **fabriquer des phrases** à partir des mots d'une langue (les mots du dictionnaire), il existe des **règles du jeu**, comme pour le tennis, le football ou encore les jeux de cartes ! L'ensemble de ces règles constitue la **Grammaire**.

La grammaire de l'anglais est-elle facile ou difficile ?

L'anglais n'a ni féminin, ni masculin, les adjectifs sont invariables et les participes passés aussi ! Il y a tout de même quelques règles à savoir. Mais pour les français qui apprennnent l'anglais, c'est plutôt la compréhension de la langue orale, la prononciation et l'accentuation des mots et des phrases qui leur donneront du fil à retordre.
Au fond, on peut dire qu'en anglais, le plus difficile, ce n'est pas la grammaire, comme vous le verrez dans ce précis que l'on peut appeler : "les règles du jeu de l'anglais".

Les mots employés dans ce précis :

- **L'énonciateur**, c'est celui qui parle.
- Les **opérateurs** sont des mots comme **be, have, do** et les **modaux** qui permettent de faire **des opérations** : en maths on pose des additions, on fait des soustractions, en langue on pose des **questions**, on fait des **négations**, par exemple.
- Les **Temps grammaticaux** porteront toujours une majuscule (Présent) pour ne pas confondre avec le temps qui passe : le présent, le passé...

Sommaire

1. *Be - have*
2. Les temps de l'anglais
3. Les modaux
4. Parler de l'avenir en anglais
5. Les énoncés interrogatifs
6. Style direct / style indirect
7. Un verbe en suit un autre
8. La voix passive
9. Le nom
10. Pronoms, possessifs, réfléchis
11. Les articles
12. *This / that*
13. Les prépositions
14. Les quantifieurs
15. Les adjectifs
16. Le comparatif et le superlatif
17. Pronoms relatifs et propositions relatives
18. Connecteurs de phrases

1 BE - HAVE

A. Be

1. Un peu de mécanique

SUJET	PRESENT	PRÉTÉRIT
I	am	was
You	are	were
he/she/it	is	was
we	are	were
you	are	were
they	are	were

Participe passé : **been** /biːn/

Prononciation

Présent

	accentué	inaccentué
am	Yes, I **am**! /æm/	Hi! I'm Kate. /m/ **Am** I late again? /əm/
are	Yes, we **are**! /ɑː/	My parents **are** late. /ə/ **Are** you happy? /ə/
is	Yes, it **is**. /ɪz/ **Is** it yours? /ɪz/	Kate's here. /s/ Bryan's at school. /z/

Prétérit

	accentué	inaccentué
was	Yes, I **was**! /wɒz/	Josh **was** late. /wəz/ **Was** she angry? /wəz/
were	Yes, we **were**! /wɜː/	My parents **were** out. /wə/ **Were** you happy? /wə/

Attention aux négations !
are + not : **aren't** (/ɑːnt/ en une seule syllabe : comme *can't* /kɑːnt/)
were + not : **weren't** (/wənt/ en une seule syllabe)

2. Emploi

Be est un verbe un peu "spécial" car il peut être **à la fois verbe et opérateur** : il n'a pas besoin d'un autre opérateur au Présent et au Prétérit pour les questions et les négations.

- **Présent** : Hi! I'**m** Josh. How **are** you? My baby brother **is** a pain. We **aren't** ready! Where **are** my jeans?
- **Prétérit** : Where **were** you last night? I **was** out. Josh's parents **weren't** at home last night. My sister **was** ill last week.

Be ne fait appel à *Do* que pour l'impératif :
Be careful! (Fais attention !)
Do be careful! (Fais bien attention !)
Don't be late!

• opérateur :
- au Présent *Be + -ing* . Voir 4
- au Prétérit *Be + -ing* . Voir 9
- au passif. Voir 64

• verbe :
- avec un modal. Voir chapitre 3.
- à tous les Temps sauf au Présent et Prétérit simple où il est à la fois verbe et opérateur.

PIÈGE !

À une construction avec *Be* en anglais, correspond quelquefois une construction avec "avoir" en français:

I'm 13. I'm 13 years old. = J'ai 13 ans.
She's hungry / thirsty. = Elle a faim/ soif.
He's cold. = Il a froid.
There is... / there are... = il y a...

2 B. *Have*

1. Un peu de mécanique

	PRESENT	PRÉTÉRIT
I	**have** /hæv/	**had** /hæd/
You	**have**	**had**
he/she/it	**has** /hæz/	**had**
we	**have**	**had**
you	**have**	**had**
they	**have**	**had**

2. Emploi

Have peut être employé comme :

• **verbe** : il se comporte comme n'importe quel verbe.

Il fait appel à l'opérateur ***do*** (*does/did)* pour les questions et les négations au Présent et au Prétérit simples, comme tous les autres verbes sauf *Be* :

- My parents **have** breakfast at 7.
- Josh **had** breakfast in bed this morning.
- I **don't have** enough money.
- My friends **did not have** time.
- When **does** she **have** her French class?
- Where **did** you **have** lunch?

• **opérateur**

Have + got : l'anglais exprime la possession de deux façons. Soit avec ***have*** comme verbe, soit avec ***have + got***, ou *have* et opérateur.

- I'**ve** got an idea.
- My sister'**s** got two hamsters.
- How many pets **have** they got ?

Have est employé comme opérateur dans d'autres cas, comme le *Present perfect*.
Voir 10

Prononciation

Have opérateur en position inaccentuée est le plus souvent réduit :

I'**ve** got a new bike. /v/
My sister'**s** got a new boyfriend. /z/
Have you got a stamp? /həv/

2 LES TEMPS DE L'ANGLAIS

L'anglais possède *deux* Temps grammaticaux : le Présent et le Prétérit. Chacun de ces deux Temps peut être combiné avec *Be + -ing*, ce qui donne deux possibilités pour chaque Temps:

Présent simple	Josh **plays** tennis.
Présent *Be + -ing*	Josh **is** [play**ing** tennis].

Prétérit simple	Josh **played** tennis.
Prétérit *Be + -ing*	Josh **was** [play**ing** tennis].

3 A. Le Présent simple

1. Un peu de mécanique

a. Énoncés affirmatifs

SUJET	VERBE	COMPLEMENT(S)
I/We/You/They	play	in the garden.
He/She/It	plays	in the garden.

Pour certains verbes, on trouve aussi la terminaison *–es* à la troisième personne du singulier:

go → go**es** /z/
wash → wash**es** /ɪz/
watch → watch**es** /ɪz/
kiss → kiss**es** /ɪz/
miss → miss**es** /ɪz/

b. Énoncés négatifs

SUJET	OPERATEUR + NOT	GROUPE VERBAL
I / you / we / they	**do not** (don't /dəʊnt/)	play in the garden.
she / he / it	**does not** (doesn't /dʌznt/)	play in the garden.

c. Énoncés interrogatifs/réponses brèves

Yes/no questions (questions fermées)

OPERATEUR	SUJET	GROUPE VERBAL
Do	I / you / we / they	play in the garden?
Does	he / she / it	play in the garden?

- **Do** you like fish?
- Yes, I **do**. / No, I **don**'t.

- **Does** Josh like fish?
- Yes, he **does**. / No, he **doesn**'t.

Wh- questions (questions ouvertes)

MOT INT.	OPERATEUR	SUJET	GR. VERBAL
Where	**do**	I / you / we /they	play?
Where	**does**	he / she / it	play?

2. Emploi

Celui qui parle, l'énonciateur, informe son interlocuteur. Il le renseigne : ce qui est important, c'est l'information en elle-même.

• Questions et réponses lorsqu'on fait connaissance :

- Where **do** you **live**?
- I **live** in London.

- What **does** your mother **do**?
- She **works** at the Royal Free Hospital.

• Pour exprimer ou interroger sur ses sentiments, ses opinions, sa volonté, ses goûts :

- I **think** it **is** too expensive.
- What **do** you **think** of this book?
- I **agree** with you.
- **Do** you **like** my cake?
- I **like** your new shoes.
- Where **do** you **want** to go?

• Pour décrire une situation :

- Listen! There **is** a funny noise in the tent. I **think** it **comes** from under my sleeping bag.

• Quand on veut simplement donner une information (date, horaire, ...)

- England **plays** against Scotland on March 15th. (rugby...)
- My train **leaves** at 5 pm.

4 B. Le Présent *Be + -ing*

1. Un peu de mécanique

C'est ***Be*** qui est l'opérateur aux trois formes : affirmative, interrogative et négative. Il est conjugué au Présent, il porte la négation et passe devant le sujet dans les questions.
-ing est collé à la base verbale.

a. Énoncés affirmatifs

- I'**m** read**ing** a book.

am est la plupart du temps réduit à /m/

- You'**re** com**ing** with me.

are est la plupart du temps réduit à /ə/

- She'**s** driv**ing**.

is est la plupart du temps réduit à /z/

b. Énoncés négatifs

- He **is** not wear**ing** a suit.

is + ***not*** est la plupart du temps prononcé soit ***'s not***, soit ***isn't*** /ɪznt/.

- They **are** not stay**ing** for tea.

are + ***not*** est la plupart du temps prononcé soit ***'re not***, soit ***aren't*** /ɑːnt/.

c. Énoncés interrogatifs

Yes/no questions

- **Am** I see**ing** things?

Am est la plupart du temps réduit à /əm/

- **Are** you com**ing**?

Are est la plupart du temps réduit à /ə/

Wh- questions

- When **are** they com**ing** back?
- Where **is** she go**ing** for the holidays?

2. Emploi

En anglais, on a déjà le Présent simple. Pourquoi un deuxième Présent ?
Rappel : Au Présent simple celui qui parle informe, renseigne. Ce qui est important, c'est l'information en elle-même.
Quand je dis:

- I **go** back on Monday (Présent simple).

Je donne ma date de retour de vacances. L'information, c'est *Monday*.

Quand je dis :

- I'**m** go**ing** back on Monday.

Je dis cela pour faire remarquer qu'il ne me reste que quelques jours de vacances, et que je n'aurai pas le temps de tout faire, etc. En fait, je parle de moi.

Avec le Présent *Be + -ing*, ce n'est pas l'information en elle-même qui est importante. Celui qui parle donne ou demande des explications, justifie, etc. Il y a toujours une raison autre que l'information elle-même pour utiliser le Présent *Be + -ing*.

Observe les exemples suivants :

- "What **are** the children do**ing**?"

On pose cette question quand :
- on n'entend plus rien depuis quelques minutes ou on ne voit plus les enfants ;
- on entend un vacarme épouvantable ;
- on a besoin d'eux (mettre la table, etc.) ;
- on téléphone à la baby-sitter pour s'assurer que tout va bien.

Au fond, on s'intéresse plutôt aux enfants qu'à ce qu'ils font.

Bob: Dinner is ready!
John: Just a minute! I'**m** *wash**ing** the car.*

En disant *"I'**m** wash**ing** the car"***,** John explique pourquoi il ne peut pas venir tout de suite. On peut dire que *"wash**ing** the car"* est son **alibi**.

Bryan : Can you come over tonight?
Chris : Tonight... Oh no, I'm busy. I'**m** *walk**ing** my neighbours' dog.*

Chris dit cela pour dire qu'il est pris. "*Walking my neighbour's dog*" est son excuse.

- She sits next to me because she says she's my best friend, but she's not! She'**s** always bully**ing** me!

Celle qui parle justifie ce qu'elle a dit juste avant en donnant une explication.

- Come on Tamara, don't cry. When I ***say*** you're not good at French, I'**m** not say**ing** you're worthless!

Avec *I* ***say*** ... (Présent simple) l'énonciateur informe. Avec *I'**m** not say**ing** you're worthless*, il se justifie = Je n'ai jamais dit cela !

5 C. Le Prétérit simple

1. Un peu de mécanique

• Le Prétérit simple s'obtient à partir de la base verbale à laquelle on ajoute la terminaison ***-ed*** ou ***-d*** pour la majorité des verbes :

arrive → arriv**ed** /d/
play → play**ed** /d/
happen → happen**ed** /d/
kiss → kiss**ed** /t/
ask → ask**ed** /t/
wash → wash**ed** /t/
want → want**ed** /ɪd/

• Un petit nombre de verbes – mais on les utilise souvent – sont des verbes dits "irréguliers". (voir liste pages 168-169)

a. Énoncés affirmatifs

• I play**ed** football last night.
• My brother miss**ed** his bus yesterday morning.

b. Énoncés négatifs

• My sister **did** not phone.
• The neighbours **did** not see me.

Prononciation : ***did + not*** est la plupart du temps réduit à ***didn't*** /dɪdnt/

c. Énoncés interrogatifs/réponses brèves

Yes/no questions

• **Did** you play in the garden? (I **did**. / I **didn't**.)
• **Did** Josh watch TV? (He **did**. / He **didn't**.)

Wh- questions

- Where **did** he play?
- He play**ed** in the garden.

- When **did** we go to London ?
- Last year.

- What **did** they watch last night?
- They watch**ed** a film on BBC2.

2. Emploi

a. Celui qui parle – l'énonciateur – renseigne son interlocuteur à propos de ce qui a eu lieu avant, dans le passé. Il y a un *décalage entre le moment où il parle et le moment où les choses ont eu lieu.* Ce qui compte, c'est l'information.

• Sir Arthur Conan Doyle creat**ed** Sherlock Holmes in 1887.
• And then Mordred rebell**ed**...
- So what **did** Arthur do?
- He **went** back to England.
• What happen**ed** to Mackenzie?
- Well, he end**ed** up at the Arctic ocean instead of the Pacific!

6 *ago* : compagnon de route du Prétérit

En français : *J'ai reçu ta lettre **il y a** 2 semaines.*
En anglais : I receiv**ed** your letter *2 weeks* **ago**.

ago se place **après** l'indication de temps exprimée sous la forme de **temps mesuré** :

a hundred and fifty years **ago**
5 years **ago**
a month **ago**
2 minutes **ago**

- **How long ago** did you phone the doctor?
(Il y a combien de temps que ...?)
- (I phon**ed** him) 20 minutes **ago**.

7 Prétérit + *for*

Le Prétérit signale que ce dont on parle a eu lieu dans le passé, et ***for* + durée mesurée** permet de dire **pendant** combien de temps.

• He liv**ed** **for** 75 years.
• He **fought** against the Romans **for** more than ten years.

La question correspondante est *How long?* :

• **How long** did he live?
• **How long** did he fight against the Romans?

8 b. Le Prétérit est aussi employé pour envisager une situation en *décalage par rapport à la réalité des faits présents.*

• If I play**ed** in a sitcom I would become rich and famous. (Si je jouais .../ je deviendrais...)
• What if you **sent** them a tape? You might be selected. (Et si tu leur envoyais...)
• She would have a heart attack if I **told** her I want**ed** to be an actress. (... si je lui disais que je voulais...)

Compare :

If I **play** in a sitcom... / If I play**ed** in a sitcom...

- If I **play**: simple hypothèse dont il est question pour la première fois ;
- If I play**ed**: celui qui parle indique que cette hypothèse a déjà été envisagée.

Voir 39

Après ***I wish*** ou encore ***If only*** on trouve le Prétérit quand l'énonciateur évoque le contraire de la situation présente (décalage avec la réalité présente).

situation actuelle	situation désirée
I don't know many people.	**I wish I knew** more people at this party.
I don't have the necessary instruments.	**If only I had** the necessary intruments.

Remarque :

Dans cet emploi du Prétérit, la conjugaison de *be* peut faire appel à ***were*** pour **toutes les personnes :**

If I was/**were** you (Si j'étais toi)

If only he **were** with me... (si seulement il était avec moi...)

9 D. Le Prétérit *Be + -ing*

1. Un peu de mécanique

C'est ***Be*** (voir 1) au Prétérit qui est l'opérateur. ***-ing*** se colle à la base verbale.

a. Énoncés affirmatifs

I **was** listen**ing** to the radio.
/wəz/
They **were** leaving.
/wə/

b. Énoncés négatifs

He **was**n't listening.
/wɒznt/
We **were**n't looking.
/wənt/

c. Énoncés interrogatifs/réponses brèves

Yes/no questions

- **Were** you danc**ing** with his girlfriend?
- Yes, I **was**.
/wɒz/
- **Was** she chatt**ing** with her neighbour?
- No, she **wasn't**.
/wɒzn'ˈt/

Wh- questions

What **were** you do**ing** in my garage?
Where **was** she go**ing**?

2. Emploi

Comme avec le Présent *Be + -ing*, dans un énoncé au Prétérit *Be + -ing* l'énonciateur utilise le groupe verbal en *-ing* pour expliquer, justifier – et non informer directement – à propos de quelque chose qui s'est déroulé dans le passé.

Observe ces exemples :

- Arthur **was** fight**ing** Lancelot in France when Mordred rebelled.

En disant *"Arthur was fighting Lancelot in France"* l'énonciateur explique ici dans quelle situation se trouvait Arthur pour dire ensuite ce qui s'est passé : *Mordred rebelled.*

- What **were** you do**ing** when Mordred rebelled?

On demande ici dans **quelle situation se trouvait** la personne que l'on interroge – on lui demande par exemple son alibi, elle doit s'expliquer.

- Arthur **was** fight**ing** Lancelot in France when Mordred rebelled. He couldn't stop the rebellion immediately.

En disant *"Arthur was fighting Lancelot in France"* l'énonciateur **explique avant tout pourquoi Arthur n'a pas pu arrêter** la rébellion immédiatement.

10 E. Le *Present perfect*

1. Un peu de mécanique

Le ***Present perfect*** se construit avec le **Présent** de ***Have*** et le **participe passé du verbe** qui suit. C'est ***Have*** *(voir* 2*)* qui est l'opérateur : il passe devant le sujet dans les questions et prend la négation.
Pour la majorité des verbes, le participe passé est semblable au Prétérit : on ajoute *-d* ou *-ed* à la fin du verbe. Pour les verbes dits irréguliers, voir la liste page 168-169 :

donner : give, gave, **given**
prendre : take, took, **taken**
voir : see, saw, **seen**

a. Énoncés affirmatifs

SUJET	HAVE	GROUPE VERBAL
I/you we/they	**have** ('ve)	open**ed** the door. (rég.)
he/she/it	**has** ('s)	**seen** a monster. (irrég.)

b. Énoncés négatifs

- I **haven't** seen that film.
- He **hasn't** open**ed** his present.

c. Énoncés interrogatifs / réponses brèves

Yes/no questions

- **Has** she post**ed** my letter?
- Yes, she **has**.

- **Have** you **brought** new batteries?
- No, I **haven't**.

Wh- questions

- What **have** they **done**?
- Where **has** she been?

2. Emploi

Le *Present perfect* est un **lien** entre le passé et le présent. Il permet à l'énonciateur de dire, de constater **maintenant, au moment présent où il parle,** qu'il (ou quelqu'un d'autre) a fait telle ou telle chose avant, que telle ou telle chose s'est produite, sans donner de date ou de repère temporel précis. **Ce qui est important, c'est d'en parler maintenant – c'est le moment présent qui l'emporte.** C'est pourquoi on peut dire que le *Present perfect* est un "satellite" du Présent : ***have*** est conjugué au Présent.

- Guess what?! I **have forgotten** the new batteries for the torch.

L'énonciateur constate et annonce maintenant l'oubli des piles – l'oubli a eu lieu avant. C'est le constat présent qui compte : la lampe torche ne marche pas !

- They say *Star Wars* is a very good film. I just don't know. I **have** not seen it.
- I'd love to go to Australia. I **have** never seen a koala.

Le constat peut comporter une négation : ***never*** ou ***not.***

- **Have** you seen *Star Wars?*
- **Have** you been to Germany?

Dans ces deux questions, l'énonciateur veut faire un **bilan présent** de ce que connaît son interlocuteur – films vus, pays visités...

11 *Present perfect* et *ever*

Ever, tel un radar, signale que l'on passe en revue une période donnée. Avec le *Present perfect,* on part du présent et on "balaie" le passé pour savoir si ce dont on parle a eu lieu au moins une fois.

1. **Have** you seen a crocodile?

Quelle différence avec :

2. **Have** you ever seen a crocodile?

1 = Simple demande de renseignements : tu as vu un crocodile ou pas ?
2 = Est-ce que dans ta vie tu as déjà vu un crocodile ?

12 *Present perfect* et *yet*

- I have**n't** caught a fish **yet**.

Yet signale que pour l'énonciateur les choses sont attendues, qu'elles auront lieu à un moment ou un autre.

Compare :

I **haven't** see**n** Josh today. (Je ne l'ai pas vu. = On ne dit pas si on le verra.)
I **haven't** see**n** Josh today **yet**. (Je ne l'ai pas encore vu. = Je m'attends à le voir.)

13 *It is the first time* + *Present perfect* *It is* + superlatif + *Present perfect*

Dire ***It is (not) the first time*** ou encore ***It is the most*** + adjectif / *the best* + nom signifie que l'énonciateur effectue un bilan au moment présent après avoir fait appel à sa mémoire, donc au passé. Voilà pourquoi c'est le *Present perfect* qui est employé dans le cas où une phrase commence par ***It is the first / second / etc. time*** ou encore ***It is the most*** + adjectif / ***the best*** + nom.

- It is the first time in the history of mankind that teenagers **have** represente**d** so much money.
- It is the most degrading thing I'**ve** ever **heard**!
- It is the best shampoo I **have** ever **used**.
- It is the smallest car I **have seen** in my whole life.

Autres exemples :

- It is the second cake I **have made** this week.
- It is not the first Japanese car I **have bought**.

14 PIÈGE !

Prétérit ou *Present perfect* ?

a. Tu sais quoi ? J'**ai** perdu mes clés. Je suis sûr que je les **ai** perdues ce matin en allant à l'école.

b. Est-ce que tu **as vu** le dernier film de Spielberg ?
- Oui, bien sûr.
- Tu l'**as vu** quand ?
- Je l'**ai vu** il y a deux semaines.

Le français offre la même conjugaison – le passé composé – face au Prétérit et au *Present perfect* de l'anglais. Comment faire pour choisir entre les deux ?

Constat présent → *Present perfect*
Récit d'événements passés → Prétérit

a. Guess what? I **have lost** my keys.
(= constat **présent** de la perte qui a eu lieu avant)
I am sure I **lost** them this morning on my way to school. (= **récit**)

b. Have you **seen** Spielberg's latest film?
(= **bilan** de ce que connaît l'interlocuteur)
- Of course I **have**.
- When **did** you **see** it?
(= **récit** – on s'intéresse au passé avec la question *When?*)
- I **saw** it two weeks **ago**. (= **récit**)

15 *Present perfect* avec *since*

Employé avec ***since*** qui signale que l'on introduit **un point de départ** (une date, un événement) le *Present perfect* permet de faire le point – faire un bilan – au moment présent : on parle de choses dont le commencement se situe dans le passé et qui sont toujours vraies au moment présent. (voir piège, 18).

- **Since** the creation of SETI in 1960, astronomers **have** looke**d** for radio signals.

Since peut être suivi :
- d'une date : **since 1960**
- d'un groupe nominal : **since the creation of SETI**
- d'une proposition au Prétérit : **since we created SETI**

16 *Present perfect* avec *for*

Employé avec ***for*** qui introduit **une durée** (ou du "temps mesuré" : *two minutes, five hours, ten years*, etc.) le *Present perfect* permet de faire le point – de faire un bilan – au moment présent : on dit **depuis combien de temps** les choses durent.

- Astronomers **have** looke**d** for radio signals **for** 40 years.

17 *Present perfect* simple et la question *How long?*

Poser une question avec *How long* suivi du *Present perfect* simple signifie qu'on s'intéresse avant tout à la durée : on fait le point.

- How long **have** you live**d** here?
- How long **has** he **had** this car? It looks new.

On répond à l'aide de ***for*** :

- (I've lived here) **for** 3 years.
- (He's had it) **for** 6 months.

Ou à l'aide de ***since*** :

- I have lived here **since** 1997.
- He has had this car **since** he got a new job.

Si c'est le point de départ qui intéresse l'énonciateur, la question ***Since when?*** est possible :

- **Since when** have you lived here?

18 PIÈGE !

1. Présent en français ➜ *Present perfect* en anglais

a. **Depuis** la création de SETI en 1960, les astronomes **sont** à la recherche de/**cherchent** des signaux radio.
➜ *Since the creation of SETI in 1960 astronomers **have looked** for radio signals.*

b. Les astronomes **cherchent** des signaux radio **depuis** 40 ans.
Cela fait 40 ans que les astronomes cherchent des signaux radio.
➜ *Astronomers **have looked** for radio signals for 40 years.*

2. Le français DEPUIS peut être traduit par ***since*** ou ***for***.
Depuis 1960 ➜ ***Since** 1960.*
Depuis 40 ans ➜ ***For** 40 years.*
Mais face à : **Cela fait 40 ans que...** seul ***for*** marche car on mesure le temps écoulé.

3. Il est là **depuis 4 heures ...**

a. depuis 4 heures = l'heure que donne la montre = point de départ
➜ *He has been here **since** 4 o'clock.*

b. depuis 4 heures = 4 x 60 minutes = temps écoulé
➜ *He has been here **for** four hours.*

19 F. Le *Present perfect Be + -ing*

1. Un peu de mécanique

Il s'agit de la combinaison du *Present perfect* et de *Be + -ing* :

• Nice smell ... you **have** *be***en** us*ing* hair conditioner. ... May I ask you what brand?

Le *Present perfect Be + -ing* se construit avec le **Présent** de ***Have*** (voir 2) suivi du **participe passé** de ***Be*** – ***been*** – et de **V-ing**. Comme pour le *Present perfect* simple (voir 10) **l'opérateur** est ***have***.

a. Énoncés affirmatifs

SUJET	HAVE	BEEN	GROUPE VERBAL en *-ing*
I/you/we/they	have	been	using hair conditioner.
he/she/it	has	been	using hair conditioner.

b. Énoncés négatifs

• I **haven't been** us**ing** hair conditioner.
• She **hasn't been** buy**ing** stuff.

c. Énoncés interrogatifs / réponses brèves

Yes/no questions

• **Have** you **been** us**ing** hair conditioner?
Yes, I **have**.
• **Has** she **been** buy**ing** stuff?
No, she **hasn't**!

Wh- questions

• How long **have** you **been** celebrat**ing** Buy Nothing Day?

2. Emploi

Comme il y a deux Présents et deux Prétérits – simples et *Be + -ing* – il y a deux *Present perfect*. Avec le *Present perfect Be + -ing*, l'énonciateur utilise le groupe verbal en *-ing* pour **dire maintenant**, au moment présent, **quelque chose à propos du sujet**. Ce dont il parle a eu lieu avant. Le but n'est pas pour l'énonciateur d'informer directement, mais de justifier, d'expliquer, de déduire, etc.

• Nice smell... you **have been** us**ing** hair conditioner. ...May I ask you what brand?

En produisant cet énoncé, l'énonciateur indique au sujet *you* (une jeune fille) qu'il a déduit/compris *(nice smell!)* qu'elle avait utilisé de l'après-shampoing. En utilisant la forme en *-ing*, il lui indique qu'il **s'intéresse à elle** avant tout.

• Sorry, I'm late. I **have been** do**ing** some shopping with mum.

L'énonciateur, après s'être excusé, explique, justifie son retard. S'il voulait, dans une autre situation, annoncer qu'il avait fait des courses pour simplement informer, il aurait employé le *Present perfect* simple :

• I **have bought** 12 bottles of Coke and five packets of crisps for the party. Do you think it is enough?

• What **have** you **been** buy**ing**?

En posant cette question l'énonciateur ne s'intéresse pas directement aux choses achetées. Non, il demande par exemple à *you* d'expliquer pourquoi il n'a plus d'argent, pourquoi il a un air mystérieux/coupable, etc. Ce qui a déclenché la question n'est pas l'envie de connaître la liste des achats, c'est autre chose, d'où l'emploi du *Present perfect Be + -ing*.

Si on veut savoir précisément ce que quelqu'un a acheté on dit tout simplement : *What have you **bought**?*
Celui qui pose cette question attend une énumération, une liste des choses achetées. La question est au *Present perfect* simple.

20 *Present perfect Be + -ing* avec *since* et *for* (voir 15 16).

Employé soit avec ***since*** qui signale que l'on introduit **un point de départ** (une date, un événement) ou encore avec ***for*** qui introduit **une durée** (ou du "temps mesuré" : *two minutes, five hours, ten years*, etc.), le *Present perfect Be + -ing* permet de faire le point – de faire un bilan – au moment présent **à propos du sujet** : on dit **depuis quand** ou **depuis combien de temps** le sujet **fait** telle ou telle chose, pour expliquer, justifier, déduire, etc. quelque chose qui le concerne.

- His English is very good now of course. He **has been** liv**ing** in England **since** 1995 you know.

Le but ici n'est pas uniquement de dire depuis quand he vit en Angleterre, mais **d'expliquer pourquoi il parle bien anglais**.

- Big deal! I'**ve been** celebrat**ing** BND **for years now**! *(BND = Buy Nothing Day)*

En disant cela l'énonciateur dit en fait qu'il n'a pas attendu un jour précis pour fêter BND, qu'il est au courant depuis longtemps, etc. Il veut dire que lui **fait déjà ce qu'il faut**.

21 *Present perfect Be + -ing* et la question *How long?*

Poser une question *How long* avec le *Present perfect Be + -ing* signifie que l'on s'intéresse au sujet avant tout.

- How long **have** you **been** learn**ing** English?

C'est la question que l'on pose très souvent quand le sujet parle très bien ou... très mal anglais, qu'il va avoir besoin de l'anglais pour son travail, etc. On demande au sujet des explications le concernant. Ce n'est pas simplement la durée qui est importante ici.

- How long **have** you **been** liv**ing** here?

On pose cette question à quelqu'un qui semble bien connaître la ville, le quartier, ou se plaint du bruit, etc. On veut en savoir un peu plus sur lui. Si on s'intéresse uniquement à la durée (renseignements administratifs par exemple) on dit simplement :

- How long **have** you live**d** here?

22 PIÈGE !

Présent en français → *Present perfect* (simple ou *Be + -ing*) en anglais

a. C'est la première fois qu'il **prend** un taxi.
b. Elle **habite** Paris depuis 5 ans maintenant (et je crois que ça lui plaît).
c. Il parle bien anglais. Normal, il **vit** en Angleterre depuis 5 ans.

Les deux langues n'ont pas la même logique : pour traduire **a.** **b.** et **c.** l'anglais fait appel au *Present perfect*.

Pour traduire b. et c. il faut non seulement choisir le *Present perfect* mais également choisir entre simple et *Be + -ing*. Les deux *Present perfect* ne s'emploient pas au hasard.

a. It is the first time he **has taken** a taxi.
b. She **has** live**d** in Paris for 5 years now *and I think she likes it.*

Ce qui importe c'est de dire où elle habite et depuis quand.

c. *He speaks very good English.* Of course, he **has been** liv**ing** in England for 5 years.

Ce qui importe c'est d'expliquer pourquoi il parle bien.

Pour traduire "il **fait** ceci **depuis** 2 ans - il **fait** ceci **depuis** 2001", il faut avant tout avoir le "**réflexe *Present perfect***". Le choix entre simple ou *Be + -ing*, dépend de ce que l'on veut dire exactement.
Si on s'intéresse **:**
- **au groupe verbal** *(lived in Paris for 5 years)* = *Present perfect* **simple**
- **au sujet** = *Present perfect **Be** + **-ing***.

23 G. Le *Pluperfect* (ou Prétérit *perfect*)

1. Un peu de mécanique

Le ***Pluperfect*** (on peut aussi dire Prétérit *perfect*) se construit avec le **Prétérit** de ***Have*** (voir 2) et le **participe passé** du verbe qui suit. C'est ***Have*** l'opérateur.

a. Énoncés affirmatifs

SUJET	HAD	GROUPE VERBAL
I/you/he/she/it/we/you/they	had	opened the door.
I/you/he/she/it/we/you/they	had	seen a monster.

b. Énoncés négatifs

- I **had** not (hadn't) seen the monster.

c. Énoncés interrogatifs / réponses brèves

Yes/no questions

- **Had** she posted my letters?

Yes, she had.

- **Had** they seen the monster?

No, they **hadn't**.

Wh- questions

- What **had** he **told** his mum?
- How long **had** he **been** there?

2. Emploi

À la différence du *Present perfect* qui, lui, permet de faire un bilan au moment présent, le *Pluperfect* signale qu'à **un moment donné du passé**, une chose avait **déjà** – ou n'avait pas – eu lieu. L'énonciateur **fait le point** – fait un bilan – à ce moment-là.

- By the time McGruder turned 29, in 2003, *The Boondocks* **had** already appear**ed** in over 250 newspapers and they **had become** the heroes of a very popular TV series.

Le moment du passé qui sert de point de repère peut être exprimé sous la forme :

a. d'une date : **in 2003**

b. d'une proposition au Prétérit : **By the time/when McGruder turned 29**

24 ***Pluperfect* et *ever, never, already,...* (voir 11 *Present perfect* et *ever*)**

Le *Pluperfect* fonctionne, comme le *Present perfect*, avec *ever, never, already*, ces adverbes de temps liés à l'expression d'un bilan.

- No other rappers **had** ever **written** like this before.
- He **had** never **written** like this before.
- When McGruder turned 29, *The Boondocks* **had** already appear**ed** in over 250 newspapers.

25 ***If* + *Pluperfect*, *would* + *have* + participe passé**

En lisant la phrase suivante :

- If he **had** *known* more about navigation he **would have** reach**ed** the right ocean.

on comprend que :

a. *he did not know enough about navigation*

et que en conséquence :

b. *he did not reach the right ocean.*

La combinaison de ***If*** – qui indique que l'on fait une hypothèse – et du ***Pluperfect*** permet d'envisager le contraire de ce qui s'est réellement passé. La suite de l'énoncé envisage la conséquence **probable** de ce que l'on vient d'imaginer.

If I **had known** *(= but I did not know)* I **would have** called you *(but I did not call you).*

Si j'avais su, je t'aurais appelé.

26 **PIÈGE !**

a. Plus-que-parfait en français ➜ *Pluperfect*

b. Imparfait en français + depuis x années ➜ *Pluperfect*

a. Quand elle est arrivée ils **avaient** déjà **appelé** un taxi.

➜ *When she arrived they **had** already **called** a taxi.*

b. Ils **étaient** fans de rap depuis des années quand...

➜ *They **had been** rap fans for years...*

3 LES MODAUX

Que veut dire “modaliser” ?

Un exemple en français :
Le bébé se réveille en pleurant au milieu de la nuit.
La maman dit : *“Il doit avoir mal aux dents.”*
En disant cela, elle dit que, **selon elle,** il est presque sûr que le bébé a mal au dents.

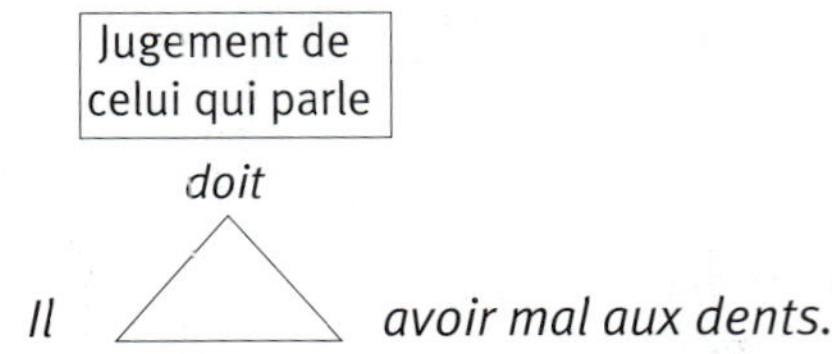

En utilisant un modal, celui qui parle donne son avis dans la phrase. “Modaliser” veut dire : donner son avis.

27 A. Généralités

Voici les modaux de l’anglais : ***may/can, shall/will, might/could, should/would, must.***

1. Un peu de mécanique

a. Les modaux sont invariables.
Ils ne changent pas selon le sujet *(I, she, they...)* C’est logique, puisqu’ils dépendent de celui qui parle (voir schéma ci-dessus).

She **can** play tennis.
They **can** play tennis.
We **can** play tennis.

b. Les modaux sont des opérateurs.

- Ils se placent entre le sujet et le verbe dans les phrases affirmatives :
  Josh **can** speak German.
  You **should** walk faster.
- Ils prennent la négation :
  You **mustn’t** climb without a rope.
  You **shouldn’t** go to bed so late.
- Ils passent avant le sujet pour les questions :
  Shall I tell my parents?
  Will it rain?
- Ils sont utilisés dans les *tags* :
  Kate will be there, **won’t** she?

2. Les modaux en système

Les modaux de l’anglais fonctionnent selon un **système** rigoureux. Voici comment leur fonctionnement est organisé :

a. *may* et *can* : le possible
b. *shall* et *will* : le très probable
c. *must* : l’obligatoire

En conséquence, un modal ne peut jamais en suivre un autre car l’énonciateur ne peut pas dire, par exemple, que les choses sont à la fois possibles et probables.

B. *may* et *can* : le possible

28 1. *may*

May a deux types d’emplois :

a. l’énonciateur **rend les choses possibles** (ou impossibles) pour le sujet **(il décide).** Il autorise le sujet à / lui permet de faire quelque chose.

Énoncés affirmatifs et négatifs

- You **may** go out tonight.
- You **may not** watch this film. It is not for young children.

Énoncés interrogatifs

Les rôles sont inversés. L’énonciateur s’en remet à son interlocuteur et lui demande si celui-ci lui accorde la possibilité de faire telle ou telle chose (demande d’autorisation).

- Dad? **May** I go out for pizza with John on Saturday night?

b. L’énonciateur émet une hypothèse **et il pense qu’il est possible** que les choses aient lieu.

- Children who are unable to join groups **may** feel rejected or excluded and they **may** become aggressive or hateful.

La traduction peut faire appel à :
__Il est possible__ que les enfants [...] se sentent rejetés...
ou à
Les enfants [...] __risquent__ de se sentir rejetés...

29 2. *can*

Avec ***can***, l'énonciateur signale qu'il **a constaté** *(ou qu'il sait)* que les choses sont possibles *(ou impossibles)*.

- I **can** help you with your maths if you like.
- I'm sure you **can** help me with my revision.
- I'm going to my first drama club meeting... I **can't** miss it.
- **Can** you drive?
- You look exhausted. **Can** I help you?
- It **can't** be a UFO. Voir 34

Remarque :

"May I...?" ou ***"Can I...?"***

En famille, avec les copains, on dit facilement :

Can I make a phone call?

Mais une **réelle** demande de permission passe par ***may*** :

May I make a phone call?

Prononciation

• **Can** est prononcé /kæn/ avec la voyelle de *cat* quand il est en fin de phrase ou accentué.
Sinon il est réduit à /kən/ voire /kn/:

Can you come tonight? /kən/
Of course, I **can**. /kæn/
He **can** speak four languages. /kn/

• ***Can*** + ***not*** : deux solutions
- soit ***cannot*** : /ˈkænɒt/
- soit ***can't*** /kɑːnt/

C. *shall* et *will* : le très probable

30 1. *shall*

Énoncés interrogatifs

L'énonciateur demande à son interlocuteur de prendre une décision. **Il lui demande de décider** si les choses auront lieu ou pas :

- **Shall** I make some coffee?
- **Shall** we go this weekend?
- **Shall** I ask my parents?

Le recours au verbe *vouloir* dans la traduction en français (est-ce que tu veux que je...) montre bien **que l'énonciateur attend que son interlocuteur prenne la décision,** impose son point de vue.

Prononciation

Shall est prononcé /ʃl/ la plupart du temps. Quand il est accentué, il se prononce /ʃæl/ avec le son /æ/ de *cat*.

(Tu verras d'autres emplois de ***shall*** plus tard, au lycée).

31 2. *will*

a. Énoncés affirmatifs et négatifs

Avec **will**, l'énonciateur **constate qu'il est fortement probable** que les choses auront lieu – ou pas. Il fait des prédictions, des pronostics, à partir de ce qu'il sait, de ses connaissances.

- Children who can't make friends **will** isolate themselves.
- Many people think that if they ever meet E.T.s they **will** be friends.
- When children become young adults they'**ll** meet all sorts of people.
- It is too late to go shopping. The shops **won't** be open.

b. Énoncés interrogatifs

- **Will** we meet E.T.?
- **Will** we go out this weekend? (Est-ce que c'est prévu ?)

≠ **Shall** we go out this weekend? (= À toi de décider.)

Prononciation

Will se prononce
- /wɪl/ en début et en fin d'énoncé → **Will** it rain? I think it **will**.
- /l/, dans tous les autres cas, ce que l'orthographe montre bien : ***I'll, you'll, she'll, they'll***, etc.
Même s'il ne s'écrit pas toujours ***'ll***, *will* se prononce /l/, comme par exemple dans : Josh **will** come.
- /wəʊnt/ : ***won't*** *(will + not)* se prononce avec la même voyelle que ***don't*** : /dəʊnt/

32 **PIÈGE !**

I **will** phone you when I **get** home.
when I ***get*** *home* = chose considérée comme acquise, sûre à 100 % : à mon retour)
I ***will*** *phone you.* (= **prédiction**, chose fortement probable – ici, une promesse)

Il est impossible de dire ici : ~~*when I will get home*~~ puisque ***will*** signifie : chose fortement probable, et non sûre à 100%.

De même, on aura :
I'll phone you **as soon as** I **am** ready.
We'll tidy our room **before** Mom **comes** home. I promise!

D. *must* et l'obligatoire

33 **a. *L'énonciateur décide* de rendre les choses *obligatoires* pour le sujet – énoncés affirmatifs – ou de lui *interdire* de faire quelque chose – énoncés négatifs.**

- You **must** put on your helmet.
- I **must** go now. (l'énonciateur s'oblige lui-même à ...)
- You **mustn't** smoke in the house.

Prononciation

Must est dans ce cas prononcé /məs/, voire /ms/. Il est donc très réduit oralement :
I **must** go now : /ms/
Le "t" de *must* n'est pas prononcé.
Must not – mustn't – est prononcé /mʌsnt/.
Le "t" de *must* n'est pas prononcé.

34 **b. *L'énonciateur s'intéresse à une situation, et dit qu'il y a de fortes chances* pour que les choses soient comme il le dit – pour lui, *"c'est obligé"* qu'il en soit ainsi.**

- She **must** be at work. (Elle ne répond pas sur son portable.)
- It **must** be a UFO! (Il y a quelque chose qui brille dans le ciel.)

Si l'on n'est pas d'accord on peut dire :

- It **can't** be a UFO!

Prononciation

Must est dans ce cas prononcé /mʌst/. (/ʌ/ est la voyelle de *mo*ther ou encore de *cou*sin).

E. Les modaux au Prétérit

may	devienneent au Prétérit	**might**
can		**could**
shall		**should**
will		**would**

Rappel :

Le Prétérit signale l'existence d'un **décalage**. Ce décalage peut être de deux natures :

a. Décalage dans le temps :

We **were** in the garden when the postman **came**.

b. Décalage par rapport à la réalité des faits :

If I **were** rich...

35 1. *might* (*may* + Prétérit)

L'énonciateur parle du moment **présent**. En utilisant ***might*** il signale que selon **son analyse** de la situation les choses sont tout à fait possibles.

- Don't make a noise! The children ***might*** hear you.
- Drake has calculated that there ***might*** be as many as 10,000 high-tech worlds...

Prononciation

Might se prononce /maɪt/ avec le même son que *by*. Les lettres ***-gh-*** ne sont pas prononcées.

36 2. *could* (*can* + Prétérit)

a. L'énonciateur parle du passé.

Il signale que **le sujet** avait – ou n'avait pas – la possibilité, la **capacité** de faire quelque chose.

- The firemen had to use dynamite to stop the fire. It was the only thing they **could** do.

b. L'énonciateur parle du présent.

Il signale avec ***could*** que **le sujet** aurait la possibilité, la capacité de faire quelque chose. Une condition est à remplir pour que les choses soient possibles.

- **Could** you help me with my maths? (sous-entendu : si tu as le temps...)
- If we had time we **could** go and see a film.
- Do you really think there **could** be intelligent life out there? (= les conditions sont-elles remplies pour que la vie soit possible ?)

Prononciation

Could se prononce /kʊd/ avec le même son que *book*. La lettre ***-l-*** n'est pas prononcée.

37 ## 3. *should* (*shall* + Prétérit)

L'énonciateur parle du moment **présent.** Il exprime un conseil, une recommandation, une suggestion. Dans une question, il demande à l'interlocuteur de prendre une décision.

- Roller-skating is dangerous you know. You **should** be more careful.
- Bullying is wrong and **should** be stopped.
- Victims **should** tell their teachers.
- You **shouldn't** talk when you are practising.
- **Should** I phone her now?
- **Should** we stop looking for "little green men"?

Prononciation

Should se prononce /ʃʊd/ avec le même son que *book*. Comme pour ***could***, le ***-l-*** n'est pas prononcé.

38 ## 4. *would* (*will* + Prétérit)

L'énonciateur parle du moment **présent**. Avec ***will***, l'énonciateur signale que les choses sont fortement probables. Avec ***would***, il y a toujours un **'if'** sous-entendu et la probabilité est donc atténuée.

- Where **would** you travel <u>if you had the money?</u>
- What **would** you like to eat?
- I'**d** like a cup of coffee, please.

Prononciation

Would se prononce /wʊd/ avec le même son que *book*. Comme pour ***could*** et ***should***, le ***-l-*** n'est pas prononcé.

39 **ATTENTION !**

1. [*if* + Présent / *will*]

Pour émettre une hypothèse au moment où l'on parle et en prévoir le résultat logique, très probable :

If you **use** your best fighters you'**ll** be able to destroy him.

2. [*if* + Prétérit / *would*]

Pour reprendre une hypothèse – par exemple :

a. ce dont on vient de parler :

If you **went** to that audition you **would** win the competition.

b. le contraire de la réalité du moment :

If I **had** enough money I **would** buy a plane ticket right now and go to that audition. (I don't have enough money.)

If I **were** you I'**d** go to that audition. (I'm not you.)

Voir 8

F. Modaux et verbes non-modaux

Avec un modal, l'énonciateur émet un jugement personnel. Quand il n'est pas en mesure de le faire – si la situation ne s'y prête pas – ou s'il ne souhaite pas le faire, il exprime le possible ou l'obligatoire au moyen de verbes ordinaires, non-modaux. C'est ainsi que :

may	cèdent la place à	**be + allowed + to + V**
can		**be + able + to + V**
must		**have + to + V**

40 1. *be + allowed + to + V*

L'énonciateur transmet ce qu'il sait. Il ne prend aucune décision. Les choses sont – ou ne sont pas – autorisées.

• Pour parler du passé :

He **was** not allowed to get on the plane with a knife. (Il n'a pas été autorisé à...)

• Pour parler du présent :

I'm sorry but you **are** not allowed to carry dangerous objects on board.

• Pour parler de l'avenir :

You **won't be** allowed to get on the plane without a ticket.

41 2. *be able + to + V*

• Pour parler du passé :

In 1996 he **was** able to cross the Atlantic on his own.

• Pour parler du présent :

A child who **is** able to make friends will be a happy adult.

• Pour parler de l'avenir :

Do you think that child **will** ever **be** able to express love?

42 3. *have + to + V*

• Pour parler du passé : *had*

L'énonciateur ne peut pas imposer une obligation après coup. ***Must*** est donc exclu pour parler du passé.

Arthur was fighting Lancelot in France when Mordred rebelled. Arthur **had** to return to England immediately.

Énoncés interrogatifs : ne pas oublier ***did***

Why **did** he have to return to England?

• Pour parler du présent : *have/has*

L'énonciateur **évoque** une contrainte, un règlement. **Mais il n'en est pas responsable.** (= c'est comme cela.)

You're too young. Look! You **have** to be sixteen!

Énoncés interrogatifs : ne pas oublier *do/does*.

How old **do** you **have** to be for that audition?

• Pour parler de l'avenir :

First you**'ll have** to find the demon.
We**'ll have** to find a secret herb.

43 4. *do/does + not + have + to + V*

You **don't** have to dress like Britney Spears, you know! (Tu n'es pas obligée de t'habiller... / Tu n'es pas tenue de...)

Voir 45

44 5. *would + rather + V / had + better + V*

Avec ces deux combinaisons, l'énonciateur porte un jugement appréciatif.

a. Avec la combinaison ***would* + *rather* + V**. l'énonciateur exprime **une préférence** parmi des choix possibles, en général deux.

- "Well, I'd **rather** play sports **than** watch sports on TV!"

L'énonciateur peut aussi s'arrêter à :

- "Well, I'd **rather** play sports."

si le deuxième élément de la comparaison est évident pour tout le monde.

On peut traduire ces énoncés au moyen de **"J'aimerais mieux** faire du sport (que de regarder le sport à la télévision)".
Oralement, *would* est réduit à /d/ après : *I*, *you*, *she*, etc. et on l'écrit donc ***'d***.

b. Avec la combinaison ***had* + *better*** + V, l'énonciateur conseille vivement de faire ce que désigne le verbe, et sous-entend une conséquence négative si on ne le fait pas. ***Better*** est le comparatif de *good* (bien/bon). (Voir 96) Le français dira : "Tu ferais mieux de...".

- You**'d better** think about it... (before it is too late).
- Don't you think she**'d better** take the train? There's a terrible storm...

C'est le Prétérit de *have* – ***had*** – qui est employé à toutes les personnes. Oralement il est réduit à /d/, et on l'écrit alors ***'d***.

45 **ATTENTION!**

You must **go.** (Tu dois y aller. = l'énonciateur l'ordonne.)

≠

You **have** to go. (Il faut que tu y ailles. = l'énonciateur rappelle la règle / ce qui a déjà été décidé.)

You **mustn't** go. (Tu ne dois pas y aller. / Interdiction d'y aller. = l'énonciateur interdit.)

≠

You **don't have** to go. (Tu n'es pas obligé d'y aller. = l'énonciateur rappelle que ce n'est pas une obligation.)

G. Modaux + *have* + participe passé

46 Avec la combinaison **modal** + **have** + **participe passé** l'énonciateur **émet un jugement** maintenant, **au moment présent** où il parle, à propos **de faits qui ont eu lieu avant**, dans le passé.

1. *must* + *have* + participe passé

Avec *must* + V, l'énonciateur dit qu'il a des fortes chances pour que les choses soient comme il le dit. Voir 34

Avec *must* + *have* + participe passé, l'énonciateur juge une situation passée : les choses ont dû se produire ainsi.

- They **must have poisoned** the dog.

2. *should* + *have* + participe passé

47 Avec ***should* + V**, l'énonciateur recommande, suggère, conseille. Voir 37. Avec ***should*** + ***have*** + **participe passé** il émet un avis après coup et peut par exemple reprocher à quelqu'un (y compris à lui-même) de ne pas avoir fait quelque chose.

- "You **should have talked** about it with friends." (tu aurais dû...)

48 ### 3. *might* + *have* + participe passé

Avec ***might* + V**, l'énonciateur signale que ce qu'il dit est tout à fait possible dans la situation présente. Voir 35

Avec ***might*** + ***have*** + **participe passé**, il dit que les choses étaient tout à fait possibles dans la situation passée dont il est question.

- Why didn't you ask your dad? You never know, he **might have said** yes. (il était tout à fait possible qu'il dise oui)
- "I **might not have affected** millions of people but I feel it was worth it."

49 ### 4. *would* + *have* + participe passé

Avec ***would*** + ***have*** + **participe passé** l'énonciateur fait une prédiction **a posteriori** (après coup).

- If he had known more about navigation he **would have reached** the right ocean. (= il est fortement probable qu'il aurait atteint...)

4 PARLER DE L'AVENIR EN ANGLAIS

50 Il existe différents procédés grammaticaux pour parler de l'avenir en anglais. Chacun d'entre eux nous signale comment l'énonciateur voit les choses.

1. Présent simple (voir 3 32)

Ce qui est annoncé est vu comme une certitude. C'est l'information en elle-même qui est importante.

– When **does** your train leave?
– It **leaves** tomorrow at 8.

• She will send you a letter when she **arrives**. *(... à son arrivée)*

2. Présent *Be + -ing* (voir 4)

L'énonciateur justifie, s'explique, mais n'informe pas directement. La phrase est produite pour d'autres raisons que la simple information.

• Sorry, I can't come this weekend. I **am** play**ing** football in Oxford.

3. *is/are going + to* + V

Il s'agit du verbe *go* au Présent *Be + -ing* suivi d'un deuxième verbe. Les choses sont en bonne voie pour se réaliser. L'énonciateur explique, justifie quelque chose.

• Give me your hand, quick! I **am going to fall.**

4. *shall* (voir 30)

• **Shall** I see you again?
(Est-ce que je vous reverrai ? = le désirez-vous ?)

5. *will* (voir 31 32)

will est souvent utilisé pour parler de l'avenir puisqu'il sert à faire des pronostics, des prédictions.

• It **will** be sunny in England next week.
• I **will** buy a car **when** I **have** enough money.
• **Will** I see you again?
(Est-ce que je vous reverrai ? – savez-vous si c'est prévu ?)

5 LES ÉNONCÉS INTERROGATIFS

Savoir poser une question en anglais – c'est-à-dire choisir puis ordonner les éléments qui la composent – c'est capital. C'est un bon moyen pour maîtriser le fonctionnement des opérateurs fondamentaux : *be, do, have,* les modaux.

Il existe **deux types de questions** :
A. Les questions dites **fermées** dont la réponse est ***yes*** ou ***no*** – ou encore ***I don't know*** ou ***maybe*** ...
Ces questions commencent toujours par un des opérateurs fondamentaux.
B. Les questions dites **ouvertes** qui portent sur le lieu, la cause, le temps, etc. Ces questions commencent par un mot en ***wh-***.

51 A. Questions fermées *(Yes-No questions)*

- avec *be* au Présent ou au Prétérit seul

Be	sujet	adjectif/nom etc.
Are	you	happy?
Were	they	late?

- avec *Be + -ing* (Présent ou Prétérit *be + -ing*)

Be	sujet	V-ing	compléments
Are	you	coming?	
Were	they	walking	their dog?

- avec *have + got*

Have	sujet	got...
Have	you	**got** a brother?
Has	she	**got** a cigarette?

- au *Present perfect* ou *Pluperfect*

Have	sujet	participe passé
Have	you	**brought** the torch?
Had	he	**called** the doctor?

- avec *have + to*

Do	sujet	have to	V	complément
Do	you	have to	get up	early?
Does	Josh	have to	go to	that audition?
Did	he	have to	return	to England?

- avec un modal

modal	sujet	verbe	complément
May	I	**help**	you?
Will	she	**become**	an actress?
Could	you	**carry**	my bag

- avec le Présent ou le Prétérit simples

Do	sujet	verbe	complément
Do	you	live	in London?
Did	you	watch	the match last night?
Does	she	like	you?
Did	they	see	you take the envelope?

Conclusion

L'ordre des mots de ces questions est : **opérateur + sujet + verbe,**
l'opérateur pouvant être *be, do, have*, ou un modal.

L'intonation des ces questions est, en contexte neutre, **montante**. On descend sur l'avant-dernière syllabe et on remonte sur la dernière : ↘↗

52 B. Questions ouvertes *(Wh- questions)*

a. Liste des mots interrogatifs :

how (comment)
what (que /qu'est ce que...)
when (quand)
where (où)
which (quel/lequel...)
who (qui)
whose (à qui)
why (pourquoi)

b. Ordre des mots dans les questions ouvertes

wh - (ou how)	opér.	sujet	verbe	complément
How	do	you	spell	your name?
What	does	she	want?	
When	did	they	go	to Sydney?
Where	is	she	going?	
Who	will	you	marry?	
Why	was	she	talking	to him?

c. Un nom/pronom peut apparaître juste après *which* ou *whose* :

Which cat do you prefer?
Which one will you buy?
Whose dog is it?

d. Questions composées avec *how*

- Pour dénombrer, interroger sur une quantité : ***How many...? / How much...?***

How many brothers and sisters do you have?
(Combien... ? + nom dénombrable au pluriel)
How much did you pay for that suit?
How much money did you spend? (Combien... ? + verbe/nom indénombrable)

Ainsi que toutes les questions avec *how* + adjectif :

How old are you?
How deep is the Grand Canyon?
How tall is your brother? etc...

- Question portant sur la durée : *How long ...?*

- *How long* + Présent simple :
  How long do we have to wait? (Combien de temps est-ce que nous devons attendre ?)
  (We have to wait) **for** about half an hour. (Environ une demi-heure.)

- *How long* + Présent *Be* + *-ing* :
  How long are you staying in London? (Combien de temps passez-vous à Londres ?)
  For two weeks. (Deux semaines.)

- *How long* + Prétérit :
  How long did you live in India? (Combien de temps avez-vous vécu en Inde ?)
  I lived there **for** 4 years. (J'y ai vécu 4 ans.)

- *How long* + *will* + V. :
  How long will you spend in New York? (Combien de temps est-ce que tu vas passer à NY ?)
  I'll be there **for** 6 months. (J'y serai pendant 6 mois.)

- *How long* + *Present perfect* simple :
  How long have you been here? (Cela fait combien de temps que tu es là ?)
  I have been here **for** 6 months, **since** Christmas. (Je suis là depuis 6 mois, depuis Noël.)

- *How long* + *Present perfect* Be + *-ing* :
  You speak very well! **How long** have you been living in England? (Tu parles très bien. Depuis combien de temps est-ce que tu vis en Angleterre ?)
  (I have been living in England) **for** more than a year now, **since** September 2003. (Je vis en Angleterre depuis plus d'un an maintenant, depuis septembre 2003.)

Pour toutes ces questions la réponse est introduite par ***for*** : *for half an hour, for six months*, etc. Seule la question au *Present perfect* peut aussi faire appel à ***since***.

- Question portant sur le temps qui nous sépare d'une date, d'un événement : *How long ago ...?* (La question et la réponse comportent *ago* et donc le Prétérit.)

How long ago did Napoleon die? (Il y a combien de temps que Napoleon est mort ?)
He died 182 years **ago**. (2003 - 1821 = 182)

- Question portant sur la fréquence : *How often ...?*

How often do you visit this site? (Vous visitez ce site tous les combien ?)

La réponse comporte l'expression d'une régularité : ***every*** *fifteen minutes*, ***every*** *hour*, ***every*** *day/week*, ***once/twice/three*** *times...* ***a*** *day/**a** week/**a** year*, *(very)* ***regularly***, *(very)* ***often***.

e. Questions ouvertes ... en deux temps

WH- | OPERATEUR + SUJET + VERBE | **PREPOSITION** ?

what ... for (Pour quoi ?)
Simon went to the kitchen **to** [???]
→**What** did he go to the kitchen **for**?
Réponse : *(He went to the kitchen)* **To** get some milk from the fridge.

where ... from (D'où ?)
Josh came from [???]
→ **Where** did he come **from**?

who ... at?
She was looking at [???]
→ **Who** was she looking **at**?

who ... with? (Avec qui ?)
Josh went out with [???]
→ **Who** did he go out **with**?

f. Questions ouvertes portant sur le sujet

[???] opened my letter.
→ **Who** opened my letter?
[???] is coming today?
→ **Who** is coming today?

L'ordre des mots est dans ce cas le même que celui d'une phrase affirmative.

On trouve aussi :
- Guess what? **Something terrible** happened!
- **What** happened?

Conclusion

L'ordre des mots est toujours le même, excepté pour les questions qui portent sur le sujet (en *who* ou *what*).

mot interrogatif + opérateur + sujet + verbe

L'intonation dans ces questions, en contexte neutre, est **descendante**. On monte sur l'avant-dernière syllabe, et on redescend sur la dernière : ↘

6 STYLE DIRECT / STYLE INDIRECT

53 Style **direct** : *"**Je** vis à Londres", dit-il.*
Style **indirect** : *[**Il** m'a dit] qu'**il** vivait à Londres.*

Construire une phrase au style indirect consiste à **rapporter** après coup les propos de quelqu'un. Cette opération entraîne quelques modifications grammaticales, comme tu le vois dans l'exemple en français ci-dessus. Voici pour l'anglais les modification auxquelles il faut penser quand on est au style indirect :

1. *say ≠ tell*

Le français possède *un* verbe "dire". L'anglais en a deux. Quelle est la différence entre les deux ?

"Good morning!" he said. → **He said** good morning.
"I don't like tea, you know" he said. → He **told** me he did not like tea.

Avec *say*, l'énonciateur rapporte ce qui a été dit.
Avec *tell*, l'énonciateur rapporte ce qui a été dit **et** à qui.

54 2. style indirect avec *ask / forbid / tell / etc. + to* V.

Pour **rapporter des propos** comme des ordres ou des interdictions, on peut utiliser des verbes comme ***ask, forbid, tell,*** etc. (Voir chapitre 7, 60)
On fait alors appel à ***to*** pour **relier *ask/forbid/tell*** à la **base verbale** qui suit.
Dans le cas où une négation est nécessaire, on place ***not*** juste **après *ask/forbid/tell***, c'est-à-dire, juste **avant *to***.

	STYLE DIRECT	→	STYLE INDIRECT
1.	"Speak English, please!" *(ask)*		They **were asked** [to] speak English. **(passif)** They **asked** them [to] speak English. **(actif)**
2.	"Wait outside!" *(tell)*	→	We **were told** [to] wait outside. **(passif)** They **told** us [to] wait outside. **(actif)**
3.	"Don't wear your tribal clothes at school!" *(forbid)*	→	We **were forbidden** [to] wear our tribal clothes at school. **(passif)** They **forbade** us [to] wear our tribal clothes at school. **(actif)**
4.	"Please, don't speak your native language in class." *(ask)*	→	They **were asked** [not] [to] speak their language in class. **(passif)** They **asked** them [not] [to] speak... **(actif)**

55 3. D'un pronom à l'autre

a. Changement de pronom sujet. Exemples :

"**I** live in London", *he* says.	*He* says **he** lives in London.
"**We** have two dogs", *they* said.	*They* said **they** had two dogs.

b. Changement de pronom complément. Exemples :

"*I* don't like **you**", *she* says.	*She* says she does not like **me**.
"*We* don't like **you**", *they* said.	*They* said *they* did not like **us**.

56 4. D'un Temps à l'autre

Quand le verbe introductif (*say, tell, ask*) est au Présent, l'énoncé rapporté reste au Présent s'il est au Présent au style direct, au Prétérit s'il est au Prétérit, etc. En revanche, quand le **verbe introductif** est au **Prétérit** :

a. Présent simple → Prétérit simple

"I **live** in London", Kate said.	Kate said *she* **lived** in London.	**live → lived**
"My sister **doesn't** like tea", Bryan said.	Bryan said *his* sister **did not** like tea.	**does → did**

b. Présent *Be + -ing* → Prétérit *Be + -ing*

"I'**m** walking my neighbour's dog", he told me.	*He* told me *he* **was** walking *his* neighbour's dog.	**am → was**
"We **are** getting married on Monday", he said.	He said *they* **were** getting married on Monday.	**are → were**

c. *Present perfect* → *Pluperfect*

"We **haven't found** any clues" the police said.	The police said they **hadn't found** any clues.	**have found → had found**

d. Prétérit → *Pluperfect*

"The vandals **cut** the fence with a pair of pliers", the authorities said.	The authorities said the vandals **had cut** the fence with a pair of pliers.	**cut → had cut**

e. *will* → *would*

"I'**ll** take the dollar", he said.	He said he **would** take the dollar.	**will → would**
"My character **will** be very clever", he said.	He said *his* character **would** be very clever.	**will → would**

f. *can* → *could*

"I **can** babysit for you", she said.	She said she **could** babysit for us.	**can → could**

57 5. Questions directes / questions indirectes

a. Questions fermées (*yes/no questions*)

"Are you English?" she asked me.	→	She asked me **if** I was English.
"Are you reading a book?" she asked him.	→	She asked him **if** he was reading a book.
"Were you in the hall?" the inspector asked me.	→	The inspector asked me **if** I was in the hall.
"Are you getting married?" he asked.	→	He asked **if** we were getting married.
"Have you found any fingerprints?" the reporters asked.	→	The reporters asked **if** they had found any fingerprints.
"Did the security patrols hear or see anything unusual?" the reporter asked.	→	The reporters asked **if** the security patrols had heard or seen anything unusual.
"Can you help us?" they asked us.	→	They asked us **if** we could help them.

Attention !

La question rapportée fait appel à ***if***. L'ordre des mots est identique à celui d'une phrase affirmative.

b. Questions ouvertes

"What time is it?" he asked.	→	He asked **what time it was.**
"Where do you live?" he asked me.	→	He asked me **where I lived.**
" When are you getting married?" he asked us.	→	He asked us **when we were getting married.**
"Why are you mad at me?" he asked them.	→	He asked them **why they were mad at him.**
"What have you done?	→	He asked me **what I had done.**
"Where did you lose it?	→	He asked me **where I had lost it.**

Attention !

L'ordre des mots dans la question rapportée est le même que celui d'une phrase affirmative.

7 UN VERBE EN SUIT UN AUTRE

Quand un verbe (V_1) est suivi d'un deuxième verbe (V_2)... sous quelle forme se présente ce deuxième verbe ? V, *to* + V, ou V *-ing* ?

58 1. *make* et *let*

Make et *let* sont toujours suivis de V.

OPÉRATEUR	sujet 1	verbe 1	sujet 2	verbe 2	COMPLÉMENTS
	These jeans	**make**	me	feel	great.
	She	**makes**	me	do	things I don't want to do.
Did	his parents	**make**	him	wear	a suit?
	They	**let**	their children	watch	what they like.
	Parents	**let**	them	play	violent games for hours.

Si le S_2 est un pronom, on utilise le pronom complément (*me*, *him, them*). Voir 73

59 2. *want*

Want est suivi de *to* + V.

OPÉRATEUR	S_1	V_1	S_2	TO	V_2	COMPLÉMENTS
1	Calvin's dad	**wants**		**to**	pick up	the fallen branches.
2	Calvin's dad	**wants**	Calvin	**to**	pick up	the fallen branches.
3 Did	he	**want**	Calvin	**to**	pick up	the fallen branches?

1. *Calvin's dad* est le sujet du V_1 ***wants***, et du V_2 ***pick up*** : il veut ramasser lui-même.
2. *Calvin's dad* est le sujet du V_1 ***wants***, Calvin est le sujet de ***pick up*** : son père veut que Calvin ramasse les branches.

60 3. *ask, expect, tell, like*

Ces V1 fonctionnent comme *want* et sont suivis de *to* + V.
Même construction qu'avec *want*.

OPÉRATEUR	S_1	V_1	S_2	TO	V_2	COMPLÉMENTS
	Calvin's dad	**asks / expects / tells**	Calvin	**to**	**pick up**	the fallen branches.
	Calvin's dad	**asks / expects / tells**	his wife	**to**	**pick up**	the fallen branches.
Does	Calvin's dad	**ask / expect / tell**	her	**to**	**pick up**	the fallen branches?

S_1	OPÉRATEUR	V_1	S_2	TO	V_2	COMPLÉMENTS
He	would	**like**	his dad	**to**	**wear**	normal clothes.

61 ! PIÈGE !

1. *Il veut partir demain.*
Le $\mathbf{V_1}$ français ***vouloir*** est suivi de $\mathbf{V_2}$. Prudence donc en anglais : n'oublie pas ***to*** !
He wants **to** leave tomorrow.

2. *Il veut qu'elle parte demain.*
Le français utilise une subordonnée au subjonctif. En anglais, on ajoute simplement le sujet du $\mathbf{V_2}$ avant ***to*** :
He wants **her** to leave tomorrow.

62 4. *see* et *hear*

Ces deux verbes peuvent être suivis de V ou de V *-ing*, selon ce que veut dire l'énonciateur. Les deux constructions ne sont pas synonymes.

Exemples avec *see/hear* + V :

I think I **saw** Fred **get** into a stranger's car.
Did you **hear** them leave?

Exemples avec *see/hear* + V *-ing* :

It's so exciting! Sometimes I **see** a strange shadow mov**ing** around or a tiny spot shin**ing** in the moonlight.
I frightened my father one day. He was reading a book and he didn't **hear** me com**ing** into the room.

- Avec *see/hear* + V, les deux verbes ont la même importance dans la phrase.
- Avec V-*ing*, l'énonciateur veut dire que **le fait de voir ou d'entendre est plus important** que ce que l'on voit ou entend.

OPÉRATEUR	sujet 1	OPÉRATEUR	verbe 1	sujet 2	verbe 2	COMPLÉMENTS
	I		**saw**	Frank	**get**	into a stranger's car.
	She		**heard**	him	**ask**	for the price.
Did	you		**hear**	them	**leave?**	
	I		**see**	a strange shadow	mov**ing**	around.
	He	did not	**hear**	me	com**ing**	into the room.
Did	you		**see**	her	gett**ing**	out of her car?

Si le Sujet 2 est un pronom, on utilise le pronom complément *(him, them...)*. Voir 73

63 5. *remember, regret,...*

Remember, regret (et d'autres verbes) sont suivis soit de *to* + V, soit de V-*ing*.
Avec *to* V, le V_2 arrive **"après"** le V1, tandis qu'avec V-*ing*, le V_2 a **précédé** le V_1 (pour "se souvenir de"... il faut que la chose ait **déjà** eu lieu, d'où V-*ing*.). Exemples :

Please remember **to** buy a newspaper. (= N'oublie pas de...)
I remember buy**ing** a newspaper but I can't find it. (= Je me souviens de...)
Do you remember com**ing** here? (= Est-ce que tu te souviens de...)
I regret **to** inform you that our plane is 2 hours late. (= Je suis au regret de vous informer ...)
I regret tell**ing** him the truth. (= Je regrette de lui avoir dit la vérité.)

8 LA VOIX PASSIVE

64 1. Un peu de mécanique

A la voix passive, comme en français, c'est ***be*** qui est conjugué. Il est suivi du participe passé du verbe.

If a child **is rejected** he may feel frustrated.
The Lakotas **were offered** a territory.
He wants to leave because he thinks he **is being rejected**.
They did not know a crime **was being committed**.
She says she **has been abducted** by aliens.

	SUJET	BE	PARTICIPE PASSÉ
Présent simple	A child	**is**	reject**ed**
Prétérit simple	The Lakotas	**were**	offer**ed**
Présent *Be + -ing*	He	**is** be**ing**	reject**ed**
Prétérit *Be + -ing*	A crime	**was** be**ing**	committ**ed**
Present perfect	She	**has** be**en**	abduct**ed**

2. Emploi

• On n'utilise pas la voix active ou la voix passive sans raison. Cela dépend du ***sujet*** que l'on veut placer en début de phrase. Ce choix dépend du thème de la conversation, de ce qui a été dit avant ...

Peace Treaty with the US army.
In this treaty **the Lakotas were offered two things...**

Dans ce contexte, on met en avant les bénéficiaires du traité plutôt que ceux qui ont offert quelque chose *(the US army)*. Si on voulait davantage mettre en avant la chose offerte, on aurait aussi pu dire :

A territory was offered to the Lakotas.

Dans un cas comme dans l'autre, il est logique de commencer la phrase par ce qui constitue le traité de paix :
– soit les Lakotas qui se sont battus pour obtenir un compromis,
– soit la chose pour laquelle ils se sont battus.

• Le passif permet de ne pas mentionner l'agent :
- soit parce qu'il est évident, donc sans intérêt,
- soit parce qu'on ne le connaît pas ou qu'on préfère ne pas citer son nom (diplomatie, articles de journaux, enquêtes policières...).

• L'agent n'apparaît en position de complément que s'il apporte une information importante :

She says she has been abducted **by aliens**.

65 3. Quelques différences français/anglais : le cas des verbes *offer, give, grant, etc.*

Les verbes comme *offer, give, grant...* fonctionnent avec **trois** éléments : **la personne qui offre** (le donateur), **la personne à qui on offre** (le bénéficiaire) et **la chose offerte**.
Il en est de même pour le verbe *offrir* en français, à la différence que l'anglais permet deux constructions à la voix "active", alors qu'une seule est possible en français. Observe :

ANGLAIS **Voix active**		**FRANÇAIS** **Voix active**
John gave a present **to** Sarah.	→	John a offert un cadeau **à** Sarah.
Donateur + verbe + cadeau + ***to*** *+ bénéficiaire.*		*Donateur + verbe + cadeau +* ***à*** *+ bénéficiaire.*

Voix active		**Voix active**
John gave Sarah a present.	→	~~John a offert Sarah un cadeau~~.
Donateur + verbe + bénéficiaire + cadeau.		Impossible en français.

Seul l'anglais fonctionne dans ce deuxième cas. Ceci a des répercussions sur la fabrication des énoncés à la voix "passive". Observe :

Voix passive		**Voix passive**
A present was given to Sarah (by John).	→	**Un cadeau** a été offert à Sarah (par John).
Sarah was given a present (by John).	→	~~Sarah a été offert un cadeau (par John)~~.
	→	Sarah **s'est vu offrir** un cadeau. **On** a offert un cadeau à Sarah.

Il y a un cas dans lequel le français fait de la résistance là où l'anglais n'en fait pas : le français ne peut pas avoir comme point de départ d'un énoncé à la voix passive la personne à qui on offre (le bénéficiaire) alors que l'anglais peut le faire. Le français, lui, a recours à : "**On** a offert...", ou encore à "**Elle s'est vu** offrir...".

Exemples en anglais d'énoncés à la voix passive avec comme sujet **la personne à qui** on offre, donne, accorde, etc. :

- offer / make a promise
In this treaty, the Lakotas were **offered** 2 things: they were **offered** a territory, and they were **made** a promise.

- give
President Andrew Jackson was **given** the right to remove the Indians.

- grant
In 1882 the Cherokee nation was **granted** sovereignty by Chief Justice John Marshall of the Supreme Court.

9 LE NOM

66 A. Types de nom

Il existe des noms "simples" (*car, boy, house,* etc.) et des noms qui sont le résultat d'un **assemblage.** Il existe différents types d'assemblage :

1. nom + nom = 3ᵉ nom

tea + cup = teacup
space + shuttle = space shuttle
tennis + ball = tennis ball
tooth + paste = toothpaste
bed + room = bedroom

2. nom + suffixe = 2ᵉ nom

music + **-ian** = musician
friend + **-ship** = friendship

3. adjectif + suffixe = nom

happy + **-ness** = happiness

67 4. verbe + suffixe = nom

play + **-er** = player
drive + **-r** = driver
clean + **-ing** = cleaning

-ing permet de transformer n'importe quel verbe en nom. Le nom obtenu fonctionne comme tous les autres noms.

Il peut être précédé :
- d'un article : Have you done **the** wash**ing** up?
- d'un démonstratif : I just can't stand **this** wait**ing**.
- d'un adjectif possessif : I cannot understand **his** marry**ing** so young.
- d'une préposition : Why don't you go out **instead of** stay**ing** in? A bully makes people insecure **by** slapp**ing** them.

Il peut aussi, comme tout autre nom, être le sujet ou le complément d'un verbe :
• Bully**ing** means hitt**ing** someone.

Enfin, dans un exemple comme le suivant :
• Bullying can mean *[mak**ing** someone do something they don't want to do].*
si le nom en ***-ing*** est ***making***, le groupe nominal ne s'arrête pas à *making* et est en fait TOUT ce qui est entre [...].

5. préfixe + nom = 2ᵉ nom

after- +noon = afternoon
sub- + marine = submarine

6. nom *of* nom = 3ᵉ nom

L'assemblage en ***of*** permet de relier deux noms. Le deuxième apporte après coup une précision à propos du premier :
a cup **of** tea
a bottle **of** beer
a packet **of** cigarettes
a box **of** matches
My best friend is the son **of** a famous musician.

68 7. nom *'s* nom = Le génitif

• L'assemblage en **'s** permet de relier deux noms. **Le deuxième est le nom dont on parle.** Le premier lui apporte une précision importante. Cet assemblage est souvent utilisé pour exprimer la possession :
It is my dad**'s** car.
I don't like my brother**'s** friends.
Where are mum**'s** glasses?

• Pour trouver l'identité du possesseur :
***whose* + chose possédée + ?**
Whose car is it? → It's John's (car)
On peut éviter la répétition.

• On désigne souvent les **commerces** au moyen de : **nom's,** le deuxième nom est sous-entendu : ***shop.***
the baker's (= *the baker's shop*)
the butcher's

et également :
the doctor's
the dentist's
C'est le mot ***surgery*** (cabinet médical) qui est sous-entendu ici.

Et lorsqu'on dit :
I think she is at Bryan's. (Je pense qu'elle est chez Bryan.),
on sous-entend le mot ***house.***

• **Quand le premier nom est au pluriel en *-s*, on ne conserve que l'apostrophe :**
my parents' bedroom
my sisters' boyfriends

Dans tous les autres cas, on garde *'s* :
the children's room (child → children)
Charles's horse

Le savais-tu ?

Quand tu dis *Tuesday, Wednesday, Thursday,* tu utilises le génitif, puisqu'à l'origine chacun de ces jours est en fait associé à un dieu particulier :

- Tuesday : day of Tiw (= Mars, dieu de la guerre)
- Wednesday : day of Woden (= Mercure, dieu des voyageurs et des commerçants)
- Thursday : day of Thor (= dieu du tonnerre)

B. Genre et nombre

69 1. Le genre *(masculin/féminin)*

Il y a en français des noms masculins (***un/le*** *siège*) et des noms féminins (***une/la*** *porte*). Cette distinction n'existe pas en anglais. Tous les noms fonctionnent avec les articles ***a*** et ***the***. La distinction masculin/féminin n'existe que pour les humains (et les animaux de la maison) :

a boy → **he**
a girl → **she**
a cousin → **he** pour un garçon ; **she** pour une fille.
a dog : → **he** pour un mâle ; **she** pour une femelle.

Pour tous les autres noms, c'est le pronom **it** qui est employé.

Where is your ball? **It** is in the garage.
I love the new Rover. **It** is very nice.

70 2. Le nombre *(singulier/pluriel)*

a. Le pluriel des noms

Il est réalisé à l'écrit au moyen de *-s* (ou *-es*) pour la quasi-majorité des noms.

Oralement, comme pour le ***-s*** du présent simple, il existe 3 prononciations possibles, en fonction du **dernier son** du nom au singulier :

- **après un son voyelle :** /z/
- **après un son consonne** : /s/, /z/, /ɪz/

CONSONNE	PRONONCIATION	EXEMPLE
/p/	/s/	ships
/t/		cats
/k/		books
/f/		roofs
/θ/		months
/b/	/z/	crabs
/d/		beds
/g/		bags
/v/		doves
/ð/		clothes
/m/		teams
/n/		sons
/ŋ/		kings
/l/		crocodiles
/s/	/ɪz/	buses
/z/		roses
/ʃ/		bushes
/ʒ/		bridges

Il subsiste quelques pluriels "à l'ancienne" : il s'agit de noms qui ont conservé la façon dont se faisait le pluriel il y a plusieurs siècles.

SINGULIER		PLURIEL	
child	/tʃaɪld/	**children**	/'tʃɪldrən/
man	/mæn/	**men**	/men/
woman	/'wʊmən/	**women**	/'wɪmɪn/
life	/laɪf/	**lives**	/laɪvz/
foot	/fʊt/	**feet**	/fi:t/
tooth	/tu:θ/	**teeth**	/ti:θ/
mouse	/maʊs/	**mice**	/maɪs/
wolf	/wʊlf/	**wolves**	/wʊlvz/

Sur le modèle de *life/**lives***, (/f/ → /vz/), on trouve aussi :

knife/kni**ves** — lea**f**/lea**ves**
*my*self/*them*selves — shel**f**/shel**ves**

Noms toujours au pluriel

- Dès qu'il y a idée de **couple** (deux), l'anglais emploie le nom au pluriel.

trousers et ***shorts*** (deux jambes !)

Where **are** my red trousers?
My shorts **are** dirty.

- ***people*** : *des/les gens, des/les personnes*

People est un nom toujours pluriel qui est invariable. Contrairement au nom français **gens**, on peut dénombrer *people*. La quantité minimum est **deux** – donc on dit ***one person***.

There **are** 2 people at the door.
How many people **are** there?

Noms qui ne prennent pas de *-s* au pluriel :

Par exemple, deux mots courants :

- **sheep** (mouton) : There are 5 sheep in the field. /There are **many** sheep in Scotland.
- **fish** (poisson) : How **many** fish did you catch? / I caught **6** fish.

La plupart des noms de poissons ne prennent pas le *-s* du pluriel :
five salmon /sæmən/, **three** carp, etc.

71 b. Les noms dits "dénombrables"

Il s'agit des noms que **la langue** permet de compter – de dénombrer. À quelques exceptions près, il s'agit de noms désignant des choses concrètes : objets, etc.
Est classé dans les dénombrables un nom qui peut être précédé de :
- l'article ***a /an*** **:**
- un **nombre :** 3, 67, 89, etc.
- ***many*** : pour exprimer une grande quantité
- la question ***how many?*** combien
- ***(a) few :*** (un) peu de = pour exprimer une petite quantité
- ***fewer :*** moins de...

72 c. Les noms dits "indénombrables"

Il s'agit de noms que la langue ne permet pas de compter – de dénombrer. Ce sont le plus souvent les noms désignant des matières (*gold*), des liquides (*milk*), des concepts (*love*), etc. Est classé dans les indénombrables un nom qui peut être précédé de:
- article Ø : article zéro = pas d'article
- ***much*** : pour exprimer une grande quantité
- la question ***how much?*** (combien)
- ***(a) little :*** pour exprimer une petite quantité
- ***less :*** moins de...

d. Quelques noms dénombrables en français et indénombrables en anglais

Ce que le **français dénombre** (1, 2, 3 etc.) **n'est pas forcément dénombrable en anglais. Le français parle** par exemple des cheveu**x**, l'anglais emploie lui un mot singulier : ***hair***.

Voici quelques mots que les deux langues traitent différemment :

fruit
Where **is** the fruit?
Où sont les fruits?

hair
Your hair **is** grey.
Tu as les cheveux gris.

luggage
Your luggage **is** very heavy.
Tes bagages sont très lourds.

news
Here **is** the news.
Voici les informations.

toast
Your toast **is** ready.
Tes tartines grillées sont prêtes.

Demander **quatre** tartines, demander **un** fruit, ou dire que l'on a **trois** nouvelles à annoncer est quand même possible en anglais. On a recours à : ***a piece of, two pieces of***, etc.
(*piece* /pi:s/)

Can I have **two pieces of** toast, please?
How many **pieces of** luggage do you have?

10 PRONOMS, POSSESSIFS, RÉFLÉCHIS

73

PRONOM SUJET	PRONOM COMPLÉMENT	ADJECTIF POSSESSIF	PRONOM POSSESSIF	PRONOM RÉFLÉCHI
I	me	my /maɪ/	mine /maɪn/	my**self**
you	you	your /jɔ:/	yours /jɔ:z/	your**self**
he	him	his	his	him**self**
she	her	her	hers	her**self**
it	it	its	its	it**self**
we	us	our /aʊə/	ours /aʊəz/	our**selves**
you	you	your /jɔ:/	yours /jɔ:z/	your**selves**
they	them /ðm/	their	theirs	them**selves**

11 LES ARTICLES

Ils sont au nombre de trois : **Ø** (article zéro), ***a*** ou ***an*** et ***the***. Selon l'article choisi, l'énonciateur ne présente pas le nom de la même façon.

74 1. Ø (article zéro)

He came by Ø car.
He likes Ø coffee.
Andrew likes Ø school.

L'énonciateur parle des choses en général :

- *Ø car* indique le moyen de transport ;

- *Ø coffee* désigne la boisson ;

- *Ø school* désigne le système scolaire (et pas une école en particulier).

75 2. *a / an*

There is **a** car in front of the house.
Can I have **a** coffee?
Josh goes to **a** school in Hampstead.

Avec ***a***, l'énonciateur désigne maintenant un élément particulier. Il s'agit d'un premier repérage.

- ***a*** *car* désigne l'objet "voiture".

- ***a*** *coffee* désigne non plus la boisson en général mais une tasse de cette boisson.

- ***a*** *school* désigne un établissement précis – les bâtiments.

Remarque :

a devient ***an*** devant les noms dont le premier **son** est une voyelle :

an animal, **an** umbrella, etc.

On dit aussi : ***an*** *hour* car le "h" de l'orthographe n'est pas prononcé. Mais on dit *a uniform* car le premier son de ce nom est un son-consonne /j/.

76 3. *the*

Where is **the** car?
Can you pass me **the** coffee?
Where is **the** school?

Avec ***the***, l'énonciateur considère que son interlocuteur sait de quoi il est question : il a déjà identifié, repéré le nom qui suit ***the*** :

- ***the*** *car* désigne celle que tout le monde connaît, celle de la famille par exemple.

- ***the*** *coffee* désigne celui qui est sur la table, que l'énonciateur et son interlocuteur ont sous les yeux.

- ***the*** *school* désigne celle où vont les enfants de la famille, celle du village, celle dont on a parlé juste à l'instant. L'interlocuteur sait forcément de laquelle il s'agit.

The fonctionne avec le **singulier** et le **pluriel** : Where is **the** dog? / Where are **the** dogs?

Remarque

Avec les noms propres, c'est Ø qui est employé. Le nom suffit à faire le repérage maximum. C'est également vrai pour les titres :

la reine Elisabeth : Ø Queen Elizabeth
le prince Charles : Ø Prince Charles
le président Bush : Ø President Bush

Si on retire le nom, on emploie ***the***

the Queen : celle du pays dont nous parlons (donc Elizabeth pour les Britanniques) ;
the Prince : celui que tout le monde connaît (Charles pour les Britanniques) ;
the President : celui du pays dont on parle (Bush pour les Américains depuis 2001).

! PIÈGE !

1. I like Ø coffee. / I like Ø children.
J'aime **le** café. / J'aime **les** enfants.
2. Can you pass me **the** coffee?
The children are waiting for me.
Tu peux me passer **le** café?
Les enfants m'attendent.

Pour employer ***the*** en anglais, il faut que le nom soit connu de l'énonciateur et de l'interlocuteur.
L'article français *le/la/les* peut être une source d'erreurs.

12 THIS/THAT

77 • Le français possède **un** démonstratif :
- ***ce*** (+ masculin) : *Tu peux me donner **ce** livre ?*
- ***cette*** (+ féminin) : *Tu peux me donner **cette** tasse ?*
- ***ces*** (+ pluriel) : *Tu peux me passer **ces** livres/tasses ?*

• L'anglais, lui, possède **deux** démonstratifs :

SINGULIER	PLURIEL
Can you pass me **this** book/cup? /ðɪs/	Can you give me **these** books/cups? /ðiːz/
Can you give me **that** book/cup? /ðæt/	Can you pass me **those** books/cups? /ðəʊz/

Deux démonstratifs : pour quoi faire?

Que ce soit avec le français ***ce/cette*** ou avec ***this*** et ***that*** en anglais, **l'énonciateur prend son interlocuteur à témoin.**

1. this

L'énonciateur **présente** un objet / une personne à son interlocuteur. **L'interlocuteur le découvre :**

- Do you know **this** man?
(= l'énonciateur désigne à son interlocuteur une personne dans un groupe sur une photo)
- You can have **this** book.
(= l'énonciateur tend à son interlocuteur un livre pris dans la bibliothèque)
- I'm not wearing **this** stupid suit.
(= un garçon dit cela à ses parents ; ils connaissent le costume en question mais il en parle à sa manière : *stupid!*)

Why don't you try on **these** nice black jeans?
(= dans un magasin de vêtements)

2. that

L'énonciateur ne présente plus un objet / une personne à son interlocuteur. **Il considère** que **son interlocuteur a déjà vu, déjà identifié** l'objet / la personne dont on parle. Il créé une **complicité** avec son interlocuteur.

- You like **that** girl, don't you?
(= l'énonciateur parle d'une fille précise – celle avec qui son interlocuteur vient de passer une heure au téléphone)
- Look at **that** black Rolls Royce... Nice car, isn't it?
(= l'énonciateur parle de la Rolls Royce noire qui est garée devant la maison et que tout le monde a forcément vue.)
- Where is **that** stupid dog?
(Où est passé cet imbécile de chien ? = pour l'énonciateur, il est acquis pour tout le monde le chien en question est *stupid*.)
- "Did you hear **those** wings? **Those** birds attacked me. They flew straight at my eyes."
(L'homme qui dit cela parle à sa femme qui vient d'être témoin de la scène.)

13 LES PRÉPOSITIONS

78 On appelle **prépositions** *(pré- = qui se place avant)* les mots tels que ***at, in, on,*** *etc.*, qui introduisent un nom dans la phrase.
Voici une liste des prépositions les plus courantes :

PRÉPOSITIONS	EXEMPLES D'EMPLOI	TRADUCTIONS
about /ə'baʊt/	It is a book **about** the war.	à propos de
across /ə'krɒs/	It is **across** the street.	en face, de l'autre côté de
after /'ɑ:ftə/	He came **after** dinner.	après
around /ə'raʊnd/	She travelled **around** the world.	dans, de par
at /ət/ *ou* /æt/	He is **at** school.	à
because /bɪ'kɒz/ **of**	They couldn't leave the island **because of** the storm...	à cause de
before /bɪ'fɔ:/	I got home **before** tea.	avant
behind /bɪ'haɪnd	Your umbrella is **behind** the door.	derrière
between /bɪ'twi:n/	Where were you **between** 10 and 11 last night?	entre, au mileu de
by /baɪ/	a film **by** Spielberg / **by** the fireplace A bully makes people insecure **by** slapping them. I have to finish this **by** Monday.	par, de, près de, etc. = au moyen de, en (les frappant) pour (lundi)
down /daʊn/	He lives **down** the street.	en bas de
during /'dju:rɪŋ/	He came **during** the night.	pendant
for /fə/ *ou* /fɔ:/	It is **for** you. / Who is it **for**?	pour
from /frəm/ ou /frɒm/	Josh is **from** New York. Where are you **from**?	de (provenance, origine)
in /ɪn/	Josh is **in** the bath. / I live **in** England.	dans, en
into /'ɪntu:/ *ou* /'ɪntə/	He fell **into** the water.	dans – avec déplacement
in front of /ɪn'frʌntəv/	He parked **in front of** the house. Don't say that **in front of** the children.	devant
instead /ɪn'sted/	I try to save my money **instead of** spending it all in one go.	au lieu de, à la place de
like /laɪk/	He plays **like** a pro.	comme (comparaison)
of /əv/ *ou* /ɒv/	a cup **of** tea / What are you scared **of**?	de, à, etc.
off /ɒf/	Keep **off** the grass. *(Pelouse interdite.)*	*idée d'éloignement*
on /ɒn/	It is **on** the fridge. / There is a good film **on** BBC 2.	sur
out of /'aʊtəv/	Get **out of** here! /**Out of** order	en dehors de, hors de
round /raʊnd/	A trip **round** the world. / We work **round** the clock. *(= 24 h sur 24)*	autour de
to /tə/ *ou* /tu:/	I am going **to** London. Who did you give your torch **to**?	à, vers, etc.
under /'ʌndə/	Put it **under** the table.	sous
up /ʌp/	He took me **up** St Paul's.	en haut de
with /wɪð/	Do you work **with** him? Sugar **with** your coffee?	avec
without /wɪð'aʊt/	You mustn't climb **without** a rope; you might fall.	sans

14 LES QUANTIFIEURS

On appelle **quantifieurs** l'ensemble des outils grammaticaux exprimant la quantité : les chiffres et les nombres (cardinaux et ordinaux), et également (pour le français) des mots tels que **un peu, beaucoup...**
Les quantifieurs peuvent porter sur des noms : too **much** rain, des adjectifs : **a little** cold, des verbes : he smokes **too much**.

79 1. Cardinaux et ordinaux

	CARDINAUX	ORDINAUX
1	one	the first
2	two	the **se**cond /'seknd/
3	three	the third
4	four	the fourth
5	five /faɪv/	the fifth /fɪfθ/
6	six	the sixth /sɪksθ/
7	**se**ven	the **se**venth
8	eight /eɪt/	the eighth /eɪtθ/
9	nine	the ninth /naɪnθ/
10	ten	the tenth
11	e**le**ven	the e**le**venth
12	twelve	the twelfth /twelfθ/
13	thir**teen**	the thir**teenth**
14	four**teen**	the four**teenth**
15	fif**teen** /fɪf'tiːn/	the fif**teenth**
16	six**teen**	the six**teenth**
17	seven**teen**	the seven**teenth**
18	eigh**teen**	the eigh**teenth**
19	nine**teen**	the nine**teenth**
20	**twen**ty	the **twen**tieth /'twentɪəθ/
21	twenty-**one**	the twenty-**first**
22	twenty-**two**	the twenty-**se**cond
23	twenty-**three**	the twenty-**third**
24	twenty-**four**	the twenty-**fourth**
25	twenty-**five**	the twenty-**fifth**
30	**thir**ty	the **thir**tieth
40	**for**ty	the **for**tieth
50	**fif**ty	the **fif**tieth
60	**six**ty	the **six**tieth
70	**se**venty	the **se**ventieth
80	**eigh**ty	the **eigh**tieth
90	**nine**ty	the **nine**tieth
100	a **hun**dred	the **hun**dredth
150	a **hun**dred and **fif**ty	the **hun**dred and **fif**tieth
153	a **hun**dred and **fif**ty-**three**	the **hun**dred and **fif**ty-**third**
1000	a **thou**sand /'θaʊzənd/	the **thou**sandth
1672	a **thou**sand **six hun**dred and **se**venty-**two**	the **thou**sand **six hun**dred and **se**venty-**se**cond
etc.		

N.B. : Les syllabes accentuées sont en gras. La prononciation n'est indiquée que dans les cas où l'orthographe risque de prêter à confusion.

80 **PIÈGE !**

Dozen, hundred, million

a. I need 2 **dozen** eggs.
b. **Dozens of** people from all over the world visit the site.

a. This magnificient oak tree is over six **hundred** years old.
b. Graffiti has been around for **hundreds of** years...

a. The damage cost ten **thousand** dollars.
b. They have spent **thousands of** dollars to repair the damage.

a. Their album sold 3 **million** copies in the USA.
b. In the 19th century **millions of** buffaloes were killed.

Précédés d'un chiffre et suivi d'un nom, *dozen / hundred / million* sont **invariables** car ils sont employés comme adjectifs – exemples **a.**
Dans les exemples **b.** ils sont employés comme noms ; **ils prennent le pluriel *-s*** et sont suivis de ***of* + nom au pluriel.**

79 bis **Prononciation**

-teen est généralement accentué mais ***-ty*** ne l'est jamais :
seven → seven**teen** → **se**venty

Les ordinaux servent par exemple à exprimer la date. On ne dit pas tout à fait ce qui est écrit :

Friday, February 16th 2002
→ Friday *the* sixteenth of February two thousand and two

jour + *the* + ordinal + *of* + mois + année

Comment exprimer l'année?

Avant 2000 :

19|53 : nineteen fifty-three (couronnement de la Reine Elizabeth II d'Angleterre)
17|76 : seventeen seventy-six (indépendance des États-Unis)
16|16 : sixteen sixteen (mort de William Shakespeare)

2000 et après... :

2000: two thousand
2004: two thousand and four

81 2. De zéro à un

NO /nəʊ/	Suivi du singulier ou du pluriel. Il fonctionne comme un article négatif. There is **no** coffee. There are **no** snakes in Ireland.
NONE /nʌn/	C'est un pronom. Il reprend un nom, au singulier ou au pluriel. There were ten little Indians... and then there were none.
ONE /wʌn/	• le numéral : I have **one** brother, not two. • le pronom reprend un nom déjà présent dans le contexte avant : Few animals survive in the wild. The Tamarin is **one** of them. I have a red gremlin and a blue **one**. Which **one** do you like best?

82 3. deux

BOTH /bəʊθ/	• ***Both*** est un pluriel **limité à deux** unités. On le trouve avec des noms de paires déjà établies : *eyes, arms, legs*, etc. • **Both** eyes are usually the same colour. I've got two cats. **Both** just love milk. • ***Both*** peut également traduire le français : **à la fois** x **et** y. If you use someone who is **both** very good at sensing chaos **and** very good at hiding, you will be able to find it.

83 4. peu de / un peu… / quelques…

Ø LITTLE /lɪtl/	• ***Ø little* + nom indénombrable** ***Ø little*** est plutôt **négatif,** comme le français **peu**. There is Ø **little** money. (peu d'argent) He eats very Ø **little**. (Il mange très peu.)
A LITTLE	• *a little* est plutôt **positif,** comme le français **un peu**. Give them **a little** love… They weigh **a little** over a kilo.
Ø FEW /fjuː/	• Ø ***few*** + **nom dénombrable** au **pluriel** Ø ***few*** est plutôt **négatif**, comme *little*. Ø **few** animals have been successfully reintroduced in the wild. (Peu d'animaux)
A FEW	• ***a few*** est plutôt **positif,** comme *a little*. I'd like to ask you **a few** questions. (Quelques…)

84 5. beaucoup… (et beaucoup trop !)

A LOT OF LOTS OF	***a lot of / lots of* + dénombrable pluriel ou indénombrable** exprime une **grande quantité.** I've got **a lot of** work to do. There are **lots of** animals in this hospital. Thanks **a lot**!
MUCH /mʌtʃ/	• ***much*** + **indénombrable** Our train leaves at 11 . We haven't got **much** time. • ***how much?*** **How much** money do you need? • ***too much*** I practice for an hour and a half when I don't have **too much** homework. He smokes **too much**.
MANY /ˈmenɪ/	• ***many* + dénombrable pluriel** **Many** animals are in danger of extinction. The weather was bad. I didn't take **many** pictures. How **many** postcards did you **buy**? • ***too many*** Don't ask **too many** questions!
MOST /məʊst/	• ***most* + dénombrable au pluriel traduit le français *"la plupart, la plus grande partie, presque tout/tous"*.** Most Golden Lion Tamarins weigh over a kilo. • ***most* employé pour le superlatif** (le plus…) 98 Dolphins are **the most** intelligent animals in the world.

85 6. *some* et *any*

Ils fonctionnent avec **les noms indénombrables et les noms dénombrables.**

SOME /sm/ Exprime une certaine quantité de ce que désigne le nom qui suit (en français : **du** café, **de la** confiture).

• **Énoncés affirmatifs :**
You should drink **some** water.
I must get **some** stamps.
• **Énoncés interrogatifs :**
What about some Coke?
Where can I get **some** stamps?

/sʌm/ • ***Some* pronom**
Where is my money? I need **some** now.
I have made some /sm/ biscuits. Do you want **some**?

ANY /ˈenɪ/ Fonctionne principalement dans les énoncés interrogatifs et négatifs.

Énoncés interrogatifs :
Is there **any** mail for me?
Do you buy **any** cosmetics?
Énoncés négatifs :
(ici, en réponse à la question : Do you buy any cosmetics?)
→ I don't buy **any** cosmetics simply because my parents don't give me **any** money!
• ***Any* pronom**
I wanted some coke but there isn't **any**. My brother has drunk it all.

86 7. Les composés de *some*, et *any* et *no*

Pour les êtres humains :

- Look! There is **somebody** in the garden!
- Where? I can't see **anybody**.

There's **nobody** home.

I need **someone** like you.
Is **anyone** home?
There's **no one** around.

Pour les choses :

I must buy **something** for my sister.
This is a very expensive shop. I haven't bought **anything**.
There's **nothing** I can do for you!

Pour les lieux :

I can't find my mobile. I know it must be **somewhere** in my room.
We won't go **anywhere** this summer.
He came from **nowhere.**

87 ## 8. *each* et *every*

Each et ***every*** ne fonctionnent qu'avec les dénombrables au singulier. Ils peuvent traduire tous les deux le français **chaque**. ***Each*** est plus proche de **chacun.** ***Every*** est plus employé pour exprimer un bilan, une régularité.

each /iːtʃ/	Match **each** question with the appropriate answer. How much are these books? £5 **each.** (£5 pièce / £5 chacun)
every /ˈevrɪ/	There is a fast train **every** morning at 7. This is Shadow. He comes to visit me **every** week. Les composés de ***every*** sont ***everybody/everyone***, ***everything***, ***everywhere***. Come on **everybody**, time to go. Make sure you take **everything** with you. Josh's been **everywhere.**

88 ## 9. *all*

ALL /ɔːl/	Fonctionne avec les dénombrables au pluriel et les indénombrables. He lost **all** his money. **All** his friends live in New York. She's read **all** her magazine. / She's read it **all**. - Do you save any money? - No, I spend it **all**." **Expressions avec *all* :** I'm **not** shy **at all.** - Do you mind if I go out? **- Not at all.** **That's all** folks! (cf. cartoons *Merry Melodies*)

89 ## 10. *too* et *also*

Ils peuvent tous les deux traduire le français **aussi.**

too /tuː/	Jury : Do you play any other instruments? Josh : I don't. But I sing in the school choir. Jury : So, you sing **too**? Josh : Yes, and I love it **too.** ***Too*** signale un simple ajout : tu joues d'un instrument + tu chantes. Réponse de Josh : je chante, et (+) j'aime cela.
also /ˈɔːlsəʊ/	Dolphins <u>are good fun</u>. They **also** <u>help children with learning problems</u>. ***Also*** **: non seulement** x, **mais aussi** y. Les éléments soulignés ont un point commun : choses positives.

90 ## 11. *enough*

enough /ɪˈnʌf/	Fonctionne avec noms et adjectifs. **Attention** à sa place dans la phrase ! • ***enough*** **+ nom** I don't think we have **enough** *food* for two days. • **adjectif +** ***enough*** This tent is not *big* **enough** for two people.

91 ## 12. *such* + nom / *so* + adjectif

On peut classer dans les quantifieurs ces deux outils grammaticaux qui permettent de mettre en relief le nom ou l'adjectif sur lequel ils portent.

• ***such*** **+ nom**

Ending up at the wrong ocean was a disappointment for Mackenzie. → pas de mise en relief

Ending up at the wrong ocean was **such** a disappointment for Mackenzie. → mise en relief du nom (une telle déception)

Ending up at the wrong ocean was **such** a disappointment **that** Mackenzie named the river "The River of Disappointment". → mise en relief du nom ET conséquence logique

Such peut être suivi de [adjectif + nom] : Makenzie was **such** a *brave man*...

- ***so* + adjectif**

Radiation and heat levels are high, and cosmic bombardments severe. → pas de mise en relief
Radiation and heat levels are **so** high, and cosmic bombardments **so** severe! → mise en relief des adjectifs.

Radiation and heat levels are **so** high, and cosmic bombardments **so** severe **that** the only life-forms that might exist would be little green bacteria. → mise en relief des adjectifs et conséquence logique

Compare :

Mackenzie was **such** [a brave man]! = on parle d'un homme brave

et

Mackenzie was **so** [brave]! = on parle de sa bravoure

92 13. Quantifieurs au comparatif

En anglais comme en français, on compare les quantités. On peut ainsi comparer :
- avec des noms : **plus** d'argent, de soucis, **moins** de problèmes, **autant** de pluie.
- avec des verbes : manger **plus**, fumer **moins**, dépenser **autant**.

Que le nom soit dénombrable ou indénombrable, le français fait appel à UN seul procédé : moins que, plus que, autant que. Il en est de même avec les verbes.

En anglais la distinction indénombrable /dénombrable est importante. On emploie les mêmes comparatifs avec les verbes et les noms indénombrables.

a. People should consume **less**.
b. I should have thought about it **more**.
c. What would happen if the Chinese consumed **as much as** we do?
d. I enjoyed myself **so much**!
e. You should use **less** sugar.
f. I spent **more** time in that shop (than you).
g. He tried to get **as much** money **as** he could.
h. There wouldn't be **so much** violence if there weren't so many guns.
i. There are **fewer** tourists than last year.
j. We need **more** knives. Can you go and get some?
k. I hate writing but I tried to send **as many** postcards **as** I could.
l. If people didn't buy **so many** guns there wouldn't be so much violence.

QUANTIFIEURS AU COMPARATIF	avec un verbe	avec un nom indénombrable	avec un nom dénombrable pluriel
moins	**less** than (a)	**less** ... than (e)	**fewer** ... than (i)
plus	**more** than (b)	**more** ... than (f)	**more** ... than (j)
autant	**as much as** (c)	**as much** ... **as** ... (g)	**as many** ... **as** ... (k)
autant / tant	**so much** (d)	**so much** (h)	**so many** ... (l)

15

LES ADJECTIFS

93 • **L'adjectif en anglais est invariable.**

À la différence du français, il n'a pas de masculin, pas de féminin, pas de pluriel :

a **nice** man → **nice** men
a **nice** girl → nice **girls**

• **L'adjectif se place avant le nom qu'il qualifie,** et non pas après, comme c'est possible en français : a **red** car - **green** buses - a **young** man

1. Ordre des adjectifs

Dès qu'il y a **plus d'un** adjectif, se pose le problème de l'ordre dans lequel on va les placer, puisqu'ils sont **tous** placés avant le nom.

Règle :
L'adjectif qui se trouve le plus près du nom est celui qui dépend le moins de l'appréciation de l'énonciateur.

Par exemple :
nom : a car
adjectifs à placer : beautiful, large, American
Comment choisir ?

1. American : la nationalité ne dépend pas de celui qui parle
2. large : la taille peut être perçue différemment selon chacun
3. beautiful : les goûts ne sont que personnels

→ **A beautiful large American car**

94 2. Fabrication d'adjectifs

De nombreux adjectifs sont le résultat d'un **assemblage**. Voici quelques exemples de fabrication :

• ***un- (valeur négative)* + adjectif**
un**hap**py, un**lu**cky

• **nom + *-ful***
beautiful, **care**ful, **use**ful

• **nom + *-less***
careless, **home**less, **pen**niless

• **nom + *-ese***
Chi**nese** , Japa**nese**

• **nom + *-ly***
friendly, **love**ly

• **nom + *-y***
dirty, **noi**sy

• **nom + *-n***
A**me**rican, Aus**tra**lian, **Rus**sian

• **nom + *-ish***
British, **Scot**tish, **Tur**kish

• **adjectif + *-ish***
foolish, **gree**nish, **red**dish, **sel**fish

• **verbe + *-ing***
a**mu**sing, **fright**ening, **in**teresting

• **verbe + *-ed***
a**mu**sed, **fright**ened, **in**terested

Les syllabes accentuées sont en gras.

95 3. Adjectifs employés comme noms

En faisant précéder un adjectif de l'article *the*, on obtient **un nom à sens pluriel** qui est invariable (il ne prend pas le *-s* du pluriel) :

rich → the rich (les riches)
poor → the poor (les pauvres)
homeless → the homeless (les sans-logis)

Les adjectifs de nationalités deviennent également des noms pour désigner les habitants d'un pays. Voici un tableau récapitulatif :

1 pays	2 adjectif de nationalité	3 nom donné à un(e) habitant(e) du pays	4 nom donné aux habitants du pays
Britain	British	a Briton / a British woman	the British
England	English	an Englishman /'ɪŋglɪʃmən/ an English woman	the English
Scotland	Scottish	a Scotsman /'skɒtsmən/ a Scotswoman	the Scottish
Wales	Welsh	a Welshman /'welʃmən/ a Welsh woman	the Welsh
Ireland	Irish	an Irishman /'aɪrɪʃmən/ an Irish woman	the Irish
America	American	an American	the Americans
Australia	Australian	an Australian	the Australians
India	Indian	an Indian	the Indians
Mexico	Mexican	a Mexican	the Mexicans
China	Chinese	a Chinese (person)	the Chinese
France	French	a Frenchman /'frentʃmən/ a French woman	the French
Japan /dʒə'pæn/	Japanese /dʒæpə'ni:z/	a Japanese (person)	the Japanese

Note que parmi les noms de la colonne 4, seuls ceux qui se terminent par ***-an*** prennent le ***-s*** du pluriel.

16 LE COMPARATIF ET LE SUPERLATIF

96 A. Le comparatif

		Comparatif		
		d'infériorité	d'égalité	de supériorité
français		moins *adj.* que	aussi *adj.* que	plus *adj.* que
anglais	une syllabe	**less** *adj.* **than**	**as** *adj.* **as**	adj. **-(e)r than**
	deux syllabes et plus			**more** *adj.* **than**

- A Jaguar is **less** expensive **than** a Rolls Royce.
- He is **as** cunning **as** a fox.
- He jumps high**er than** his brother.
- Skating is **more** exciting **than** cycling.

Remarque

On emploie plus volontiers [***not as*** + adj. + ***as***] que [***less*** + adj. + ***than***] :

- Kate is **not as** tall **as** Josh.
- Coffee is **not as** expensive **as** tea.

ATTENTION !

1. Quelques adjectifs ne suivent pas le procédé décrit dans le tableau :

good → **better**
- Josh is **better** at tennis **than** Bryan.

bad → **worse**
- American coffee is **worse than** English coffee.

2. Modifications orthographiques : pour les adjectifs d'une syllabe terminés par une consonne précédée d'une seule voyelle, on double la consonne finale :

hot → hot**ter**
big → big**ger**

3. Quelques adjectifs **de deux** syllabes peuvent fonctionner **comme ceux d'une syllabe :**

clever → clever**er**

C'est aussi le cas de quelques adjectifs en ***-y*** :

pretty → pretti**er**
friendly → friendli**er**
dirty → dirti**er** À noter : **y → i**

97 B. Accroissement progressif (ou comparatif double)

a. Their territory became small**er**.
a.' Their territory became small**er and** small**er**.

b. Pressure groups are becoming **more** insistent.
b.' Pressure groups are becoming **more and more** insistent.

c. Today **more** Lakotas want the Black Hills back.
c.' Today **more and more** Lakotas want the Black Hills back.

Le comparatif de supériorité peut porter sur un adjectif et également sur un nom *(Lakotas)*. Les phrases **a., b.,** et **c.** présentent des exemples de comparatifs traduits à chaque fois par ***plus*** pour les adjectifs (**a.** et **b.**) et ***plus de / davantage de*** pour les noms (**c.**).
Le comparatif portant sur un nom est le même que celui des adjectifs de deux syllabes et plus : ***more***.

- There are **more** people than last year.
- I've got **more** DVDs than you.

Les phrases **a.'**, **b.'**, et **c.'** signalent que le changement se fait par étapes, qu'il est en pleine évolution, d'où l'étiquette **accroissement progressif**. On traduit en français par ***de plus en plus*** + ***adjectif***, et de ***plus en plus de*** + ***nom***. Le procédé de fabrication est simple :

- adjectifs d'une syllabe (voir 96) :

adjectif + ***(e)r and*** adjectif + ***(e)r***

nice**r and** nice**r**, bigg**er and** bigg**er**, etc.

- adjectifs de deux syllabes et plus :

more and more + adjectif

more and more difficult, **more and more** expensive, etc.

- noms (dénombrables ou indénombrables) :

more and more + nom

more and more money, **more and more** friends, etc.

ATTENTION !

good → better and better

Her English is getting **better and better**, don't you think?

bad → worse and worse

I am very worried. Paul's maths results are getting **worse and worse**.

98 C. Le superlatif

	superlatif	
	minimum (le moins)	**maximum** (le plus)
adjectif d'1 syllabe	**the least** *adj.*	**the** *adj.*- **(e)st**
adjectif de 2 syllabes et +		**the most** *adj.*

- This is the clean**est** hospital I've ever visited.
- This is **the least** expensive restaurant in New York.
- The dolphin is **the most** intelligent animal in the world.

ATTENTION !

1. Quelques adjectifs ne suivent pas le procédé décrit dans le tableau.

good → the **best** (le meilleur)
bad → the **worst** (le pire/le plus mauvais)

2. Modifications orthographiques :

hot → hott**est** - big → bigg**est**

3. Quelques adjectifs **de deux syllabes** fonctionnent **comme ceux d'une syllabe** :

clever → the clever**est**
pretty → the pretti**est**

17 PRONOMS RELATIFS ET PROPOSITIONS RELATIVES

99 La raison d'être d'une proposition relative est **d'apporter des précisions**, des informations supplémentaires, à propos d'un nom. Pour ne pas répéter ce nom, on fait appel à un pronom relatif.

1. He gives hope to children ***who** are mentally and physically handicapped.*
2. According to parents ***whose** kids have spent a few hours with dolphins,* the therapy has brought great results.

Les deux propositions en italiques ci-dessus sont appelées **propositions relatives**. Elles sont **en relation** avec le nom qu'elles complètent : *children* et *parents* – et qu'on appelle **l'antécédent.**
Si on supprime les propositions relatives de 1 et 2, on change complètement le sens des phrases, car en 1 tous les enfants et en 2 tous les parents sont alors concernés.

Voici les principaux pronoms relatifs :

who	**what**	**when**	**Ø**
whose	**which**	**where**	**that**
		why	

Les pronoms relatifs tiennent compte de la distinction humain/non humain :

	HUMAIN	NON-HUMAIN	HUMAIN ET NON HUMAIN
sujet	**who**	**what/which**	**that**
complément d'objet	**who**	**what/which**	**Ø/that**
complément du nom	**whose**	**whose**	
complément de lieu		**where**	
complément de cause		**why**	

who **: sujet**	He gives hope to children ***who** are mentally and physically handicapped.*
whose **: complément du nom**	According to parents ***whose** kids have spent a few hours with dolphins,* the therapy has brought great results. (les parents dont les enfants...)
which **: sujet**	It produces an enormous amount of sound energy ***which** can affect the human body.*
where **: complément de lieu**	Some dolphins are released back in the wild ***where** they do not know how to survive.*
that **: sujet**	Few of the dolphins ***that** are released back in the wild* have a happy ending.
Ø **: complément d'objet**	It is the dirtiest hospital ***Ø** I have ever seen.*

What / Which

Face au français ce qu(e) / ce qui, l'anglais offre ***what /which*** :

- So I'm using **what** they love... (**ce qu**'ils aiment)

What n'a pas d'antécédent direct dans la phrase.

- That relaxation helps stimulate the immune system, **which** explains why... (**ce qui** ...)

Which remplace **toute** une proposition.

18 CONNECTEURS DE PHRASES

100 Un connecteur est un outil grammatical qui permet de relier –d' établir une connexion – entre deux propositions. Quelques exemples en français : *parce que, tandis que, pendant que*, etc. En anglais tu connais : ***as soon as, because, how, when***, etc.

Nous ne regroupons ici que quelques connecteurs qui ont en commun de signaler une **opposition**, une **différence**, un **conflit** entre deux propositions : ***although, however, while, whereas, and yet.***

1. *although* /ɔːlˈðəʊ/ -gh- n'est pas prononcé

- **Although** they were granted to the Lakotas in 1868, the Black Hills have been constantly exploited by non-Indians. (Bien que ...)

Although permet d'abord de rappeler une situation pour ensuite dire quelque chose qui est en totale contradiction. Il se place **au début** de la proposition qu'il introduit. Le français *bien que* (+ subjonctif) traduit ***although***.

2. *however* (composé de *how + ever*)

- In the past four decades, they've spent more than $ 100 million and they haven't detected a beep! **However**, Drake, who founded SETI, remains optimistic.

However permet d'introduire une contradiction à une phrase qui précède. Il se place au début de la phrase qu'il introduit. Il est traduit par *cependant*.

3. *while*

- Forty-four percent of the respondents say that if they meet E.T.s from a galaxy far, far away, they'll be friends, **while** 26 percent think they'll be enemies.

While permet d'introduire un fait qui se déroule au même moment qu'un autre et avec lequel il est en opposition. On oppose ici 26% aux 44% du début. Le français traduit cet emploi de ***while*** avec *tandis que/alors que*.

4. *whereas* /weəˈræz/

- [The real Arthur fought against the Saxons] **whereas** [the legendary Arthur fought against the Romans].

Placé entre deux propositions, *whereas* permet d'opposer deux personnes, deux choses. Il est surtout employé à l'écrit. Dans la langue parlée, c'est ***while*** qui pourrait être employé ici.

5. *and yet...*

- The region is very arid **and yet** the company wastes huge quantities of water.

Utilisé comme connecteur après ***and***, ***yet*** signale que ce qui suit est inattendu, surprenant.
and yet se traduit par : *et pourtant*.

verbes irréguliers

	BASE VERBALE	PRÉTÉRIT	PARTICIPE PASSÉ	TRADUCTION
B	**be** [iː]	**was** [ɒ]	**been** [iː]	*être*
	bear [eə]	**bore** [ɔː]	**borne** [ɔː]	*porter, supporter, naître* (born)
	beat [iː]	**beat** [iː]	**beaten** [iː]	*battre*
	become [ɪ/ʌ]	**became** [ɪ/eɪ]	**become** [ɪ/ʌ]	*devenir*
5	**begin** [ɪ/ɪ]	**began** [ɪ/æ]	**begun** [ɪ/ʌ]	*commencer*
	bend [bend]	**bent** [e]	**bent** [e]	*courber, (se) pencher*
	bet [e]	**bet** [e]	**bet** [e]	*parier*
	bite [aɪ]	**bit** [ɪ]	**bitten** [ɪ]	*mordre*
	bleed [iː]	**bled** [e]	**bled** [e]	*saigner*
10	**blow** [əʊ]	**blew** [uː]	**blown** [əʊ]	*souffler*
	break [eɪ]	**broke** [əʊ]	**broken** [əʊ]	*casser*
	bring [ɪ]	**brought** [ɔː]	**brought** [ɔː]	*apporter*
	build [ɪ]	**built** [ɪ]	**built** [ɪ]	*construire*
	burn [ɜː]	**burnt** [ɜː]	**burnt** [ɜː]	*brûler*
15	**burst** [ɜː]	**burst** [ɜː]	**burst** [ɜː]	*éclater, exploser*
	buy [aɪ]	**bought** [ɔː]	**bought** [ɔː]	*acheter*
C	**cast** [ɑː]	**cast** [ɑː]	**cast** [ɑː]	*jeter, lancer*
	catch [æ]	**caught** [ɔː]	**caught** [ɔː]	*attraper*
	choose [uː]	**chose** [əʊ]	**chosen** [əʊ]	*choisir*
20	**come** [ʌ]	**came** [eɪ]	**come** [ʌ]	*venir*
	cost [ɒ]	**cost** [ɒ]	**cost** [ɒ]	*coûter*
	cut [ʌ]	**cut** [ʌ]	**cut** [ʌ]	*couper*
D	**deal** [iː]	**dealt** [e]	**dealt** [e]	*distribuer, donner, faire le commerce*
	dig [ɪ]	**dug** [ʌ]	**dug** [ʌ]	*creuser*
25	**do** [uː]	**did** [ɪ]	**done** [ʌ]	*faire*
	draw [ɔː]	**drew** [uː]	**drawn** [ɔː]	*dessiner, tirer (les rideaux)*
	dream [iː]	**dreamed(t)** [iː]	**dreamed(t)** [iː]	*rêver*
	drink [ɪ]	**drank** [æ]	**drunk** [ʌ]	*boire*
	drive [aɪ]	**drove** [əʊ]	**driven** [ɪ]	*conduire*
E 30	**eat** [iː]	**ate** [e]	**eaten** [iː]	*manger*
F	**fall** [ɔː]	**fell** [e]	**fallen** [ɔː/ə]	*tomber*
	feed [iː]	**fed** [e]	**fed** [e]	*nourrir*
	feel [iː]	**felt** [e]	**felt** [e]	*se sentir, toucher*
	fight [aɪ]	**fought** [ɔː]	**fought** [ɔː]	*se battre, se disputer*
35	**find** [aɪ]	**found** [aʊ]	**found** [aʊ]	*trouver*
	flee [iː]	**fled** [e]	**fled** [e]	*s'enfuir*
	fly [aɪ]	**flew** [uː]	**flown** [əʊ]	*voler*
	forbid [ə/ɪ]	**forbade** [ə/eɪ]	**forbidden** [ə/ɪ]	*interdire*
	forget [ə/e]	**forgot** [ə/ɒ]	**forgotten** [ə/ɒ]	*oublier*
40	**freeze** [iː]	**froze** [əʊ]	**frozen** [əʊ]	*geler*
G	**get** [e]	**got** [ɒ]	**got** [ɒ]	*obtenir, devenir, recevoir*
	give [ɪ]	**gave** [eɪ]	**given** [ɪ]	*donner*
	go [əʊ]	**went** [e]	**gone** [ɒ]	*aller*
	grow [əʊ]	**grew** [uː]	**grown** [əʊ]	*croître, faire pousser, grandir*
H 45	**hang** [æ]	**hung** [ʌ]	**hung** [ʌ]	*accrocher, pendre, suspendre*
	have [æ]	**had** [æ]	**had** [æ]	*avoir*
	hear [ɪə]	**heard** [ɜː]	**heard** [ɜː]	*entendre*
	hide [aɪ]	**hid** [ɪ]	**hidden** [ɪ]	*(se) cacher*
	hit [ɪ]	**hit** [ɪ]	**hit** [ɪ]	*frapper*
50	**hold** [əʊ]	**held** [e]	**held** [e]	*tenir*
	hurt [ɜː]	**hurt** [ɜː]	**hurt** [ɜː]	*(se) blesser, (se) faire mal*
K	**keep** [iː]	**kept** [e]	**kept** [e]	*garder*
	kneel [iː]	**knelt** [e]	**knelt** [e]	*s'agenouiller*
	know [nəʊ]	**knew** [njuː]	**known** [nəʊn]	*savoir, connaître*
L 55	**lead** [iː]	**led** [e]	**led** [e]	*mener, conduire à*
	lean [iː]	**leant** [e]	**leant** [e]	*s'appuyer*
	learn [ɜː]	**learned(t)** [ɜː]	**learned(t)** [ɜː]	*apprendre*
	leave [iː]	**left** [e]	**left** [e]	*partir, quitter, laisser*

		BASE VERBALE	PRÉTÉRIT	PARTICIPE PASSÉ	TRADUCTION
		lend [e]	**lent** [e]	**lent** [e]	*prêter*
	60	**let** [e]	**let** [e]	**let** [e]	*prêter*
		lie [aɪ]	**lay** [eɪ]	**lain** [eɪ]	*être allongé*
		lose [uː]	**lost** [ɒ]	**lost** [ɒ]	*perdre*
M		**make** [eɪ]	**made** [eɪ]	**made** [eɪ]	*faire, fabriquer, rendre*
		mean [iː]	**meant** [e]	**meant** [e]	*signifier, vouloir dire*
	65	**meet** [iː]	**met** [e]	**met** [e]	*rencontrer*
P		**pay** [eɪ]	**paid** [eɪ]	**paid** [eɪ]	*payer*
		put [ʊ]	**put** [ʊ]	**put** [ʊ]	*mettre*
Q		**quit** [ɪ]	**quit** [ɪ]	**quit** [ɪ]	*quitter, abandonner*
R		**read** [iː]	**read** [e]	**read** [e]	*lire*
	70	**ride** [aɪ]	**rode** [əʊ]	**ridden** [ɪ]	*aller à cheval, à bicyclette, en moto*
		ring [ɪ]	**rang** [æ]	**rung** [ʌ]	*sonner*
		rise [aɪ]	**rose** [əʊ]	**risen** [ɪ]	*s'élever, se lever*
		run [ʌ]	**ran** [æ]	**run** [ʌ]	*courir*
S		**say** [eɪ]	**said** [e]	**said** [e]	*dire*
	75	**see** [iː]	**saw** [ɔː]	**seen** [iː]	*voir*
		seek [iː]	**sought** [ɔː]	**sought** [ɔː]	*chercher*
		sell [e]	**sold** [əʊ]	**sold** [əʊ]	*vendre*
		send [e]	**sent** [e]	**sent** [e]	*envoyer*
		set [e]	**set** [e]	**set** [e]	*poser, se coucher (soleil)*
	80	**shake** [eɪ]	**shook** [ʊ]	**shaken** [eɪ]	*secouer, trembler, serrer la main*
		shine [aɪ]	**shone** [ɒ]	**shone** [ɒ]	*briller*
		shoot [uː]	**shot** [ɒ]	**shot** [ɒ]	*tirer, tourner un film*
		show [əʊ]	**showed** [əʊ]	**shown** [əʊ]	*montrer*
		shut [ʃʌt]	**shut** [ʃʌt]	**shut** [ʃʌt]	*fermer*
	85	**sing** [ɪ]	**sang** [æ]	**sung** [ʌ]	*chanter*
		sit [ɪ]	**sat** [æ]	**sat** [æ]	*être assis*
		sleep [iː]	**slept** [e]	**slept** [e]	*dormir*
		slide [aɪ]	**slid** [ɪ]	**slid** [ɪ]	*glisser*
		smell [e]	**smelt** [e]	**smelt** [e]	*sentir (odeur)*
	90	**speak** [iː]	**spoke** [əʊ]	**spoken** [əʊ/ə]	*parler*
		spell [e]	**spelt** [e]	**spelt** [e]	*épeler*
		spend [e]	**spent** [e]	**spent** [e]	*dépenser de l'argent, passer du temps*
		spill [ɪ]	**spilt** [ɪ]	**spilt** [ɪ]	*renverser*
		split [ɪ]	**split** [ɪ]	**split** [ɪ]	*fendre, (se) séparer, partager*
	95	**spoil** [ɔɪ]	**spoilt** [ɔɪ]	**spoilt** [ɔɪ]	*gâcher, gâter (enfant), pourrir*
		spread [e]	**spread** [e]	**spread** [e]	*étaler, étendre, se répandre*
		spring [ɪ]	**sprang** [æ]	**sprung** [ʌ]	*jaillir, bondir, provenir de*
		stand [æ]	**stood** [ʊ]	**stood** [ʊ]	*se tenir debout, supporter, tolérer*
		steal [iː]	**stole** [əʊ]	**stolen** [əʊ/ə]	*voler*
	100	**stick** [ɪ]	**stuck** [ʌ]	**stuck** [ʌ]	*coller, épingler*
		swear [eə]	**swore** [ɔː]	**sworn** [ɔː]	*jurer*
		sweep [iː]	**swept** [e]	**swept** [e]	*balayer*
		swim [ɪ]	**swam** [æ]	**swum** [ʌ]	*nager*
T		**take** [eɪ]	**took** [ʊ]	**taken** [eɪ/ə]	*prendre*
	105	**teach** [iː]	**taught** [ɔː]	**taught** [ɔː]	*enseigner*
		tear [eə]	**tore** [ɔː]	**torn** [ɔː]	*déchirer*
		tell [e]	**told** [əʊ]	**told** [əʊ]	*dire, raconter*
		think [ɪ]	**thought** [ɔː]	**thought** [ɔː]	*penser, croire*
		throw [əʊ]	**threw** [uː]	**thrown** [əʊ]	*lancer, jeter*
U	110	**understand** [ʌ/ə/æ]	**understood** [ʌ/ə/ʊ]	**understood** [ʌ/ə/ʊ]	*comprendre*
		undertake [eɪ]	**undertook** [ʊ]	**undertaken** [eɪ/ə]	*entreprendre*
W		**wake (up)** [eɪ]	**woke (up)** [əʊ]	**woken (up)** [əʊ/ə]	*réveiller, s'éveiller*
		wear [eə]	**wore** [ɔː]	**worn** [ɔː]	*porter (vêtements)*
		win [ɪ]	**won** [ʌ]	**won** [ʌ]	*gagner*
	115	**write** [aɪ]	**wrote** [əʊ]	**written** [ɪ]	*écrire*

expressions

A big cheer for...	Un grand bravo pour...
a good turn	une bonne action
Any time!	N'importe quand ! Quand vous voulez !
April fool!	Poisson d'avril !
Are you nuts?	Tu es fou/folle ?
at the time	à l'époque
Be quiet!	Silence ! Tais-toi !
Behave yourself!	Tiens-toi bien !
Big deal!	Tu parles !
Bye for now !	Maintenant, au revoir !
catch one's death of cold	attraper la mort
Come off it!	Redescend sur terre !
Come on!	Allez ! Allons !
Come on in!	Entrez donc !
draw the line on	refuser
Enjoy yourself!	Amuse-toi bien !
for fun	pour le plaisir
get a big kick out of something	s'éclater
Get off my back!	Laisse-moi tranquille !
get one's mind off (something)	penser à autre chose
Go ahead!	Vas-y ! Allez-y !
Good for you!	Tant mieux pour toi !
Good luck!	Bonne chance !
green with envy	malade de jalousie
hands up	haut les mains
Hard luck!	Pas de chance !
Help yourself!	Sers-toi !
Here we are!	Nous voici !
Honest!	Juré !
I can't believe it!	Je n'y crois pas !
I don't think so.	Je ne crois pas.
I get it!	Je comprends (tout) !
I look forward to seeing you!	Je suis impatient de vous revoir !
I'm hopeless!	Je suis incorrigible !
I owe you one.	Je te revaudrais ça.
in the flesh	en chair et en os
It's a piece of cake!	C'est du gâteau !
It's no fun!	C'est pas drôle !
It's none of your business!	Ça ne te regarde pas !
It's not fair.	Ce n'est pas juste.
It seems to me that ...	Il me semble que...
It serves her right!	Bien fait pour elle !
Keep up the good work!	Poursuis tes efforts !
lend a hand	prêter main forte
Let me see...	Voyons...
Let's say...	Disons que...
make ends meet	joindre les deux bouts
Make yourself at home!	Fais comme chez toi !
Make yourself comfortable!	Mettez-vous à l'aise !

most of the time	la plupart du temps
Never mind!	Ça ne fait rien ! Tant pis !
no big deal	ce n'est pas un problème
no fear	out of the question
No way!	Pas question !
No wonder!	Pas étonnant !
No worries!	Pas d'inquiétude ! Ne vous inquiétez pas !
Not another word!	Plus un mot ! Pas un mot de plus !
Off we go!	C'est parti !
one by one	un par un
Out of the question!	Hors de question !
Pull your socks up!	Mets-toi au travail ! Retrousse tes manches !
right now	immédiatement
See you on Tuesday!	A mardi !
'Seems a shame	Quel dommage !
smash someone's face in	casser la figure à quelqu'un
snail mail	courrier postal
so-so	comme-ci, comme ça
Sure!	Bien sûr !
Take it easy!	Du calme ! Ne vous en faites pas !
Thank goodness!	Dieu merci !
That's all!	C'est tout !
That's final!	Un point c'est tout !
That/It doesn't matter!	Ça n'a pas d'importance !
The good old days!	Le bon vieux temps !
the pros and cons	le pour et le contre
There's no point in...	Ça ne sert à rien de...
There you go!	Voilà !
Think twice!	Réfléchis bien !
Time's up!	C'est fini !
to top it all	pour couronner le tout...
Trick or treat!	Une farce ou des bonbons (Hallowe'en).
Well done!	Bravo !
Well then...	Bon alors...
What a relief!	Quel soulagement !
What about you?	Et toi ?
What are you up to?	Qu'est-ce que vous fabriquez ?
What's got into you?	Qu'est-ce qui te prend ?
What's keeping you?	Qu'est-ce qui te retient ?
What's the matter? What's wrong?	Qu'est-ce qui ne va pas ?
What's up?	De quoi s'agit -il ? Que ce passe -t-il ?
You know what?	Tu sais quoi ?
You must be joking/kidding!	J'espère que tu plaisantes !
You're a pain!	Tu es pénible !
You're pulling my leg!	Vous me faites marcher !
You reckon?	Tu crois ?
You see...	Vois-tu...

lexique anglais-français

Si tu cherches un verbe et que tu ne le trouves pas dans le lexique ci-dessous, regarde dans la liste des verbes irréguliers pp. 168-169. Les mots transparents (ex : *ambulance*) ne figurent que dans le lexique français-anglais (p. 190).

A

abandon	abandonner
abandoned	abandonné
abduct	enlever
ability	aptitude
able to (be)	pouvoir, être capable de
abolish	abolir
Aborigine	aborigène
abroad	à l'étranger
absently	distraitement
absent-minded	distrait
absolutely	absolument
absurd	absurde
abused	maltraité
accelerate	accélérer
acceptable	acceptable
acceptance	acceptation, reconaissance
access	accès
accessory	accessoire
accomplice	complice
according to	selon
acquire	acquérir
across	de l'autre côté, en travers de
acrostic	acrostiche
act *(v.)*	jouer (un rôle), agir
Act *(n.)*	décret
acting talent	talent d'acteur
active	actif
activist	activiste
activity(ies)	activité
actor(tress)	acteur(trice)
adapt	adapter
add	ajouter
addict *(n.)*	fanatique, intoxiqué
addicted *(adj.)*	accro
address *(v.)*, *(n.)*	s'adresser ***(v.)***, adresse ***(n.)***
admit	admettre
adopt	adopter, choisir
advance	avancer
advantage	avantage
adventure	aventure
advertise	promouvoir, faire la publicité
advertisement, advert, ad	publicité, petite annonce
advertiser	annonceur
advertising	publicité
advice	conseil
advise	conseiller
aeroplane	avion
affect	toucher, produire un effet
afford	s'offrir, avoir les moyens
afraid (be)	avoir peur, avoir bien peur (que…)
Africa	Afrique
Afro	afro (coiffure)
after, after that	après, ensuite, après cela
afterlife	vie après la mort
afternoon	après-midi
afterwards	ensuite
again	encore, à nouveau
against	contre
age	âge
aged	âgé de
aggressive	agressif
ago (... two months ago)	il y a (deux mois)
agree	être d'accord
agreeable	agréable
aid	aide
AIDS	SIDA
aim (at/to) *(v.)*, *(n.)*	viser, aspirer (à) ***(v.)***, but, objectif ***(n.)***
Air Force	Armée de l'air, aviation
aircraft	appareil, avion
alarm	frayeur
alarm clock	réveil
Algeria	Algérie
Algerian	algérien
alibi	alibi
alien	extra-terrestre
all	tout, tous, toutes
all day	toute la journée
all over	partout
all right	d'accord, bien
all the time	tout le temps
all the way	tout le long (du chemin)
all together	tous ensemble
allow	permettre
allowed to (be)	avoir le droit de
allusion	allusion
almost	presque
alone	seul
along	le long (de)
along with	ainsi que
aloud	à haute voix
already	déjà
also	aussi
alternative	alternatif
although	bien que
always	toujours
amazed	stupéfait
amazing	stupéfiant, étonnant
ambitious	ambitieux
American	américain
among, amongst	parmi
amount	montant, somme, quantité
amused	amusé
analyse	analyser
ancient	ancien
angel	ange
anger	colère
angry	fâché
anguish	angoisse
ankle	cheville
annex *(v.)*	annexer
annihilation	anéantissement
announce	annoncer
annoy	embêter
annual	annuel
annually	annuellement, chaque année
another	un(e) autre
answer *(v.)*, *(n.)*	répondre, réponse
antelope	antilope
anti-conformist	anti-conformiste
anti-nuclear	anti-nucléaire
anti-smoking	anti-tabagisme
antidote	antidote
antique	antiquité
anyway	de toute façon
apparently	apparemment
appeal *(v.)*, *(n.)*	attirer, plaire à, lancer un appel ***(v.)*** ; appel ***(n.)***
appear	apparaître
appearance	apparition
apple	pomme
apple tree	pommier
apply	appliquer, postuler
apprentice	apprenti
approach	approcher
aqueduct	aqueduc
architect	architecte
area	endroit
argue	débattre
argument	argument, raisonnement
arid	aride
arm	bras
armchair	fauteuil
around	autour, à peu près
arrow	flèche
art work	oeuvre d'art
artificial	artificiel
artillery	artillerie
artistic	artistique
as soon as (possible)	dès que (possible)
as though	comme si
ascend	gravir
ashamed (be)	honteux, avoir honte
Asia	Asie
Asia Minor	Asie Mineure
ask for help	demander de l'aide
ask one's way	demander son chemin
ask someone out	inviter quelqu'un à sortir
asleep	endormi
aspect	aspect
assassinate	assassiner
assembly	assemblée, parlement
asset	atout
associate	associer
assure	assurer
astonished	étonné, surpris, stupéfait
astronaut	astronaute
astronomer	astronome
astronomy	astronomie
at first	tout d'abord
at least	au moins
at once	à la fois
at one point	à un moment
ate, prét. de **eat**	manger
athlete	athlète
athletics	athlétisme
Atlantic Ocean	Océan Atlantique
atmosphere	ambiance
atomic	atomique
attach	s'attacher
attack *(v.)*, *(n.)*	attaquer ***(v.)***, attaque ***(n.)***
attentive	attentif
attic	grenier
attitude	attitude
attract	attirer
attractive	attirant, séduisant
audience	public, spectateurs
auditorium	auditorium
August	août
aunt, auntie	tante, tata
Australia	Australie
Australian-Aussie	australien
author	auteur
authority *(n.)*	autorité
automatically	automatiquement
autumn	automne
available	disponible

average	moyen
avoid	éviter
awaited	attendu
award *(v.)*, *(n.)*	attribuer (une récompense) *(v.)*, récompense *(n.)*
awards	cérémonie de remise de prix
aware	conscient
away *(adj.)*	absent, parti
awful	affreux, terrible
awfully	terriblement
awkward	maladoit
axe	hache

B

back *(n.)*	dos
back (at the)	arrière (à l')
back door	porte arrière
back seat	siège arrière
back (to)	retour à (de)
background	arrière-plan, fond
backpack	sac à dos
bacteria (pl.)	bactéries
bad	mal, mauvais
bad point	défaut
baggy	ample, bouffant
bagpipe	cornemuse
bake	cuire (au four)
baked beans	haricots blancs cuits
baker's	boulangerie
ball court	terrain de basket
ballerina	ballerine, danseuse
balloon	ballon, bulle (BD)
Bangladesh	Bangladesh
bank	bord, rive
bank account	compte bancaire
banner ad	bannière (publicitaire)
bar *(n.)*	barre
bare	nu
bargain	bonne affaire
bark	aboyer
barn	grange
barrier reef	barrière de corail
bar(s)	barreau(x)
based in	basé à
battery(ies)	pile
battle	bataille
bay	baie
be* around	exister, être là
be* off	partir
be* on	être à l'affiche
be* on air	être à l'antenne
be* set (story, film)	se passer (histoire, film)
be* worth *(v.)*	valoir
beach	plage
bead	perle
bear *(n.)*	ours
beard	barbe
beast	bête
beat *(n.)*	mesure, temps *(n.)*
beautiful	beau
beautifully	magnifiquement, à la perfection
beaver	castor
become* extinct	disparaître, en voie d'extinction
bedtime	heure du coucher
bee	abeille
beer	bière
beetle	scarabée
before	avant
beginner	débutant
beginning	début
behave	se comporter
behead *(v.)*	décapiter
behind	derrière
believe	croire
bell	cloche
bell tower	clocher
bell-bottomed trousers	pantalons pattes d'éléphant
belong	appartenir
beloved	bien-aimé
below	ci-dessous
belt	ceinture
bench	banc
benefit	avantage
berries (pl.)	baies
beside	à côté de
besides	en outre
best	meilleur
best-known (the...)	plus connu (le)
betray	trahir
between	entre
beyond	au-delà
bill	facture
billion	milliard
bin	poubelle
binoculars	jumelles
biology	biologie
bird	oiseau, (argot) fille
biro	stylo à bille
birth	naissance
birthday	anniversaire
birthplace	lieu de naissance
bison	bison
bit of	un peu (de), un morceau (de)
bite* one's nails	se ronger les ongles
bits and pieces	morceaux, bidules, machins
black	noir
blackmail	chantage
blame	reprocher, faire porter la faute à…
blanket	couverture
bless	bénir
blind	aveugle
blinding	aveuglant
block	bloquer
blood	sang
bloodthirsty	assoiffé de sang, sanguinaire, cruel
bloody	cruel, ensanglanté
blouse	chemisier
blue	bleu
blue-eyed	yeux bleux (qui a les …)
Blues	Blues (musique)
blurred	floue
board	tableau (blanc ou noir)
boarding-school	internat
boastful	vantard
boat	bateau
body	corps
boil	bouillir
boiling hot	suffocant
bold (letters)	gras (lettre, caractère)
bole	tronc
bomb	bombe
bombardment	bombardement
bone	os
bonfire	feu de joie
bonnet	capot
book *(n.)*, *(v.)*	livre *(n.)*, réserver *(v.)*
(be a...) bore	être casse-pieds, ennuyeux
(be) bored	s'ennuyer
(be) bored stiff	s'ennuyer à mourir
boredom	ennui
boring	ennuyeux
borough	ville, municipalité
borrow	emprunter
both (...and...)	tous les deux, à la fois
bother	embêter, ennuyer
bottom	fond, bas
bow	arc
bow tie	noeud papillon
bowl	bocal
boycott *(v.)*	boycotter
bracket	parenthèse
brain	cerveau
brainless	stupide
brainwash *(v.)*	lavage de cerveau (faire un)
branch	branche
brand	marque
brand new	flambant neuf
brave	courageux
brave *(n.)*	une personne courageuse
bravely	courageusement, avec courage
breach	enfreindre, percer
bread	pain
break *(n.)*	récréation, pause
break* a record	battre un record
break* down	tomber en panne
break* into	pénétrer par effraction
break* out	éclater, se déclarer (guerre)
break* the law	enfreindre la loi
break* the rules	enfreindre le règlement
breath	souffle
breathless	époustouflant, à couper le souffle
bribe	pot-de-vin
bride	mariée
bridge	pont
briefly	brièvement
bright	brillant, intelligent
bright-red	rouge vif
brilliant	génial
bring* out	faire ressortir
Britain	Grande-Bretagne
British	britannique
British Isles	Iles Britanniques
broadcast *(v.)*, *(n.)*	diffuser *(v.)*, diffusion, radiodiffusion *(n.)*
brush *(n.)*	brosse, pinceau
bubble	bulle
buffalo	bison
building	bâtiment, construction
bully *(v.)*, *(n.)*	harceler *(v.)*, tyran, brute *(n.)*
bum	clochard
bunch	bouquet
bungee-jumping	saut à l'élastique
burglar	cambrioleur

burgle	cambrioler
business	entreprise, affaires
busy	occupé
butcher's	boucherie
butler	majordome
butter	beurre
buying power	pouvoir d'achat
by	en, pas plus tard que
by the time	lorsque, le temps que

C

cab	taxi
cabbage	chou
caber (Scottish)	tronc
cake	gâteau
calculate	calculer
call *(v.)*, *(n.)*	appeler, nommer ***(v.)***, appel ***(n.)***
call for help	appeler au secours
caller	personne qui appelle
calm, calmly	calme, calmement
camera	appareil photo
camp	camper
campaign *(v.)*, *(n.)*	militer ***(v.)***, campagne (militaire) ***(n.)***
campaigner	militant
camper	campeur
camping trip (be on a…)	camping (faire du…)
can *(n.)*	boîte à ordures, de peinture, canette
can opener	ouvre-boîte
Canada	Canada
Canadian	canadien
candle	bougie
canteen	cantine
capital letter	lettre majuscule
caption	légende
captivity	captivité
capture	capturer
car park	parking
card	carte
cardboard	carton
care	soins, attention
career	carrière
careful	prudent
careful (be)	attention (faire)
carefully	soigneusement
careless	négligent
caricatural	caricatural
carpet	tapis
Carribean islands	Iles des Carraïbes
carry	porter, transporter
carry-out-place	restaurant avec plats à emporter
carve	sculpter
case	valise
case	affaire, procès
cast* a spell	jeter un sort
caster sugar	sucre en poudre
casual	décontracté
catch *(n)*	hic, piège
caterpillar	chenille
Catholic	catholique
cattle	bétail
cattle-thief	voleur de bétail
cauldron	chaudron
cause *(v.)*, *(n.)*	causer ***(v.)***, cause ***(n.)***
cavity	cavité
cease-fire	cessez-le-feu
ceiling	plafond
celebrate	célébrer
celebration	fête
celebrity	célébrité
cell	cellule
cellar	cave
Celt	Celte
Celtic	celtique, celte
centre forward	avant-centre
century	siècle
chain	chaîne
chalk	craie
challenge	défi
challenging	stimulant
championship	championnat
change *(v.)*, *(n.)*	changer ***(v.)***, changement ***(n.)***
change one's ways	changer sa manière d'être
channel	chaîne
Channel (the…)	Manche (la)
character	personnage
characteristic	caractéristique
charge (in… of)	responsable (de)
charismatic	charismatique
charity	œuvre de bienfaisance, organisation caritative
chart	hit-parade
chase	poursuivre
chat	bavarder
cheap	bon marché
cheat *(v.)*, *(n.)*	tricher ***(v.)***, tricheur ***(n.)***
check	vérifier
cheek	joue
cheeky	insolent
cheer up	remonter le moral
cheerful	joyeux
cheese	fromage
chemical *(n.)*	produit chimique
chemist	pharmacien
chemistry	chimie
cherry	cerise
chess	échecs
chest	coffre
chew	mâcher
chief	chef
child (children)	enfant(s)
child labour	travail des enfants
childhood	enfance
childish	enfantin
chimney	cheminée (extérieure)
chin	menton
china	porcelaine
Chinese	chinois
chips (pl.)	frites
choice	choix
chopped	hâché, pilé
chores	corvées
Christ	Christ
Christian	chrétien
Christianity	christianisme
Christmas	Noël
Christmas carol	chant de noël
Christmas eve	veille de Noël
chronology	chronologie
church	église
circle *(v.)*, *(n.)*	entourer***(v.)***, cercle ***(n.)***
citizen	citoyen
city	ville
Civil Rights	droits civiques
civilization	civilisation
claim	prétendre, affirmer
clap (one's hands)	taper dans ses mains
clash *(v.)*, *(n.)*	heurter (se) ***(v.)***, heurt, opposition ***(n.)***
classic	classique
classmate	copain de classe
classroom	salle de classe
clause	proposition
clay	argile
clean *(v.)*	nettoyer, effacer
clear *(adj.)*	clair
clear the table	débarrasser la table
clearly	clairement
clench	serrer
clerk	employé de bureau
clever	intelligent, malin
click	cliquer
cliff	falaise
climate change	changement climatique
climb (up)	grimper, escalader
climbing wall	mur d'escalade
clinical	clinique
clique	clique, petit groupe qui exclu les autres
clock	horloge
cloning	clonage
close (down) *(v.)*	fermer
close (to)	proche, près de
close-cropped	coupé ras
close-up	gros plan
closely	de près
clothes	vêtements
clothes shop	magasin de vêtements
cloud, cloudy	nuage, nuageux
club	trèfle (cartes), club
clue	indice
clumsiness	maladresse
clumsy	maladroit
coal	charbon
coast, coastal	côte, côtier
coat	manteau
coconut	noix de coco
coffee	café
coffee-bar	cafétéria
cold *(n.)*, *(adj.)*	rhume ***(n.)***, froid ***(adj.)***
Cold War	Guerre Froide
collaborator	collaborateur
collect	collectionner, ramasser
college	université
colony	colonie
color/colour *(v.)*	teindre
colour	couleur
coloured	coloré (peau)
colourful	coloré, multicolore
colourless	incolore
comb	peigne
come* and go*	aller et venir
come* back	revenir
come up with…	produire, faire surgir
comedy	comédie
comfort *(v.)*, *(v.)*	réconforter, consoler ***(v.)***, confort ***(n.)***
comfortable	confortable
comic-strip	bande dessinée, BD
comics (pl.)	bande dessinée, BD
comment *(v.)*, *(n.)*	commenter ***(v.)***, commentaire ***(n.)***

commercial *(adj.)*	commercial
commercial *(n.)*	spot publicitaire *(n.)*
commit	commettre
Commonwealth	Commonwealth
communicate	communiquer
communism	communisme
community	communauté
company	entreprise, compagnie
compare	comparer
comparison	comparaison
compass	boussole
compete (against)	être en compétition (avec), rivaliser
competent	compétent
complain	se plaindre
complaint	plainte
complete *(v.)*, *(adj.)*	compléter *(v.)*, complet *(adj.)*
completely	complètement
compose	constituer, composer
composer	compositeur
compromise	faire un compromis
computer	ordinateur
computer skills	connaissances informatiques
conceited	vaniteux
concentrate	(se) concentrer
concern *(v.)*, *(n.)*	concerner *(v.)*, intérêt, inquiétude *(n.)*
conclude	conclure
conditioner	après-shampoing
conduct	diriger, conduire
confidence	confiance
confident	confiant, sûr de soi
confirm	confirmer
conflict	conflit
conform	conformer (se)
confront	confronter, affronter
congratulations	félicitations
conical	conique
connect	connecter
conquer	conquérir
conquest	conquête
consequence	conséquence
conservation	préservation
conservationist	défenseur de l'environnement
conservative	conservateur
consider	envisager, prendre en considération
considerably	considérablement
considerate	respectueux
considering	étant donné
consist	consister
conspiracy	conspiration
constantly	constamment
consternation	consternation
construct	construire
consume	consommer
consumer	consommateur
consumerism	consumérisme
contaminate	contaminer
contented	satisfait
contest	compétition
contestant	candidat
continue	continuer
contract	contrat
contrary (on the)	contraire (au)
contrast *(v.)*	opposer

contribute	contribuer
contribution	contribution
control *(v.)*, *(n.)*	contrôler *(v.)*, contrôle *(n.)*
convention	convention
conventional	conventionnel, classique
convict	forçat, prisonnier
convince	convaincre
convincing	convaincant
convoy	convoi
cook *(v.)*, *(n.)*	cuisiner *(v.)*, cuisinier *(n.)*
cooker (gas)	cuisinière (à gaz)
cooking (do the)	cuisine (faire la)
cooking pot	marmite
cool *(adj.)*	sympa, décontracté, à la mode, calme
cool *(v.)*	refroidir
cool *(adj.)*, *(n.)*	frais *(adj.)*, frais *(n.)*
cooperate	coopérer
copper	cuivre
copy	copier
copy book	cahier
coral	corail
core *(adj.)*	central, principal
core *(n.)*	cœur, noyau, centre
corn (US)	maïs
corner	coin
Cornish	cornouaillais
corporate	de l'entreprise
corporation	compagnie, entreprise
correct *(v.)*, *(adj.)*	corriger *(v.)*, correct, juste *(adj.)*
correctly	correctement
correspond	correspondre
corresponding	correspondant
corridor	couloir
corrupt	corrompu
corruption	corruption
cosmetic	produit de beauté
cosmic	cosmique
cost *(n.)*	coût *(n.)*
cough *(v.)*, *(n.)*	tousser, toux
Council	mairie
councillor	conseiller, maire
count	compter
country	pays, campagne
country road	route de campagne
county	comté
couple (a… of)	quelques
courageous	courageux
court	terrain (tennis, basketball)
cousin	cousin, cousine
cover *(n.)*	couverture
cover up *(v.)*	couvrir, cacher
cover-up *(n.)*	affaire étouffée
cow	vache
crack	résoudre, pénétrer
crack a joke	raconter une blague
crack down on	prendre des mesures énergétiques contre...
crash *(n.)*	accident
crash into *(v.)*	percuter
crash-land	atterrir brutalement
crawl	ramper
crazy (about)	fou (de)
create	créer
creativity	créativité
creator, creature	créateur, créature
credit management	gestion de crédit
creepy-crawlies	insectes

crew	équipe, bande
crimestopper	personne qui arrête les crimes
crime, criminal	crime, criminel
cringe	avoir un mouvement de recul
crisis	crise
crisps (pl.)	chips
critic	détracteur
crooked	tortueux
cross *(v.)*, *(n.)*	traverser *(v.)*, croix *(n.)*
cross *(adj.)*	fâché
crosswords	mots croisés
crowd, crowded	foule, bondé
crown, crowned	couronne, couronné
crucial	crucial
crucify	crucifier
crude	grossier
cruel	cruel
cruelty	cruauté
cry	pleurer
cry (cries) *(n.)*	cri
culprit *(n.)*	coupable
culture, cultural	culture, culturel
cunning	rusé
cup	tasse, coupe
cupboard	placard
cure *(n.)*	traitement
curious	curieux, étrange
curly	frisé
current	actuel
cushion	coussin
custom	coutume
customer	client
cut* down	abattre
cut* someone's head off	décapiter quelqu'un
cynical	cynique

D

D-day	le jour J
daffodil	jonquille
dagger	poignard
daily	quotidien
dam	barrage
damage *(n.)*	dégâts
dance *(v.)*, *(n.)*	danser, danse
danger	danger
dangerous	dangereux
dangerously	dangereusement
daring	audacieux
dark	sombre, foncé, noir
dark	nuit
dark (in the)	obscurité (dans l'…)
dark-blue	bleu foncé
dark-skinned	peau matte (ayant la)
darts	fléchettes (jeu de)
date of birth	date de naissance
daughter	fille
dawn	aurore
dead	mort
dead (+adj) *(adv.)*	très+adj
deadline	date limite, date butoir
deadly	mortel
deal *(n.)*	accord, marché *(n.)*
deal (a great … of)	beaucoup de
deal* with *(v.)*	traiter de, avoir affaire à
dealer	marchand
dear	cher

dearly	tendrement
death ***(n.)***	mort
debris	débris
debt	dette
decade	décennie
decide	décider
deckchair	chaise longue
declare	déclarer
decline	décliner
decolonisation	décolonisation
decorate	décorer
decrease	diminuer
dedicated	dévoué
deep ***(adj.)***	profond
deeply	profondément
defeat ***(v.), (n.)***	vaincre ***(v.)***, défaite ***(n.)***
defend	défendre
defense	défense
deficient	défectueux
define	définir
definite	définitif
degradation	déterioration
degrading	dégradant, humiliant
delicate	délicat
delicious	délicieux
deliver	livrer
demolish	démolir
demonstrate	manifester
demonstration	manifestation
den	repère (animal)
denim	tissu de jean
denounce	dénoncer
department	département
departure	départ
depend on	dépendre de, compter sur…
dependable	sûr, sur qui on peut compter
depending	selon
depressed	déprimé
depressing	déprimant
deprivation	privation
descendant	descendant
describe	décrire
desert island	île déserte
deserted ***(adj.)***	désert
deserve	mériter
design ***(v.), (n.)***	concevoir ***(v.)***, dessin, plan ***(n.)***
desk	bureau
despair	désespoir
desperately	desespérément
despite	malgré, en dépit de
destroy	détruire
detached	détaché
detect	détecter
detective story / film	roman, film policier
detention (in…)	retenue (en…)
determined	déterminé, volontaire
detribalization	acculturation
devastate	anéantir
devastating	dévastateur
develop	développer
developing country	pays en voie de développement
development	développement
device	procédé
devolution	dévolution
devoted	dévoué
diamond	carreau (cartes), diamant
diary	agenda, journal
die	mourir
differ	se distinguer de, différer
differently	différement
difficult	difficile
digger	qui creuse, chercheur (d'or)
dignity	dignité
dilemma	dilemme
dimensional	dimensionnel
dining hall	cantine, salle à manger
dinner ***(n.)***	dîner
direct ***(v.)***	réaliser (film)
direct ***(adj.)***	direct
directly	directement
director	réalisateur
dirty	sale
disabled	infirme
disadvantaged	défavorisé
disagree	ne pas être d'accord
disagreeable	disagréable
disappear	disparaître
disappoint	décevoir
disappointed	déçu
disappointment	déception
discourage	décourager
discover	découvrir
discovery	découverte
discrepancy	écart
discrimination	discrimination
discuss	discuter
disease	maladie
disgusting	dégoûtant, écoeurant
disillusion ***(n.)***	désillusion
dislike	ne pas aimer
disobedient	désobéissant
disorder	désordre
distant	éloigné
distress	détresse
dive	plonger
diversity	diversité
divide	diviser
do* (one's) best	faire de son mieux
doll	poupée
dolphin	dauphin
dominate	dominer
dominion	dominion, territoire sous domination…
donation	don
donkey	âne
doubt	douter
dove	colombe
down, downstairs	bas, en bas
downtown	centre ville
dowry	dot
dozen	douzaine
drag	traîner
dramatically	de manière spectaculaire
draw* conclusions	tirer des conclusions
drawer	tiroir
drawing	dessin
dream ***(n.)***	rêve ***(n.)***
dress ***(v.), (n.)***	s'habiller ***(v.)***, robe ***(n.)***
dress style	style d'habillement
dress up (as a…)	se déguiser
drill	forer
drink ***(n.)***	boisson
drive* back	rentrer (en voiture)
drop dead	tomber raide mort
drop (out)	laisser tomber, quitter
drown	(se) noyer
drowsy	somnolent
drug(s)	drogue
drug-dealer	vendeur de drogue
drum band	groupe jouant des tambours
drums, drummer	batterie, batteur, tambour
drunk ***(adj.)***	soûl
dry	sec
duck	canard
dump	décharger
duplicate ***(n.)***	double
duration	durée
during	pendant
dustbin	poubelle
dusty	poussiéreux
dye, dyed	teindre, teint

E

each	chaque
eagle	aigle
ear	oreille
early	tôt
(the) early …	le début de (année)
earn	gagner (argent)
earnings	salaire
earth, Earth	terre, la terre
earthling	terrien
earthquake	tremblement de terre
ease up ***(v.)***	se calmer
easily	facilement
east	est
Easter	Pâques
easy	facile
easy-going	facile à vivre
eccentric	excentrique
ecology	écologie
ecosystem	écosystème
edge	bord, côté, tranchant
edgeless	émoussé
educated (be …at)	faire ses études à
effect	effet
effective	efficace
efficiently	efficacement
egg	œuf
egotistical	égocentriste
elbow	coude
elder	aîné
elderly ***(adj.)***	âgé
elderly ***(n.)***	personne âgé
elected	élu
eliminate	éliminer
else	autre, d'autre, de plus
elsewhere	ailleurs
embark	s'embarquer
embarrass	embarrasser
embarrassing	gênant, embarrassant
emblem	emblème
embrace ***(n.)***	étreinte
emerge	émerger
emergency	urgence
emigrate	émigrer
empire	empire
empty	vide
enable ***(v.)***	permettre
encampment	campement

enchant	enchanter
enchanting	enchanteur, ravissant
enchantress	enchanteresse
encourage	encourager
encyclopedia	encyclopédie
end ***(v.)***, ***(n.)***	finir ***(v.)***, fin ***(n.)***
end up	aboutir à
endanger	mettre en danger
endangered species	espèce en voie d'extinction
ending	fin, dénouement
endorsement	endossement, appui
enemy	ennemi
engage in	se lancer dans, s'adonner à
engine	moteur
engineer	ingénieur
England	Angleterre
English, Englishman	anglais ***(adj.)***, ***(n.)***
enjoy	apprécier, aimer
enormous	énorme
enough	assez (de)
enrol	s'inscrire
enslave	asservir
enter (a room)	entrer (dans une pièce)
entertain	divertir
entertaining	distrayant
entertainment	divertissement
enthusiastic	enthousiaste
entire	entier
entirely	entièrement
entrance, entry	entrée
envelop	envelopper
envelope	enveloppe
environment	environnement
environmental	écologique
environmentalist	écologiste
epic	épique
equal	égal
equal rights	égalité des droits
equality	égalité
equip	équiper
equipment	équipement
era	ère
escape	s'enfuir
escort ***(v.)***	accompagner
especially	particulièrement
essay	rédaction
essential	essentiel
establish	établir
estate agent	agent immobilier
esteem	estimer, respecter
estimate	estimer
eternal	éternel
ethnic food	nourriture exotique
ethnic shop	magasin d'articles exotiques
ethnicity	ethnicité
European	européen
even (if)	même (si)
evening (in the)	soir (le)
evening/night out ***(n.)***	sortie en soirée
event	évènement
ever	déjà, jamais
ever since	depuis
every	chaque, tous les …
everybody, everyone	tout le monde
everything	tout
everywhere	partout
evil ***(n.)***	le mal
evoke	évoquer
evolve (into)	évoluer vers, devenir
exactly	exactement
exaggerate	exagérer
exam	examen
examine	examiner
except	sauf, excepté
exceptional	exceptionnel
excessively	excessivement
exchange ***(v.)***, ***(n.)***	échanger ***(v.)***, échange ***(n.)***
excited	surexcité
excitement	excitation, agitation
exciting	passionnant, enthousiasmant
exclude	exclure
execute	exécuter
executive	cadre dirigeant
exercise ***(v.)***,***(n.)***	faire de l'exercice ***(v.)***, exercice ***(n.)***
exercise book	cahier
exhausted	épuisé
exhibition	exposition
exist, existence	exister, existence
exit	sortie
expand	étendre
expect	s'attendre à
expensive	cher
experience ***(v.)***	faire l'expérience de
experiment ***(v.)***	faire des expériences
expertise	savoir-faire
explain	expliquer
explanation	explication
explode	exploser
exploit ***(v.)***, ***(n.)***	exploiter ***(v.)***, exploit ***(n.)***
exploited	exploité
explore	explorer, étudier
explorer	explorateur
explosive	explosif
exposure	exposition
express	exprimer
expropriate	exproprier
extensive	répandu
extinction	extinction
extract ***(v.)***, ***(n.)***	extraire ***(v.)***, extrait ***(n.)***
extraordinary	extraordinaire
extraterrestrial	extra-terrestre
extremely	extrêmement
eye	œil
eyebrow	sourcil
eyelash	cil

F

fabulous ***(adj.)***	fabuleux, chouette
face ***(v.)***, ***(n.)***	faire face à ***(v.)***, visage ***(n.)***
face down	à l'envers
face paint	peinture pour visage
facility	aménagement
fact	fait
factor	facteur = élément
factory	usine
fade	faiblir, s'affaiblir, s'effacer, diminuer
fail	échouer, rater
faint ***(v.)***	s'évanouir
fair, blond	blond
fair play	bon joueur
fairly	assez
fairy ***(n.)***	fée
fairy land	pays enchanté
faith, faithful	foi, fidèle
fall* in love with	tomber amoureux de
fall* off	tomber de
fall (US) ***(n.)***	automne
falls ***(n.)***	chutes d'eau
false	faux
fame	renommée
family(ies)	famille
famine	famine
famine relief	lutte contre la famine
famous	célèbre
fanatical, fan	fanatique, fan
fantastic	fantastique
fantasy	film fantastique
far (away)	loin
farewell	adieu
farm ***(v.)***	labourer
farther	plus loin
fascinate	fasciner
fascinating	fascinant
fashion	mode
fashionable	à la mode
fast	vite, rapide
fast food restaurant	restaurant de restauration rapide
fat	gros, gras
fate	destin
father-in-law	beau-père (père du mari/femme)
favourite	préféré
fear	peur
feather	plume
fed up (be)	en avoir marre
feeling ***(n.)***	sentiment
female	femelle, femme
fence	barrière
fencing	escrime
festival	fête, festival
festivity	festivité
fetch	aller chercher
few (+*(n.)* pl.)	peu (de)
fewer (+*(n.)* pl.)	moins de
field	terrain, champ
fierce, fiercely	féroce, férocement
fight ***(n.)***	bataille ***(n.)***
fighter	combattant
fighter-pilot	pilote de chasse
figure	chiffre, silhouette
Fiji islands	Iles Fiji
file	dossier
fill in	remplir
filling	plombage
film	film, pellicule (photo)
film-maker	réalisateur
finally	finalement
find* out	découvrir
fine ***(adj.)***	bien, parfait
fine ***(n.)***	amende
finger	doigt
fingerprint	empreinte digitale
finish	finir
fire (on)	feu (en)
fireman	pompier
fireplace	cheminée (intérieure)
firewood	bois pour le feu
fireworks	feux d'artifice
first	d'abord

first of all tout d'abord
fish *(v.)*, *(n.)* pêcher *(v.)*, poisson *(n.)*
fish hook hameçon
fishing *(n.)* pêche
fishing rod canne à pêche
fist poing
fit *(adj.)* en pleine forme
fix réparer, faire
flag drapeau
flash éclair
flask gourde
flat *(n.)* appartement
flavouring parfum, essence
flex fléchir
flight vol (avion)
float char de carnaval
floor sol, étage
flour farine
flourish fioriture
flow s'écouler, couler
flower, flowered, flowery fleur, fleuri
fly* off s'envoler
flying saucer soucoupe volante
focus concentrer (se)
foe ennemi
folk folk (musique)
folklore folklore
follow suivre
follower partisan
following suivant
fond of (be) prendre plaisir à, aimer
food nourriture
fool idiot
fool *(v.)* tromper, duper
foolish insensé
foot (on) (pl. feet) pied (à)
foot-note note de bas de page
football pitch terrain de foot
footprint empreinte de pied
footstep *(n.)* pas
for, for hours pour, pendant des heures
for instance par exemple
for real pour de vrai
forbidden interdit
force forcer
foreground premier plan
forehead front
foreign étranger
foreign policy politique étrangère
forest forêt
forever pour toujours
foreword préface
form *(v.)*, *(n.)* former *(v.)*, questionnaire, forme *(n.)*
formal formel
formula formule
fort *(n.)* fort
fortunate qui a de la chance
fortune prospérité, chance
fortune-teller diseur de bonne aventure
found *(v.)* fonder
foundation fondation
Founding Father membre de la convention constituante (U.S.A.)
fox renard
fragile fragile
frame cadre
France France
free libre, gratuit
free time temps libre
freedom *(n.)* liberté
freely librement
freezing glacial
French *(adj.)* français *(adj.)*
Frenchman *(n.)* français *(n.)*
fresh frais, nouveau
fresh air air pur
friendly gentil, amical
friendship amitié
frighten faire peur
frightened effrayé
frightening effrayant
fringe bordure, lisière
front door porte d'entrée
frown froncer (les sourcils)
frustrated frustré
full (of) plein (de)
fully-equipped totalement equipé
fumes fumées d'usine
fun (be) sympa, drôle
fund-raising (do) récolter des fonds
fundamental fondamental
funds fonds (argent)
funnel passage étroit
funny amusant, drôle, bizarre
funny-looking air drôle, bizarre (qui a l'…)
fur fourrure
furious furieux
furlough permission
fussy difficile, capricieux
future avenir
futuristic futuriste

G

gaily gaiement
galaxy galaxie
gallop galoper
gamble jouer de l'argent
gambling jeux d'argent
game jeu, partie, match, gibier
games sports, jeux
games arcade salle de jeux
gang (of friends) groupe (d'amis)
gangster voyou, truand
gantry escaliers mobiles
garbage ordures
garbage can poubelle
garden *(v.)*, *(n.)* jardiner *(v.)*, jardin *(n.)*
gardener jardinier
gardening jardinage
gate portail
gather cueillir, réunir
gathering cueillette, regroupement
gear équipement
generate générer
genius génie
gentleman homme bien élevé
gently doucement
German allemand
Germany Allemagne
gesture geste
get* along with s.o. s'entendre avec qqu'un
get* dressed s'habiller
get* hurt se blesser
get* into monter dans
get* off descendre
get* on well bien s'entendre
get* rid (of) se débarasser (de)
get* some sleep dormir un peu
get* something away éloigner
get* to se rendre à
get* together se réunir
get* up se lever
get-the-guy attitude allumeuse
ghost fantôme
giant géant
gift cadeau
give*... a thought penser à quelquechose
give* advice donner des conseils
give* back rendre
give* sb a (sporting) chance donner sa chance à qqn
give* someone a lift emmener quelqu'un en voiture
give* up renoncer à
give* voice to exprimer
glad content
glass verre
glasses lunettes
glen vallée
global mondial, global
glossy en papier glacé
glove gant
glowing incandescent
glue colle
go* across traverser
go* along suivre (une rue)
go* forward *(v.)* avancer
go* on continuer, se passer
go* out sortir, s'éteindre (lumières)
go* together with aller de pair avec
goat chèvre
God Dieu
godfather parrain
godmother marraine
gold doré, or
gold rush ruée vers l'or
gold-digger chercheur d'or
gold-plated plaqué or
golden doré
goldfish poisson rouge
good *(n.)* bien *(n.)*
good point qualité
good-hearted généreux, qui a bon cœur
good-looking beau, séduisant
grade classe (US)
gradually petit à petit
grant *(v.)*, *(n.)* accorder *(v.)*, bourse, subvention *(n.)*
grass herbe
grateful reconnaissant
great génial, super, grand
great grandchild arrière petit-fils
greedy gourmand
Greek grec
green vert
greengrocer's marchand de fruits et légumes
greenhouse effect effet de serre
grey gris
grid grille
groaningly en poussant des gémissements
groom marié *(n.)*
ground sol, terrain (football…)

ground floor	rez-de-chaussée
ground water	eau souterraine
grounded (be)	interdit de sortie (être)
grow* up	grandir (pour une personne)
grown-up ***(n.)***	adulte
growth	croissance
gruelling	épuisant
grumpy	grognon
guarded	gardé
Guatemala	Guatémala
guess	deviner
guessing-game	jeu de devinettes
guest	invité
guide ***(v.), (n.)***	guider ***(v.)***, guide ***(n.)***
guilty ***(adj.)***	coupable
gun	revolver, arme à feu
gunfire	coups de feu
guy	mec
guys!	les gars! les filles !

H

habit	habitude
habitat	habitat
hair	cheveux
hair conditioner	après-shampoing
hair-cut	coupe de cheveux
hairy	poilu
half	moitié
half an hour	demi-heure
half-brother	demi-frère
half-empty	à moitié vide
half-sister	demi-soeur
hall	entrée, salle de réunion
hammer	marteau
hand, by hand	main, à la main
hand... in ***(v.)***	rendre
handkerchief	mouchoir
hang* out	traîner, passer son temps
hanging	suspendu
happen	arriver, se passer
happily	heureusement
happiness	bonheur
happy	heureux
hard	dur, difficile
hardship	épreuve
hardworking	travailleur, qui travaille dur
harm ***(n.)***	mal
harmless	inoffensif
harmony	harmonie
harp	harpe
hat	chapeau
hate	détester
hateful	haineux, détestable
have* a good time	(bien) s'amuser
have* a party	faire la fête
have* a shave	se raser
have* a try	essayer
have* a wash	se laver
have* access to	avoir accès à
have* fun	s'amuser
have*…on	porter (un vêtement)
head	tête
Head(teacher)	le principal
headache	mal de tête
headline	gros titre
headquarters	quartier général
headshot	portrait photo
heal	guérir
healer	guérisseur
health	santé
health education	éducation sur la santé
heap	tas
heart	cœur
heart attack	crise cardiaque
heat ***(n.)***	chaleur
heating	chauffage
heavily	fortement, lourdement
heavy	lourd
hedge	haie
height	hauteur, taille
heir	héritier
helicopter	hélicoptère
hell	enfer
helmet	casque
help	aide ***(n.)***, aider ***(v.)***
helpful	serviable
helpless	impuissant, sans défense
hen	poule
herd	troupeau
here	ici, présent
heretical	hérétique
heritage	patrimoine
hero	héro
heroic	héroïque
hesitant	hésitant
hesitate	hésiter
hidden	caché
hide ***(n.)***	peau (d'animal) ***(n.)***
hideous	hideux
high ***(adj.)***	haut
high school	école secondaire
high-level	haut niveau
high-tech	haute technologie
highlight ***(v.)***	surligner
hilarious	hilarant, très drôle
hill	colline
Hindu	Hindou
hip ***(adj.)***	à la mode
hipsters	pantalon taille basse
hire	louer
historian	historien
historical	historique
hit ***(n.)***	succès ***(n.)***
hitch hike (hitch)	faire du stop
hitchhiker	auto-stoppeur
HIV, HIV-positive	sida, séro-positif
hold* out	tendre
hold* together	maintenir ensemble
holiday(s)	jour férié, vacances
hollow	creux
holy	saint
Holy Grail	Saint-Graal
home	maison, foyer
home page	page d'accueil
home-base	base de départ
home-made	fait à la maison
homeless	sans abri
homeward	vers sa maison/son pays
homicide	homicide
honest	honnête
honestly	honnêtement
honesty	honnêteté
honey	miel
honour ***(v.), (n.)***	honorer ***(v.)***, honneur ***(n.)***
honoured	honoré
hoof (-ves)	sabot
hop ***(v.)***	sauter
hope	espérer
hopeful	plein d'espoir
hopeless, hopelessly	sans espoir
horde	horde
horn	cor, klaxon, corne
horrible	odieux
horrid	horrible
horrifying	abominable
horror-movie	film d'horreur
horse	cheval
horse-riding	équitation
horse-shoe	fer à cheval
hospital	hôpital
hot	bouillant, très chaud
hot-water bottle	bouillotte
hotline	téléphone rouge
hotly	vivement, avec passion
hound	chien
hour	heure
house	maison
housework	ménage
how come?	comment se fait-il?
how far	à quelle distance
how long	combien de temps
how long ago	il y a combien de temps
how many (+pl.)	combien
how much	combien
how often	à quelle fréquence
however	toutefois
huge	énorme
hum ***(v.)***	fredonner
human ***(adj.)***	humain
human being	être humain
human body	corps humain
human right	droit de l'homme
humanitarian	humanitaire
humanoid	humanoide
humiliating	humiliant
humour	humour
hundred	cent(aine)
hunger	faim
hungry (be)	affamé, avoir faim
hunt, hunter	chasser, chasseur
hunting ***(n.)***	chasse
hurry (in a)	à toute vitesse, pressé
hurry (up)	dépêcher (se)
hurt	blessé
hurtful	blessant
husband	mari
husband-to-be	futur époux
hut	refuge
hypnosis	hypnose
hypocritical ***(adj.)***	hypocrite

I

ice	glace
ice cube	glaçon
ice-rink	patinoire
ice-skating	faire du patin à glace
idea	idée
ideal	idéal
idealise	idéaliser
idealism	idéalisme
identification	identification
identify	identifier
identity	identité
idol	idole
if, if only	si, si seulement

ill	malade
ill-at-ease	mal à l'aise
ill-treat	maltraiter
illegally	illégalement
illness	maladie
illustrate	illustrer
imaginary	imaginaire
imitate	imiter
immediately	immédiatement, tout de suite
immigrant	immigré
immigration	immigration
immortal	immortel
immortality	immortalité
immune system	système immunitaire
impact	impact
implore	implorer
impolite	impoli
impress	impressioner
impressed	impressionné
impressive	impressionnant
improve	améliorer
in early 2003	au début de l'année 2003
in fact	en fait
in front of	devant
in hiding	caché (vivre)
in hope of	dans l'espoir de
in love with	amoureux de
in my opinion	à mon avis
in one go	d'un seul coup
in order to	afin de
in particular	particulièrement
in real time	en temps réel
in search of	à la recherche de
in that case	dans ce cas
in the course of	au cours de/du
in the distance	au loin
in the meantime	pendant ce temps
in what way?	de quelle manière ?
inborn	inné
incident	incident
include	comprendre, inclure
including	y compris
incoherent	incohérent
incorporate	incorporer
incorrect	incorrect, faux
increase	augmenter
increasing	croissant
incredible	incroyable
independence	indépendance
independent	indépendant
indestructible	indestructible
India	Inde
Indian	indien
indicate	indiquer
individual ***(n.)***	individu
individually	individuellement
Industrial Revolution	Révolution Industrielle
industry	industrie
infantile	infantile
infected	infecté
infectious	contagieux
infer	inférer, deviner
infiltrate	s'infiltrer
infinite	infini
influence ***(v.)*, *(n.)***	influencer ***(v.)***, influence ***(n.)***
inhabitant	habitant
inhuman	inhumain
injection	piqûre
injure	blesser
inn	auberge
inoffensive, inoffensively	inoffensif, de manière inoffensive
insecure	anxieux, qui manque d'assurance
inside	intérieur (à l')
insist (on)	insister
insistent	insistant
inspect	examiner
inspiration	inspiration
inspire	inspirer
install	installer
instead (of)	à la place, au lieu de…
institute	institut
instructor	moniteur
insufficient	insuffisant
insurance	assurance
insurance policy	police d'assurance
integral	intégral
integrate	intégrer
integration	intégration
intellectual	intellectuel
intend	avoir l'intention de
interact	échanger, être en contact
interaction	interaction
interest	intérêt
interested	intéressé
interesting	intéressant
interestingly	de façon intéressante
intergalactic	intergalactique
internet café	cyber café
Internet (Net)	internet
interpreter	interprète
interrogate	interroger
interview ***(v.)*, *(n.)***	interroger ***(v.)***, entretien ***(n.)***
interviewer	interviewer
introduce	présenter
introductory	introductif
invade	envahir
invasion	invasion
inverted commas	guillemets
investigate	enquêter
investigation	enquête
invincible	invincible
invite	inviter
involuntarily	involontairement
involve	impliquer
involvement	participation
invulnerability	invulnérabilité
Ireland	Irlande
Irish, Irish man	irlandais ***(adj.)*, *(n.)***
iron ***(v.)*, *(n.)***	repasser ***(v.)***, fer ***(n.)***
ironic	ironique
irony	ironie
Islam	islam
island	île
isolate	isoler
issue	question, problème
Italian	italien
Italy	Italie
item	article

J

jacket	blouson
jail	prison
jam	confiture
Jamaica	Jamaïque
Japan	Japon
Japanese	japonais
jaw	mâchoire
jealous	jaloux
jealousy	jalousie
jerk	secouer
jersey	maillot
jewel	bijou
jeweller	bijoutier
jewellery	bijoux, bijouterie
job	métier, travail
jobless	sans travail
join	s'inscrire à, se joindre à
join forces	unir ses forces
join in	se joindre à
joke ***(v.)***	plaisanter
jot down	prendre note
journal	journal, magazine
journey	voyage
joyfully	joyeusement
joystick	manette de jeu
juice	jus
July	juillet
jumbo jet	avion géant
jump	sauter
jumper	pullover
junction	croisement
June	juin
junk	bric-à-brac
just	juste, seulement
justify	justifier

K

keen on (be)	passioné de, amateur de
keep* alive	garder en vie
keep* in mind	garder en tête
keep* off	rester à distance de
keep* quiet	se taire
keep* someone company	tenir compagnie à quelqu'un
keep* (something) on	garder qqchose sur soi
keep* up with fashion	suivre la mode
keeper	gardien
key	clé
key-word	mot-clef
keyboard	clavier d'ordinateur
kick ***(v.)*, *(n.)***	frapper avec le pied ***(v.)***, coup de pied ***(n.)***
kid	enfant, jeune, gamin
kidnap	kidnapper
kill	tuer
kill oneself	se suicider
killing	meutre
kind	gentil
kind of	sorte de
kind-hearted	gentil
kindly	gentiment
kindness	gentillesse
king	roi
kingdom	royaume
kingship	royauté
kiss ***(v.)*, *(n.)***	embrasser ***(v.)***, baiser ***(n.)***
kitchen	cuisine
kite	cerf-volant
knee	genou
knickers	culotte
knife (pl. knives)	couteau

knight *(n.), (v.)*	chevalier *(n.)*, faire chevalier *(v.)*
knock	frapper
knock down	démolir
knock over	renverser
knowledge	connaissance
known as	connu sous le nom de

L

label	étiquette, label
labyrinth	labyrinthe
lack	manque
ladder	échelle
ladybird	coccinelle
lake	lac
lamb	agneau
land *(v.), (n.)*	atterrir, toucher le sol *(v.)*, terre *(n.)*
landmark	point de repère
landscape	paysage
lane	allée
language	langue
laptop	ordinateur portable
large	grand, spacieux
largely	en grande partie
last *(adj.)*	dernier
last *(v.)*	durer
last night	hier soir
late	tard, en retard
later still	plus tard encore
lately	dernièrement
latest	dernier en date
laugh	rire
laugh at	se moquer
launch *(v.), (n.)*	lancer *(v.)*, lancement *(n.)*
law	loi
lawn	pelouse
lawyer	avocat
lay (prét de lie)	être allongé
lay the table	mettre la table
lazy	paresseux
leader	meneur, dirigeant
leading	principal
leaf (pl. leaves)	feuilles
lean* over	se pencher
leap *(n.)*	bond
learning	apprentissage
leash *(n.)*	laisse
leather	cuir
left, on the left	gauche, à gauche
leg	jambe
legal	légal
legend	conte, légende
legendary	légendaire
leisure	loisir
lemon	citron
length, the... of	longueur, tout au long de
leprechaun	lutin
less	moins
lethal, non lethal	mortel, pas mortel
letter, letter-box	lettre, boîte aux lettres
lettuce	salade verte
level	niveau
liar	menteur
liberal	libéral
library	bibliothèque
lie *(v.)*	mentir
lie* still	être couché et immobile
life (pl. lives)	vie
lifespan	durée de vie
lifestyle	style de vie
lift *(v.)*	soulever
light *(adj.)*	léger
light *(v.)*	allumer
light(s) *(n.)*	lumière(s)
light-brown	marron clair
lighter	briquet
like *(adv.)*	comme, semblable à
like *(v.)*	aimer
like best	préférer
limit	limiter
line	ligne
link *(v.), (n.)*	relier *(v.)*, lien *(n.)*
link-word	mot de liaison
lip	lèvre
list *(v.), (n.)*	énumérer *(v.)*, liste *(n.)*
listen (to)	écouter
literature	littérature
little *(adj.)*	petit
little, a little	peu de..., un peu de...
live *(v.)*	vivre, habiter
live on something	se nourrir de...
livestock	bétail
living *(adj.)*	vivant
load *(v.)*	charger
loads of...	des masses de...
loathe	détester, avoir en horreur
lobby for	faire pression en faveur de
locate	localiser
location	emplacement, extèrieur (film)
lock *(v.)*	fermer à clé, enfermer
locker	casier
lonely	isolé, seul
lonesome	seul, solitaire
long	long, longtemps
long before	bien avant
long for *(v.)*	désirer
long-term	long terme
look *(n.)*	apparence, regard
look (at)	regarder
look (+adj.) *(v.)*	sembler, avoir l'air
look after	s'occuper de
look around	regarder autour de soi
look away	détourner les yeux
look for	chercher
look forward to	attendre avec plaisir
look (have a) *(n.)*	regarder, jeter un œil
look like	ressembler
look something up	rechercher une information
look up to s.o.	respecter qqu'un
loose	ample
lord	seigneur
lost *(adj.)*	perdu
lots of	beaucoup de
loud	bruyant, vulgaire
love *(v.), (n.)*	aimer, adorer *(v.)*, amour *(n.)*
lovely	joli, adorable
lover	amant, amoureux
low *(adj.)*	bas
loyal	fidèle
Loyalist	loyaliste
lucky (be)	avoir de la chance
ludicrous	risible
lung	poumon
lyric	lyrique

M

mad	fou
madly	follement
madman *(n.)*	fou
madness	folie
magic *(adj.)*	magique
magic *(n.)*	magie
magic wand	baguette magique
magical	magique
magnificent	magnifique
magnifying glass	loupe
mail *(n.)*	courrier
main	principal
mainly	principalement
make *(n.)*	marque
make* aware	rendre conscient
make* fun of	se moquer de
make* money	gagner de l'argent
make* sure	s'assurer de quelque chose
make-up	maquillage
making	fabrication
male	homme
mall	centre commercial
manage	réussir, se débrouiller
manhood	virilité
manipulate	manipuler
mankind	humanité
manner	manière
map	carte, plan
march	marche de protestation
March	mars
mark *(v.), (n.)*	noter *(v.)*, trace, marque *(n.)*
market	marché
marmalade	confiture d'orange
marry, married	se marier, marié
marshall	officier de police
marshmallows	shamallows
martial arts	arts martiaux
Martian	martien
martyr	martyr
mask	masque
massacre *(v.), (n.)*	massacre, massacrer
massive	énorme, imposant
massively	massivement
master	maître
match *(v.) (n.)*	associer *(v.)*, allumette(s), compétition *(n.)*
matter	question, problème, affaire
matter-of-fact	neutre
maybe	peut-être
maybe so but...	peut-être bien mais...
mayor	maire
maze	labyrinthe
meal	repas
mean *(adj.)*	méchant
meaning	signification, sens
meaningful	significatif
means of transport	moyens de transport
meanwhile	pendant ce temps
measure *(v.)*	mesurer
meat	viande
mechanic *(n.)*	mécanicien
medal	médaille
mediator	animateur
medicine	médicament
meeting	réunion
meeting-place	lieu de rendez-vous

melt	fondre
member	membre
membership card	carte de membre
memory	mémoire, souvenir
mentally deficient, mentally handicapped	handicapé mental
mention *(v.)*	mentionner
merchant	marchand
merciless	impitoyable, sans merci
merely	simplement
merit *(n.)*	mérite
merry	joyeux
mess (in a…) *(n.)*	désordre (en…), dans un triste état
mess up *(v.)*	tout rater
messy	désordonné, mal tenu
metalwork	travail des métaux
method	méthode
Mexican	mexicain
midday	midi
middle	milieu
Middle ages	moyen âge
middle-class	classe moyenne
midnight	minuit
midriff	taille (robe)
mighty	puissant
mile	mille (≈1,6 km)
military *(n.)*	armée
milk	lait
mill	moulin
mime *(v.)*	mimer
mind something *(v.)*	faire attention à qqchose
mine *(n.)*	mine
minority	minorité
mirror	miroir
mischievous	malicieux
miserable	malheureux
misgiving	crainte, doute
miss *(v.)*	manquer, rater
missing	manquant, absent
mistake	erreur
mistreated	maltraité
mix	mélanger
moan	gémir
mobile	portable (téléphone)
mobilize *(v.)*	mobiliser
model	modèle, mannequin
moderate	modérer
modify	modifier
monarch	monarque
money	argent
moneyless	fauché, sans le sou
monitor *(v.)*	surveiller
monkey	singe
monster	monstre
monstrous	monstrueux
month	mois
moon	lune
moonlight	clair de lune
morals	moralité
more	plus
moreover	de plus
moron	idiot, débile
mosquito	moustique
mostly	principalement
mother-in-law	belle-mère (mère du mari/femme)
motion picture	film
motivate	motiver
motto	devise
mountain	montagne
mouse (pl. mice)	souris
mouth	bouche
move *(v.)*, *(n.)*	déménager, bouger *(v.)*, déménagement *(n.)*
move around	bouger, remuer
movement	mouvement
movie	film
movie-theatre	cinéma
moving	émouvant
mow the lawn	tondre le gazon
mug *(v.)*	agresser
multi-ethnic	multi-ethnique
multicultural	multiculturel
multiculturalism	multiculturalisme
mural	mural (graffiti)
murder *(v.)*, *(n.)*	assassiner *(v.)*, meurtre *(n.)*
murderer	meurtrier
murderous *(adj.)*	féroce, cruel, meurtrier
museum	musée
musical *(adj.)*	musicien
musical *(n.)*	comédie musicale
musician	musicien
muslim	musulman
mutual	mutuel
mysterious	mystérieux
mystery	mystère
mythical	mythique

N

nag	enquiquiner
nail *(v.)*	clouer
naked	nu
name *(v.)*, *(n.)*	nommer *(v.)*, nom *(n.)*
nap	sieste
narrative	narration
narrow	étroit
nasty	désagréable
native *(adj.)*	originaire, natif
natural	naturel
naturally	naturellement
naughty	vilain
near, nearby	près de
nearly	presque
necessarily	nécessairement
necessary	nécessaire
neck	cou
need *(v.)*, *(n.)*	besoin (avoir) *(v.)*, besoin *(n.)*
needy	nécessiteux
neglected	négligé, délaissé, abandonné
negociate	négocier
neighbour	voisin
neighbourhood	quartier
nest	nid
nestle	se blottir
never	jamais
nevertheless	néanmoins
New Zealand	Nouvelle-Zélande
new, news	nouveau, nouvelles
newsagent's	marchand de journaux
newsletter	lettre d'information
newspaper	journal
next	prochain, prochainement
next door	à côté
next to	à côté de, près de
nickname	surnom
night-club	discothèque
nightmare	cauchemar
no longer	plus
no one	personne
Nobel Peace Prize	Prix Nobel de la Paix
noble	noble
nobody	personne
noise, noisy	bruit, bruyant
nominate	nominer
non-believer	non-croyant
non-governmental	non gouvernemental
non-official	non-officiel, officieux
none	aucun
north	nord
Northern Ireland	Irlande du nord
nose	nez
nostalgia	nostalgie
nostalgic	nostalgique
nothing	rien
nothing at all	rien du tout
notice *(v.)*	remarquer
noticed	remarqué
novel	roman
now	maintenant
nowadays	aujourd'hui
nowhere	nulle part
nuclear	nucléaire
nude	nu
number *(v.)*, *(n.)*	numéroter *(v.)*, nombre, numéro *(n.)*
number plate	plaque numéralogique
nurse	infirmière
nut	noisette

O

O.B.E. (Officer of the Order of the British Empire)	Chevalier de l'Ordre du Mérite
oak tree	chêne
obedient	obéissant
obey	obéir
object *(n.)*	objet
objectify	déshumaniser
obscene	obscène
observe	observer
obsessed	obsédé
obtain	obtenir
occupation	profession
odd	bizarre
odd jobs	petits boulots
odds	chances
of course	bien sûr
offence	délit
offensive	choquant
offer	offrir, proposer
office	bureau
official *(adj.)*	officiel
official *(n.)*	responsable
often	souvent
oil	huile, pétrole
old	vieux
old age	vieillesse
old-fashioned	démodé
oldie	vieux tube
omnipresent	omniprésent
on (one's) own	seul, tout seul
on time	à l'heure

on top of that en plus de ça
on-campus sur le campus
once une fois
oneself soi-même
online en ligne (Internet)
only seulement
only child enfant unique
onto sur
open *(v.), (adj.)* ouvrir *(v.)*, ouvert *(adj.)*
open-air en plein air
opening ouverture
opening day jour d'ouverture
opening scene scène de présentation
openly ouvertement
opportunity occasion, opportunité
opposite en face
oppress opprimer
oppressor oppresseur
or else ou bien, sinon, autrement
orchard verger
order *(n.)* ordre
ordinary ordinaire
originally à l'origine
orphan orphelin
other autre
Ouch! Aie!
out of parmi, sur, hors de
out there là-bas dans l'espace
out-of-body hors du corps
outback intérieur du pays
outdoor *(adj.)* extérieur
outdoors dehors, à l'extèrieur
outfit tenue
outlaw *(v.)* mettre hors-la-loi
outraged outré
outrageous scandaleux, monstrueux
outside à l'extérieur
outstanding remarquable
oven four
over a period of... sur une période de…
over (o'er) au-dessus, plus de…
over-the-top excessif
overtime prolongation
overwhelm submerger, dépasser
own propre, à soi
own *(v.)* posséder
owner propriétaire

P

P.E. (physical education) éducation physique
Pacific Islands Iles du Pacifique
Pacific Ocean Océan Pacifique
pacifist pacifiste
pack mettre dans sa valise
packed with rempli de
packet paquet
pad protection
paddle pagayer
pain *(n.)* douleur
pain (be a...) pénible, enquiquinant, (être)
paint *(v.), (n.)* peindre *(v.)*, peinture *(n.)*
painter peintre
painting tableau
Pakistan Pakistan
Pakistani pakistanais
pale face visage pâle
panther panthère
paper papier, journal
paper copie
Papua New Guinea Papouasie-Nouvelle-Guinée
parade défilé
paradise paradis
paralyze paralyser
paranoia paranoïa
park parc *(n.)*, garer *(v.)*
parking ticket contravention
parliament parlement
parody *(n.), (v.)* parodie *(n.)*, parodier *(v.)*
part *(n.)* partie, rôle
part *(v.)* **se** séparer
part-time temps partiel
participate participer
particular particulier
particularly particulièrement
partition division
party fête
pass away disparaître
pass (something) passer, donner (quelque chose)
pass (test) réussir (examen)
passenger passager
passive passif
past *(n.)* passé
patch période
path chemin
patient patient
patron saint saint patron
pattern modèle
pause *(v.)* faire une pause
pavement trottoir
pay paiement *(n.)*
pay* attention faire attention
peace paix
peaceful pacifique, en paix
peacefully paisiblement
peanut cacahuète
peer *(v.)* scruter du regard
pen-knife canif
penetrate pénétrer
penetrative approfondi, pénétrant
penniless fauché, sans le sou
penny sou
penultimate avant-dernier
people, people (pl.) peuple, gens
per par
percent pour cent
percentage pourcentage
perfect parfait
perfectly parfaitement
perform réaliser, interpréter
performer interprète
perfume parfum
perhaps peut-être
period période, heure de cours
persecute persécuter
personal personnel
personality personnalité
personally personnellement
pet animal de compagnie
petition *(v.)* adresser une pétition
petrified with fear pétrifié de peur
petrol essence
phenomenon phénomène
phone call coup de fil
physical physique
physically handicapped handicapé physique
piano player pianiste
pick *(v.)* choisir
pick on s'en prendre à
pick out identifier, trouver
pick (someone) up prendre en voiture
pick (up) *(v.)* ramasser
pickup truck camionnette
picture *(v.), (n.)* imaginer *(v.)*, image, photo *(n.)*
pictures (go to the) cinéma (aller au)
picturesque pittoresque
pie tarte, tourte
piece morceau
piles of... des tas de...
pilgrim pèlerin
pill pilule, médicament
pinball machine flipper
pineapple ananas
pink rose
pioneer pionier
pipe tuyau, canalisation, pipe
pitch dark noir comme dans un four
pity *(v.), (n.)* avoir pitié de *(v.)*, dommage *(n.)*
pizza parlour pizzeria
place *(v.), (n.)* placer *(v.)*, lieu, endroit *(n.)*
plain plaine
plan *(v.), (n.)* prévoir, projeter *(v.)*, projet *(n.)*
plane avion
planet planète
planned (as) prévu (comme)
plant *(v.), (n.)* planter, plante
plate assiette
platinum platine
play *(v.), (n.)* jouer *(v.)*, pièce de théâtre *(n.)*
play a part jouer un rôle
play in teams jouer par équipe
play on words jeu de mots
player joueur
playful joueur, espiègle
playfully en jouant, d'un ton taquin
playground cour de récréation
playwright dramaturge
pleased content
plentifulness abondance
plenty of beaucoup de
pliers tenailles
plot trame d'une histoire
plugged branché
plumber plombier
pluralism pluralisme
plus en plus, et
pocket poche
poem poème
poet poète
poetry poésie
point of view point de vue
pointed pointu
poison empoisonner
poisonous venimeux, vénéneux
pole perche
police officer officier de police
policeman policier
policy politique
polite poli
politely poliment

lexique anglais-français

politeness	politesse
politician	politicien
poll	sondage d'opinion
pollute	polluer
polluting	polluant
pollution	pollution
pom-pommy	anglais
pond	mare
pony-tail	queue de cheval
poor	pauvre
pope	pape
popular	connu et aimé
positive	affirmatif, sûr
post office	poste
post-war	après-guerre
postcard	carte postale
poster	affiche
potlatch	fête du "don"
potato	patate
potential	potentiel
pouch	poche (marsupiaux)
pound (£)	livre (monnaie anglaise)
pound	livre (453 grammes)
pour (with rain)	pleuvoir à verse
poverty	pauvreté
power *(n.)*	pouvoir
powerful	puissant
practical	pratique
practical joke	farce
practice *(n.)*	entraînement
practise *(v.)*	s'entraîner
prairie	prairie
praise	louange
pray	prier
precede	précéder
preciousness	valeur
precursor	précurseur
predict	prédire
prediction	prédiction
prejudiced	plein de préjugés
present *(v.)*, *(n.)*	présenter ***(v.)***, cadeau ***(n.)***
pressure group	groupe de pression
pretend	faire semblant
prevent	empêcher
prevention	prévention
preview	aperçu
prey	proie
price	prix
pride	orgueil
primary school	école primaire
print	imprimer
prisoner	prisonnier
private *(n.)*	simple soldat
prize	prix
probably	probablement
procession	défilé
procure	procurer
produce	produire
producer	producteur
product	produit
professional	professionnel
professional training	formation professionnelle
profile	portrait
profound	profond
prohibition	prohibition
project	projet
promise *(v.)*, *(n.)*	promettre ***(v.)***, promesse ***(n.)***
promote	promouvoir, faire la promotion de
pronunciation	prononciation
protect	protéger
protected	protégé
protest *(v.)*, *(n.)*	protester ***(v.)***, protestation ***(n.)***
Protestant	protestant
protester	protestataire
proud	fier
prove	prouver
provide	procurer, fournir
provocative	provocateur *(adj.)*
provoke	provoquer
pseudonym	pseudonyme
psychological	psychologique
psychologist	psychologue
public baths	bains municipaux
public opinion	opinion publique
public school	école privée
publication	publication
publish	publier
pumpkin	citrouille
punctuation	pontuation
puncture	crevaison
punish	punir
pupil	élève
puppy	chiot
purity	pureté
push	pousser
pussycat	chat
put* pressure on	mettre la pression sur
put* together	assembler
put* up	dresser
puzzle	étonner, rendre perplexe, s'interroger
puzzled	perplexe

Q

quantity	quantité
quarrel *(v.)*	se disputer
quarter	quart-temps, quart, quartier
queen	reine
queer *(adj.)*	étrange
quest	quête
question*(v.)*	interroger
questionnaire	questionnaire
queue	faire la queue
quick	vite, rapide
quickly	vite, rapidement
quiet *(n.)*, *(adj.)*	tranquillité ***(n.)***, tranquille ***(adj.)***
quietly	silencieusement
quite	assez, très
quote	citer

R

rabbit	lapin
race *(v.)*, *(n.)*	faire la course ***(v.)***, course, ***(n.)***
race, racial	race, racial
racism	racisme
racist	raciste
radiation	radiation
radical	radical
radioactive	radioactif
rag	chiffon, haillon
rage	rage
raid *(v.)*	faire un raid
rail	rambarde
railway	chemin de fer
rain *(v.)*, *(n.)*	pleuvoir ***(v.)***, pluie ***(n.)***
rainbow	arc-en-ciel
raincoat	imperméable
rainforest	forêt tropicale
rainy	pluvieux
raise	augmenter, lever
raise money	réunir de l'argent
rally	manifestation
ran, prét. de **run**	courir
rancher	propriétaire de ranch
ranger	garde-forestier
rapidly	rapidement
rapper	chanteur de rap
rare, rarely	rare, rarement
rat *(n.)*	rat
rat (on) *(v.)*	moucharder, dénoncer (qqu'un)
rather	plutôt
ratify	ratifier
rattle	hochet
rattled	ébranlé, bouleversé
raw	cru
ray-gun *(n.)*, *(v.)*	fusil à rayons (tirer avec…)
razor blade	lame de rasoir
reach	atteindre
react	réagir
reader	lecteur
reading	lecture
ready	prêt
real	vrai, véritable
real-life	véritable, réel, authentique
realise	(se) rendre compte, réaliser
realistic	réaliste
reality	réalité
really	vraiment
reappear	reapparaître
reason	raison
rebel *(v.)*, *(n.)*	rebeller (se) ***(v.)***, rebelle ***(n.)***
rebellion	rébellion
rebellious	rebelle
recall	se rappeler
receive	recevoir
recipe	recette
recognize	reconnaître
reconquer	reconquérir
record *(v.)*, *(n.)*	enregistrer ***(v.)***, disque ***(n.)***
record *(adj.)*	record
recording	enregistrement
recovery	récupération
recruit	recruter
red	rouge
red-haired	cheveux roux (qui a les…)
redecorate	redécorer, retaper
redman	homme à la peau rouge
reduce	résorber, réduire
reduction	réduction
refer	référer (se… à), faire référence
referee	arbitre
reflect	refléter
refugee	réfugié

refusal	refus
refuse *(v.)*	refuser
regarding	en ce qui concerne
region	région
regret *(v.)*, *(n.)*	regretter *(v.)*, regret *(n.)*
regular	régulier
regularly	regulièrement
regulation	règlement
reign	régner
reinforce	renforcer
reintroduce	réintroduire
reject	rejeter
rejoin	rejoindre
related to	lié à
relationship	relation, lien
relative	parent
relax	détendre (se)
relaxed	détendu
relaxing	reposant
release *(v.)*, *(n.)*	sortir (film-CD) *(v.)*, sortie *(n.)*
released *(adj.)*	libéré, sorti
relieve	soulager
relieved	soulagé
relocate	réimplanter
rely	compter sur
remain	rester
remarkable	remarquable
remember	souvenir (se)
remind	rappeler
remote	éloigné
remotest (the... idea)	moindre (la ... idée)
removal	déménagement
remove	enlever
rent	louer
repair	réparer
repeat	répéter
repeatedly	à maintes reprises
rephrase	reformuler
reply	répondre
report *(v.)*, *(n.)*	rapporter des faits *(v.)*, rapport *(n.)*
reporter	journaliste
require	demander
rescue *(v.)*, *(n.)*	secourir *(v.)*, secours, opération de secours *(n.)*
rescue team / service	équipe de secours
rescue worker	sauveteur
research (do)	recherches (faire des)
researcher	chercheur
reservation	réserve
resident	résident
resigned	résigné
resort	station (balnéaire)
respectable	respectable
respectful	respectueux
respond	répondre
respondent	personne interrogée
responsability	responsabilité
response	réponse, réaction
responsible	responsable
restrict	limiter
result	résultat
retirement	retraite
retract	rétracter
return *(v.)*, *(n.)*	renvoyer, rendre, retourner, revenir *(v.)*, retour *(n.)*
revise	réviser
revival	renouveau
revolting	révoltant
revolutionary	révolutionnaire
revolutionize	révolutionner
reward	récompense
rewrite	réécrire
rhyme, *(n.)*, *(v.)*	vers (poésie), rimer
rib	côte
rib shack	baraque à frites
ribbon	ruban
rice	riz
ridicule	ridiculiser
ridiculous	ridicule
right away	tout de suite
right (on the)	droite (à)
right-hand	droite (à..., côté...)
risk *(n.)*	risque
risk-free	sans risque
risky	risqué
ritual	rituel
river	rivière, fleuve
road (Rd)	rue, route
roam	errer
roast	rôtir
rob	voler (dérober)
robber	voleur
robbery	vol
rock	roc, rocher, rock (musique)
rocket	fusée
rodent	rongeur
roll	rouler
roll over	peindre au rouleau
Roman	romain
roof	toit
room	chambre, pièce
rope	corde
rosy	rosé
rotten	pourri
rough sea	mer agitée
round	autour
round *(n.)*	tournée
round *(adj.)*	rond
roundabout	rond-point
route	itinéraire
row (in a)	rangée, à la suite
rower	rameur
RSPCA	SPA
rubber	gomme
rubbish (be... at)	nul, très mauvais (être... en)
rude	impoli, grossier
rudely	impoliment, grossièrement
ruin *(v.)*	ruiner, abîmer, gâter
rule *(v.)*	gouverner, dominer
ruler *(n.)*	dirigeant, souverain
rules *(n.)*	règles, règlement
rumble	grondement
ruminate	ruminer
rumor/rumour	rumeur
rumpled	froissé
run* after	courir après
run* away	s'enfuir
run* out of	être à court de
run* over	écraser
runner	coureur
rush	se dépêcher

S

sacred	sacré
sacrifice	sacrifier
sad	triste
sadly	tristement
sadness	tristesse
safe *(n.)*, *(adj.)*	coffre-fort *(n.)*, sûr *(adj.)*
safe and sound	sain et sauf
safer	plus sûr, plus en sécurité
safety	sécurité
safety instructions	consignes de sécurité
sail	faire de la voile
salary	salaire
sale	solde (en)
salt	sel
salute	saluer
same	même
sample	échantillon
sand	sable
Santa Claus	Père Noël
satisfactory	satisfaisant
saucepan	casserole
savage	sauvage
savagely	sauvagement
save	sauver
save money	économiser de l'argent
savings	économies
Saxon	saxon
saxophone	saxophone
scan	lire rapidement, parcourir
scandalous	scandaleux
scar	cicatrice
scared	effrayé
scared to death	terrifié
scarf	écharpe
scary	effrayant
scene	scène, lieu
scenery	paysage
school-mate	copain d'école
scientist	scientifique
score *(v.)*, *(n.)*	marquer *(v.)*, partition (musique) *(n.)*
Scot, Scottish	écossais
Scotland	Ecosse
scratch	gratter
scream	crier
screen *(v.)*, *(n.)*	masquer *(v.)*, écran *(n.)*
screenplay	scénario
sea	mer
seal	phoque
search, *(n.)*, *(v.)*	recherche, chercher, rechercher
seaside	bord de mer
seat	siège
second-hand	d'occasion
secondary school	collège, lycée
secretary	secrétaire
secretly	secrètement
seed	graine
seem	sembler
segregation	ségrégation
seldom	rarement
select	sélectionner
selected	selectionné
self-awareness	conscience de soi
self-government	autonomie
self-regulate	s'autoréguler
self-reliant	autonome
self-respect	respect de soi

selfish	égoiste
senate	sénat
sense	sens
sense of humour	sens de l'humour
sensible	raisonnable
sensitive	sensible
sentence	phrase
separate	séparer (se)
serious	sérieux
seriously	sérieusement
serve (as)	servir (de)
session	séance
set *(n.)*	décor, paire
set* a goal	fixer un but
set* off	se mettre en route
set* (someone) free	libérer (quelqu'un)
set* the scene	situer la scène
set* up	monter (une entreprise)
setting	décor
settle	s'installer
settler	colon
several	plusieurs
severe	sévère
sexual	sexuel
shadow	ombre
shame	honte
shampoo	shampooing
shamrock	trèfle
shape *(v.)*, *(n.)*	former *(v.)*, forme *(n.)*
share *(v.)*	partager
shark	requin
sharp	pointu, tranchant
sharp	pile (heure)
sharply	brusquement
shave *(n.)*, *(v.)*	rasage, se raser
shed	abri, cabane de jardin
sheep	mouton
sheet	fiche
shelf(ves)	étagère
shell	coquille
shelter	centre d'accueil
shield	bouclier
ship	bateau, vaisseau
shirt	chemise
shock *(v.)*, *(n.)*	choquer *(v.)*, choc *(n.)*
shocked	choqué, scandalisé
shocking	choquant
shoe	chaussure
shoe-maker	fabricant de chaussures
shooting	tournage, fusillade
shop *(v.)*, *(n.)*	faire les courses *(v.)*, magasin *(n.)*
shop-lifting	vol à l'étalage
shopkeeper	commerçant
shopping centre	centre commercial
short	court
short story	nouvelle
shot *(n.)*	plan (film)
shoulder	épaule
shout	crier
shove	bousculer, pousser
show-off *(n.)*	quelqu'un qui frime
showbiz	showbiz
shower	averse
shower (have a)	douche (prendre une)
shy	timide
shyness	timidité
sick	malade
side	côté
sight	vue
sighting	fait d'avoir vu qque chose
sign *(v.)*, *(n.)*	signer *(v.)*, panneau *(n.)*
sign language	language des signes
sign up	s'inscrire
silently	silencieusement
silk	soie
silly	stupide
silver	argent (métal, couleur)
similar	semblable
similarity	ressemblance
since (then)	depuis (ce moment -là)
singer	chanteur
sinister	sinistre
siren	sirène
sister	sœur
sit* up	se redresser, s'asseoir bien droit
site	emplacement, site
size	taille
skate *(n.)*	patin
skating ring	piste de skate
skill	compétence, talent
skin *(n.)*	peau
skinny	maigre
skip	sautiller
skip (...school)	manquer (l'école)
skirt	jupe
skull	crâne
sky	ciel
skyscraper	gratte-ciel
slacks	pantalons
slap *(v.)*	donner une claque
slate	ardoise
slaughter	massacrer
slave, slavery	esclave, esclavage
slayer	tueur
sleep in	faire la grasse matinée
slightly	un peu
slim	mince
slimy	visqueux
slipper	chausson
slow, slowly	lent, lentement
small	petit
smart	intelligent
smash	fracasser
smell *(n.)*	odeur
smile	sourire
smoke *(v.)*, *(n.)*	fumer *(v.)*, fumée *(n.)*
smooth *(v.)*, *(n.)*	lisser, lisse
snack	en-cas
snail	escargot
snake	serpent
sneaker	chaussure de sport
snooker	billard
snow *(v.)*, *(n.)*	neiger *(v.)*, neige *(n.)*
so far	jusqu'à présent
society	société
sock	chaussette
soda	boisson gazeuse sucrée
sofa	divan
soft	doux
soft drink	boisson non alcoolisée
softly	doucement
software	logiciel
soil	sol
soldier	soldat
solstice	solstice
solve	résoudre
somebody	quelqu'un
someday	un jour
somehow	d'une façon ou d'une autre
someone (else)	quelqu'un (d'autre)
something	quelque chose
sometime	un jour
sometimes	quelquefois
somewhat	quelque peu
somewhere	quelque part
son	fils
song	chanson
songwriter	compositeur
soon	bientôt
sorrow	tristesse
sort *(n.)*	sorte
sound *(n.)*	son
sound (+adj.) *(v.)*	sembler, paraître
sound energy	énergie sonique
sound mix	montage sonore
source	source
south	sud
South Africa	Afrique du Sud
sovereignty	souveraineté
Soviet	soviétique
space	place, espace
space suit	combinaison d'astronaute
space travel	voyage dans l'espace
spaceship	vaisseau spatial
spacious	spacieux
spade	bêche, pelle, pique (cartes)
Spain	Espagne
Spanish	espagnol
special	spécial, particulier
specialised	specialisé
species	espèce
spectacles	lunettes de vue
spectacular	spectaculaire
spectator	spectateur
speech	discours
speed	vitesse
spider	araignée
spin	tourner sur soi-même
spinach	épinard
spirit	esprit
spoilt brat	enfant gâté
sponsor *(v.)*	sponsoriser
sponsored	sponsorisé
sponsorship	sponsorat
spooky	hanté
spoon, spoonful	cuillère, cuillerée
sportsperson	sportif *(n.)*
sportswear	vêtement de sport
sporty	sportif (adj.)
spot *(v.)*, *(n.)*	repérer *(v.)*, point *(n.)*
spray *(v.)*	vaporiser
spray paint	peinture vaporisée
spring	printemps, source
spy	espion
squirrel	écureuil
St Lucia	Ste Lucie
stadium	stade
staff room	salle des professeurs
stage	étape, scène
stagecoach	diligence
stairs	escaliers
stake	bûcher, pieu
stamp *(n.)*	timbre

stamp (one's feet) taper des pieds
stand* in line faire la queue
stand* still se tenir immobile
stand* up se lever
star étoile, star
star *(v.)* jouer (film)
start commencer, démarrer, lancer
starting point point de départ
starve to death mourir de faim
state, States état, États-Unis
statement déclaration
station gare, caserne, station
status statut
stay rester
stay cool rester calme
stay home, stay in rester à la maison
steep pentu
stem tige
step pas
step-father beau-père (nouveau mari de la mère)
step-mother belle-mère (nouvelle femme du père)
sterile stérile
stick *(n.)* bout de bois ***(n.)***
sticky collant
still encore, toujours
stimulate stimuler
stir remuer
stockade trou (prison)
stomach estomac
stomach ache mal au ventre
stone pierre
stop someone doing something empêcher qq'un de faire qqchose
stopover escale
store *(v.)*, *(n.)* stocker ***(v.)***, magasin ***(n.)***
storm orage, tempête
stormy orageux
story(ies) histoire(s)
straight raide, franche
straight into droit sur
strange étrange
stranger étranger, inconnu
strangle étrangler
strategy stratégie
strawberry fraise
stream ruisseau
street rue
strength force
stretch s'étendre
strict sévère
strictly strictement
strike *(n.)* grève
stripe bande
strong fort
strong-willed volontaire, déterminé
strongly fortement, avec force
structure structure
struggle *(v.)* débattre (se)
stubborn têtu
stuck bloqué
student étudiant, élève
study *(v.)*, *(n.)* étudier ***(v.)***, étude, bureau ***(n.)***
stuff trucs
stuntman cascadeur
sub-genre sous -catégorie
subject matière
submarine sous-marin
submission soumission
submissive soumis
submit soumettre (se)
subsist subsister
suburb, suburbia banlieue
subway métro
succeed réussir
success succès
success story réussite
successful (be) réussir, avoir du succés
successfully avec succés
such si, tellement
such as tel que
suddenly soudain
suffer subir
suffering souffrance
sufficient suffisant
sugar sucre
sugar cane canne à sucre
suggest suggérer
suit *(n.)* costume, tailleur
suitcase valise
sum up récapituler, résumer
summary résumé
summer été
sun, sunny soleil, ensoleillé
sunbathe prendre un bain de soleil
sunset coucher de soleil
suntanned bronzé
supernatural surnaturel
superstitious superstitieux
supplement *(v.)* augmenter
supply *(n.)* provision
support *(v.)*, *(n.)* soutenir (une équipe) ***(v.)***, soutien ***(n.)***
supporting role second rôle
suppose supposer
supposedly soi-disant
sure sûr
surf the internet naviguer sur le web
surname nom de famille
surprise *(v.)*, *(n.)* surprendre ***(v.)***, surprise ***(n.)***
surprised surpris
surprising étonnant
survey enquête
survive survivre
suspect *(v.)*, *(n.)* soupçonner ***(v.)***, suspect ***(n.)***
suspend suspendre
swallow avaler
swamp marécage
swap échanger
swear-box boîte à jurons
sweat *(v.)* transpirer
sweater pullover
sweet *(n.)*, *(adj.)* bonbon ***(n.)***, gentil, agréable ***(adj.)***
sweet-smelling odorant, qui sent bon
swimmer nageur
switch off éteindre (lampe)
switch on allumer (lampe)
sword épée
symbolic symbolique
symbolise symboliser
sympathize with someone partager la douleur de quelqu'un

T

tackle plaquer (rugby)
tagger taggeur
tail queue
take* a break faire une pause
take* a look (at) jeter un coup d'oeil
take* away retirer
take* care of prendre soin de
take* off décoller
take* out sortir de
take* over prendre le contrôle
take* part in prendre part à
take* place avoir lieu
take* root prendre racine
take* someone to emmener qqu'un
take-away restaurant restaurant qui fait des plats à emporter
tale conte
talk *(n.)* exposé
talk (about) *(v.)* parler (de)
talk show débat télévisé
talkative bavard
talked-about dont on parle
talkie / sound picture film parlant
tall grand, haut
tame docile
tank char
tap-dancing claquettes
tape cassette
target *(v.)*, *(n.)* cibler ***(v.)***, cible ***(n.)***
tartan tissu écossais à carreaux
task tâche
taste *(v.)* goûter, sentir le goût de
tasty appétissant
tatoo tatouage
tea thé, repas du soir
teach* enseigner
teacher professeur
team équipe
team spirit esprit d'équipe
tear *(n.)* larme ***(n.)***
teaspoon cuillère à café
technician technicien
technological technologique
teddy bear nounours
teenager (teen) adolescent
teens (be in one's) être adolescent
telepathy télépathie
tempt tenter
tendency tendance
tense temps grammatical
tepee wigwam
term trimestre, terme
terribly terriblement
terrified terrifié
terrifying terrifiant
territory territoire
terror terreur
test *(v.)*, *(n.)* tester, expérimenter ***(v.)***, examen ***(n.)***
text book *(n.)* manuel
text message texto
texture texture
thanks to grâce à
that's why c'est pourquoi
theft vol
theme thème, sujet
then puis, ensuite, alors
theory théorie

therapist	thérapeute
therapy	thérapie
there	là, là-bas
therefore	donc
thick	épais
thief (pl. -ves)	voleur(s)
thin	maigre, mince
thing	chose
think* about	réfléchir
third, a third	troisième, un tiers
Third-world	Tiers-Monde
thirsty (be)	assoiffé - avoir soif
thistle	chardon
thought ***(n.)***	pensée
thousand(-s)	mille, milliers
thread	fil
threat	menace
threaten	menacer
threatening	menaçant
three-quarters	trois-quarts
through	par, à travers
throughout	tout au long de …
thumb	pouce
tick ***(v.)***	cocher
ticket	billet
tidy ***(adj.)***	rangé, ordonné
tidy (up) ***(v.)***	ranger
tie ***(v.), (n.)***	ligoter ***(v.)***, cravate ***(n.)***
tiger	tigre
tight ***(adj.)***	serré
tights	collants
till, until	jusqu'à ce que
time	heure, temps, fois
time machine	machine à remonter le temps
time oneself ***(v.)***	se chronométrer
time table	emploi du temps
time travel	voyage dans le temps
tin	boîte de conserve
tin opener	ouvre-boîte
tiny	minuscule
tip ***(n.)***	conseil, tuyau
tired	fatigué
tiring	fatigant
title	titre
tobacco	tabac
today	aujourd'hui
toe	doigt de pied, orteil
toffee	caramel
together	ensemble
tomahawk	hache de guerre
tomato(-es)	tomate
tomorrow	demain
tone	ton
tongue	langue
tonic	tonique
tonight	ce soir
too	trop, aussi
tooth (teeth)	dent(s)
top (at the)	sommet, haut (en), en premier
topic	sujet, thème
torch	lampe-torche
torn ***(adj.)***	déchiré
tortoise	tortue
torture	torturer
tot up	additionner
totally	totalement, complètement
totem pole	mât totémique
touch	toucher
touch down	essai
touch screen	écran tactile
touchy	susceptible
tough	dur
tour	escursion
tournement	tournoi
towards	envers, vers
towel	torchon
tower	tour
town	ville
townspeople	citadins
toxic	toxique
toy	jouet
trace	trace, vestige
trade	métier
trader	marchand
traditional	traditionnel
traffic jam	embouteillage
traffic lights	feux tricolores
trail	sentier
trainers	chaussures de sport
training centre	centre de formation
training course	stage de formation
transfer	transférer
transform (into…)	transformer (se) (en…)
translation	traduction
trapped	piégé
travel ***(v.)***	voyager
travel round the world	faire le tour du monde
traveller	voyageur
treachery	trahison
treasure	trésor
treasure hunt	chasse au trésor
treat ***(v.), (n.)***	traiter ***(v.)***, cadeau ***(n.)***
treaty	traité
tree	arbre
trendy	branché
trial	procès
tribal	tribal
tribe	tribu
trick, -s	farce, farces et attrapes
Trinidad	Ile de la Trinité
trip	voyage, excursion
trouble ***(v.)***	troubler
trouble (be in) ***(n.)***	avoir des ennuis
trouble (get into) ***(n.)***	se mettre dans les ennuis
trousers	pantalon
truancy	absentéisme scolaire
truant	élève qui fait l'école buissonière
true	vrai
trumpet	trompette
trunk	tronc
trust ***(n.), (v.)***	confiance, faire confiance
truth	vérité
try	essayer
try one's luck	tenter sa chance
tube	métro
Tuesday	mardi
tune in	se brancher sur une station
turkey	dinde
turn ***(n.)***	tour, tournant
turn ***(v.)***	tourner, passer (un certain âge), devenir
turn… away… from ***(v.)***	s'éloigner de
turn into	se transformer en
turn on/off	ouvrir, fermer (robinet)
turn oneself in	se rendre, se livrer
TV coverage	couverture télévisuelle
TV series	série télé
twice	deux fois
twin	jumeau, jumelle
twist ***(v.), (n.)***	tordre ***(v.)***, tournure, chute (d'une histoire) ***(n.)***
typical	typique

U

U.S.	Etats-Unis
ugly	laid
Ulster	Ulster, Irlande du Nord
umbrella	parapluie
unable	incapable
unacceptable	inacceptable
unbelievable	incroyable
uncivilized	non civilisé, barbare
uncle	oncle
uncomfortable	inconfortable
unconscious	évanoui, inconscient
uncontrolled	incontrôlé
under	sous, dessous
underground ***(n.)***	métro
underline	souligner
underpay	sous-payé
underprivileged	défavorisé
understandable	compréhensible
underwear	sous-vêtements
undress	se déshabiller
uneasily	avec inquiétude
uneasy	mal à l'aise
unemployment	chômage
unexpected	inattendu
unexplained	inexpliqué
unfashionable	démodé
unfortunate	malchanceux
unfortunately	malheureusement
unfriendly	peu sympathique
unhappy	malheureux
unholy	profane
unidentified	non-identifié
unify	unifier
unimportant	sans importance
Union Jack	drapeau britannique
unite	s'unir
United Kingdom	Royaume-Uni
unity	unité
unknown	inconnu
unlike	à la différence de
unnatural	anormal
unnaturally	anormalement
unnerving	destabilisant
unpack	défaire sa valise
unpleasant	déplaisant
unpredictable	imprévisible
unreal	irréel
unrealistical	irréaliste
unrealistically	exagérément, de manière irréaliste
unrecognisable	méconnaissable
unsafe	pas en sécurité
unsure	incertain
until	jusqu'à (+moment)
untroubled	paisible
unusual	inhabituel
up ***(n.)***	haut

up to	jusqu'à (+nombre)
upscale	huppé, riche
upside-down	à l'envers
upstairs	étage (à l'...)
upstanding	vertueux
uranium	uranium
urban	urbain
urban area	zone urbaine
urgent, -ly	urgent, de manière urgente
use *(v.)*, *(n.)*	utiliser *(v.)*, utilité *(n.)*
useful, useless	utile, inutile
usual	habituel
usually	habituellement, d'habitude
utensil (cooking)	ustensile (de cuisine)

V

vacation	vacances
valley	vallée
value	valeur
value *(v.)*	apprécier, tenir à...
van	camionnette
variety	variété
various	divers
vast	vaste
vastly	immensément
VCR	magnétoscope
vegetable	légume, personne qui mène une vie végétative
vehicle	véhicule
vein	filon
velvet	velours
vending machine	distributeur automatique
vermin	vermine
versus	contre
victimize	persécuter, s'en prendre à
victory	victoire
Vietnam	Vietnam
view	vue, panorama
vivid	vif, éclatant, clair
voice *(n.)*	voix
volunteer *(n.)*	volontaire
voracious	vorace
vulgar	vulgaire

W

wagon	chariot
waiscoat	gilet
waist	taille
wait (for)	attendre
Wales	Pays de Galles
walk *(v.)*, *(n.)*	marcher (v), marche *(n.)*
wall	mur
wallet	portefeuille
walnut	noix
want	vouloir
war	guerre
ward	pavillon (hôpital)
warder	gardien
wardrobe	armoire
warehouse	entrepôt
warm	chaud, chaleureux
warmth	chaleur
warn	prévenir
warning	avertissement
warrior	guerrière
wash	laver
waste *(v.)*, *(n.)*	gaspiller, perdre *(v.)*, déchets *(n.)*
watch	regarder (T.V.), surveiller
watch *(v.)*, *(n.)*	observer *(v.)*, surveillance *(n.)*
watcher	observateur
water	eau
waterfall	cascade
wave	vague
way	chemin, façon, manière
way of life	mode de vie
weapon	arme
weather	temps (météorologique)
weave* (wove, woven)	tisser
web	toile
web site	site web
webcam	webcam (caméra)
wedding	mariage
wee	petit (langue ecossaise)
week	semaine
weekly	hebdomadaire
weigh	peser
weight	poids
weirdo	type bizarre
welcome *(v.)*, *(n.)*	accueillir *(v.)*, bienvenue *(n.)*
welfare	bien-être
well *(n.)*	puits
well-equipped	bien équipé
well-known	connu
well-off	aisé
well-respected	respecté
Welsh, Welshman	gallois
west	ouest
West Indies	Antilles
Western	occidental
whatever	quoi, n'importe quoi
whenever	quand, chaque fois
while	pendant que, alors que
whimsical	fantaisiste
whip	fouet
whisk away	emporter rapidement
whistle *(v.)*, *(n.)*	siffler *(v.)*, sifflet *(n.)*
whiteness	blancheur
who	qui
whole	entier, tout
whose	à qui. dont
wide	large
wield	manier
wife (pl. wives)	épouse, femme
wild *(adj.)*	sauvage
wild (in the)	nature (dans la)
wilderness	nature sauvage
wildlife	nature
wind	vent
window	fenêtre
wine	vin
wing	aile
winter	hiver
wisdom	sagesse
wise	sage
wisely	sagement
wish *(v.)*, *(n.)*	souhaiter *(v.)*, souhait *(n.)*
witch	sorcière
witch-hunt	chasse aux sorcières
witchcraft	sorcellerie
with	avec
without	sans
witness	témoin
wizard	sorcier
wizardry	magie, sorcellerie
woe	malheur, chagrin
wolf (pl. wolves)	loup(s)
womanhood	féminité
wonder	émerveillement
wonderful	merveilleux
wood	bois, forêt
wooden, woody	en bois
wool	laine
woolly	laineux
word	mot
work	travailler, fonctionner, marcher
worker	travailleur
working day	journée ouvrable
workman	ouvrier
workplace	lieu de travail
worksheet	fiche d'exploitation
world	monde
world-famous	célèbre dans le monde entier
worldwide	à travers le monde
worn	porté
worn-out	usé
worried	inquiet
worry	s'inquiéter
worse, worst (the)	pire, le pire
worship	adorer
worth, be worth	valeur, valoir
worthless	sans valeur
wounded	blessé
wrap	envelopper
wreck *(v.)*	démolir, anéantir
wrestle	lutter
wrestling	la lutte
wring*	tordre
wrist	poignet
writer	écrivain
written	écrit
wrong	faux, mal

Y

Yankee	habitant des États-Unis du nord de l'Amérique
yard	jardin, cour, chantier
yawn	bailler
year	année, an, classe (GB)
yellow	jaune
yesterday	hier
yet	encore, déjà
young	jeune
youngster	jeune
yourself	toi
youth	jeunes, jeunesse

Z

zebra	zèbre
zoo-keeper	gardien de zoo

lexique français-anglais

A

à côté de	next to, beside
à côté (maison, porte)	next door
à l'étranger	abroad
à l'extérieur	outside
à l'heure	on time
à la différence de	unlike
à la mode	fashionable, hip, cool, trendy
à travers	through
abandonner, abandonné	abandon, abandoned
abattre (arbres)	cut* down
abattre qqn	shoot*, slaughter, murder
abeille	bee
abolir	abolish
abominable	horrifying
abondance	plentifulness
aborigène	Aborigine
aboutir à	end up
aboyer	bark
abri de jardin	shed
absent	missing, away
absentéisme scolaire	truancy
absolument	absolutely
absurde	absurd
académie	academy
accélérer	accelerate
accentué	stressed
acceptable	acceptable
acceptation	acceptance
accepter	accept
accès	access
accessoire	accessory
accident	crash
accompagner	escort, accompany
accord (commercial)	deal *(n.)*
accorder	grant
accro	addicted
accueillir	welcome
acculturation	detribalization
accuser	accuse
acheter	buy*
acquérir	acquire
acrostiche	acrostic
actif	active
action	action
activiste	activist
actuel	current
adaptation	adaptation
adapter	adapt
additionner	tot up, add up
adieu	farewell
admettre	admit
admirable	admirable
admiration	admiration
admirer	admire, look up to
adolescent	teenager, teen
adopter	adopt
adorer	worship, adore
adresse, s'adresser à	address *(n.)*, *(v.)*
adulte	adult, grown-up
aéroport	airport
affaire étouffée	cover-up
affaires (les)	business
affamé, avoir faim	hungry (be)
affiche	poster
affirmatif	positive
affreux	awful
afin de	in order to
Afrique	Africa
Afrique du Sud	South Africa
afro (coiffure)	Afro
âge	age
âgé	elderly
âgé de	aged
agenda	diary
agenouiller (s')	kneel*
agent du FBI	FBI agent
agent immobilier	estate agent
agneau	lamb
agréable	agreeable
agresser	mug
agressif	aggressive
agriculture	agriculture
Aïe !	Ouch!
aigle	eagle
aile	wing
ailleurs	elsewhere
aimer	like, enjoy
aimer, adorer	love
aîné	elder
ainsi que	as well as
air, air pur	air, fresh air
aisé	well-off
ajouter	add
Algérie	Algeria
algérien	Algerian
alibi	alibi
allée	lane
Allemagne	Germany
allemand	German
aller	go* (to)
aller à cheval, vélo, moto	ride*
aller à la pêche	go* fishing
aller chercher	fetch
aller de pair avec	go* together with
aller et venir	come* and go*
allumer	switch on, light*
allumette(s)	match(es)
allumeuse (attitude d')	get-the-guy attitude
allusion	allusion
alors, donc	so
alors, ensuite	then
alors que	while
alternatif	alternative
ambiance	atmosphere
ambitieux	ambitious
ambulance	ambulance
améliorer	improve
aménagement	facility
amende	fine
américain	American
amical	friendly
amitié	friendship
amoureux de, un amoureux	in love with, lover
ample, bouffant	loose, baggy
amusant	funny
amusé	amused
amuser (bien s')	have a good time
amuser (s')	have fun
analyser	analyse
ananas	pineapple
ancien	ancient
âne	donkey
anéantir	devastate
anéantissement	annihilation
ange	angel
anglais *(adj.)*, *(n.)*	English, Englishman, pom-pommy
Angleterre	England
angoisse	anguish
animateur	mediator
annexer	annex
anniversaire	birthday
annoncer	announce
annonceur	advertiser
annuel	annual
annuellement, chaque année	annually
anormal	unnatural
anormalement	unnaturally
anti-conformiste	anti-conformist
anti-nucléaire	anti-nuclear
anti-tabagisme	anti-smoking
antidote	antidote
Antilles	West Indies
antilope	antelope
antiquité	antique
anxieux, qui manque d'assurance	insecure
août	August
aperçu	preview
apparaître	appear
appareil, avion	aircraft
appareil photo	camera
apparemment	apparently
apparence, regard	look
apparition	appearance
appartement	flat
appartenir	belong
appel	call, appeal
appeler au secours	call for help
appeler, nommer	call
appétissant	tasty
appliquer, postuler	apply
apporter	bring*
apprécier	value, enjoy
apprendre	learn
apprenti	apprentice
apprentissage	learning
approcher	approach
appuyer (s')	lean*
après	after
après-guerre	post-war
après-shampoing	hair conditioner
aptitude	ability
aqueduc	aqueduct
araignée	spider
arbitre	referee
arc	bow
arc-en-ciel	rainbow
architecte	architect
architecture	architecture
ardoise	slate
argent, … de poche	money, pocket money
argent (métal, couleur)	silver
argile	clay
argument, raisonnement	argument
aride	arid
arme	weapon
armée	army, military
Armée de l'air, aviation	Air Force
armoire	wardrobe
arrangeur	arranger
arrêter	stop, arrest
arrière (à l')	back (at the)
arrière-petit-fils	great grandchild
arrière-plan, fond	background
arrivée	arrival
arriver	arrive
arriver à la maison	get home
arriver, se passer	happen
article	item
artificiel	artificial
artillerie	artillery
arts martiaux	martial arts
Asie, … Mineure	Asia, … Minor
aspect	aspect
aspirer (à)	aim (to)
assassiner	assassinate, murder
assemblée, parlement	assembly
assembler	put together
asseoir (s')	sit* (down)
asservir	enslave
assez	quite, fairly

assez (de)	enough
assiette	plate
associer	match, associate
assoiffé, avoir soif	thirsty (be)
assoiffé de sang, sanguinaire	bloodthirsty, bloody
assurance	insurance
assurer	assure
astronaute	astronaut
astronome	astronomer
astronomie	astronomy
athlète	athlete
athlétisme	athletics
atout	asset
attacher (s')	attach
attaque, attaquer	attack *(n.)*, *(v.)*
atteindre	reach
attendre	wait (for)
attendre à (s')	expect
attendre avec plaisir	look forward to
attendu	awaited
attentif	attentive
attention (faire)	careful (be)
atterrir en catastrophe	crash-land
atterrir, toucher le sol	land
attirant, séduisant	attractive
attirer	attract, appeal (to)
attitude	attitude
attraper	catch*
attribuer (une récompense)	award
au moins	at least
au-delà	beyond
au-dessus, plus de...	over (o'er)
auberge	inn
aucun	none
audacieux	daring
augmenter	increase, rise*, raise
aujourd'hui	today ,nowadays
aurore	dawn
aussi, aussi... que	also, as + adj. + as
Australie	Australia
australien	Australian-Aussie
auteur	author
auto-stoppeur	hitchhiker
automatiquement	automatically
automne	autumn, fall (US)
autonome	self-reliant
autonomie	self-government
autoréguler (s')	self-regulate
autorité	authority
autour	round
autre, d'autre	other, else
avaler	swallow
avancer	go on, go forward, advance
avant	before
avant-centre	centre forward
avant-dernier	penultimate
avantage	advantage, benefit
averse	shower
avertissement	warning
aveuglant	blinding
aveugle	blind
avis, opinion	opinion
avocat	lawyer
avoir accès à	have access to
avoir l'intention de	intend
avoir le droit de	allowed to (be)
avoir lieu	take place
avoir peur, avoir bien peur (que)	afraid (be)

B

bactéries	bacteria (pl.)
bagarre	fight
baguette magique	magic wand
baie	bay
baies (fruits)	berries
bailler	yawn
bains municipaux	public baths
baiser, bise	kiss
balayer	sweep*
baleine	whale
ballerine, danseuse	ballerina
ballon, ballon de baudruche	ball, balloon
banc	bench
bande	stripe
bande dessinée, BD	comics (pl.), comic-strip
bande-annonce	trailer
Bangladesh	Bangladesh
banlieue	suburb, suburbia
bannière (publicitaire)	banner ad
banque	bank
baraque à frites	rib shack
Barbade	Barbados
barbare	uncivilized
barbe	beard
barrage	dam
barre	bar
barreaux	bars
barrière	fence
barrière de corail	barrier reef
bas	down, low
bas (en)	downstairs
basé à	based in
base de départ	home-base
bataille	battle, fight
bateau, vaisseau	boat, ship
bâtiment	building
batterie, batteur	drums, drummer
battre	beat*
battre (se)/se disputer	fight*
battre un record	break* a record
bavard	talkative
bavarder	chat
beau	beautiful, good-looking
beau-père (nouveau mari de la mère)	step-father
beau-père (père du mari/femme)	father-in-law
bébé	baby *(n.)*, babyish *(adj.)*
bêche	spade
belle-mère (mère du mari/femme)	mother-in-law
belle-mère (nouvelle femme du père)	step-mother
bénir	bless
besoin, avoir besoin	need
bétail	livestock, cattle
bête	beast
beurre	butter
bibliothèque	library
bicyclette	bike, bicycle
bien	good, well, fine
bien avant	long before
bien équipé	well-equipped
bien que	although
bien s'entendre	get on well
bien sûr	of course, sure
bien-aimé	beloved
bien-être	welfare
bientôt	soon
bienvenue	welcome
bière	beer
bijou	jewel
bijouterie, bijoux	jewellery
bijoutier	jeweller
bilingue	bilingual
billard	snooker
billet	ticket
biologie	biology
biscuit	cookie
bison	buffalo, bison
bizarre	odd, funny
bizarre (qui a l'air ...), air drôle	funny-looking
blancheur	whiteness
blessant	hurtful
blessé	wounded, hurt, injured
blesser (se)	hurt*, get hurt
bleu foncé	dark-blue
blond	fair, blond
bloqué	stuck
bloquer	block
blottir (se)	nestle
blouson	jacket
bocal	bowl
boire	drink*
bois (en)	wooden
bois, les bois	wood, woods
bois pour le feu	firewood
boisé	woody
boisson	drink
boisson gazeuse sucrée	soda
boisson non alcoolisée	soft drink
boîte à jurons	swear-box
boîte à ordures, boîte de peinture, canette	can
boîte de conserve	tin
bombardement	bombardment
bon marché	cheap
bonbon	sweet
bond	leap
bondé	crowded
bonheur	happiness
bonne affaire	bargain
bord	edge
bord de mer	seaside
bordure, lisière	fringe
botte, grosse chaussure	boot
bouche	mouth
boucherie	butcher's
bouclier	shield
bouger, remuer	move around, budge
bougie	candle
bouillant, très chaud	hot
bouillir	boil
boulangerie	baker's
bouleversé	rattled
bouquet	bunch
bourse, subvention	grant
bousculer	shove
boussole	compass
bout de bois	stick
bouteille	bottle
boxer	box
boycotter	boycott
branche	branch
branché (à la mode)	trendy
branché (à une prise)	plugged
brancher sur une station (se)	tune in
bras	arm
brave *(n.)*, **guerrier indien**	brave
bric-à-brac	junk
brièvement	briefly
brillant	bright
briller	shine*
briquet	lighter
britannique	British
bronzé	suntanned
brosse, ... à dents	brush, toothbrush
bruit	noise
brûler	burn*
brusquement	sharply
brute, tyran	bully
bruyant	noisy, loud
bûcher	stake
bulldog	bulldog
bulle, bulle (BD)	bubble, balloon
bureau	desk, office

bus	bus
but, objectif	goal, aim

C

c'est pourquoi	that's why
cabane, cabane en rondins	shed, log cabin
cacahuète	peanut
caché	hidden
caché (vivre)	in hiding
cacher (se)	hide*
cadeau	present, gift, treat
cadre	frame
cadre dirigeant	executive
café (boisson)	coffee
café (lieu)	pub
cafétéria	coffee-bar, cafeteria
cahier	exercise book, copy book
calculer	calculate
calme	calm, cool
calmement	calmly
calmer (se)	ease up
cambrioler	burgle
cambrioleur	burglar
camionnette	van, pickup truck
campagne	country
campagne (de pub ou militaire)	campaign
campement	encampment
camper, campeur	camp, camper
camping (faire du)	camping trip (be on a)
Canada	Canada
canadien	Canadian
canalisation	pipe
canard	duck
cancer	cancer
candidat	contestant
canif	pen-knife
canne à pêche	fishing rod
canne à sucre	sugar cane
canoë	canoe
cantine, salle à manger	dining hall, canteen
capacité	capacity
cape	cape
capitaine	captain
capitalisme	capitalism
capot	bonnet
captivité	captivity
capturer	capture
caractéristique	characteristic
caramel	toffee
caricatural	caricatural
caricature	caricature
carnaval	carnival
carrière	career
carte	card, map
carte de membre	membership card
carton, carton rouge	cardboard, red card
cascadeur	stuntman
casier	locker
casque	helmet
casse-pieds (être)	bore (be a)
casser	break*
casserole	saucepan
castor	beaver
catastrophe	catastrophe
catch, lutte	wrestling
catholique	Catholic
cauchemar	nightmare
cause, causer	cause
cave	cellar
cavité	cavity
ceinture	belt
célèbre, … dans le monde entier	famous,world-famous

célébrer	celebrate
célébrité	celebrity
cellule	cell
Celte	Celt
celtique, celte	Celtic
cent(aine)	hundred
central, principal	core
centre	centre, center
centre commercial	shopping centre, mall
centre d'accueil	shelter
centre d'orientation	careers room
centre de formation	training centre
centre-ville	downtown
cercle	circle
cérémonie	ceremony
cérémonie de remise de prix	awards
cerf-volant	kite
cerise	cherry
certain, sûr	certain, positive
certainement	certainly
certificat	certificate
cerveau	brain
cessez-le-feu	cease-fire
chaîne	chain, channel (TV)
chaise	chair
chaise longue	deckchair
chaleur	warmth, heat
championnat	championship
chance, avoir de la chance	luck, be lucky
chances	odds
changement, changer	change
changement climatique	climate change
changer sa manière d'être	change one's ways
chant de noël	Christmas carol
chantage	blackmail
chanter, chanteur	sing*, singer
chanteur de rap	rapper
chapeau	hat
chaque	each, every
char	tank
char de carnaval	float
charbon	coal
chardon	thistle
charger	load
chariot	wagon
charismatique	charismatic
chasse	hunting
chasse au trésor	treasure hunt
chasse aux sorcières	witch-hunt
chasser, chasseur	hunt, hunter
chaud, chaleureux	warm
chaudron	cauldron
chauffage	heating
chaussette	sock
chausson	slipper
chaussure	shoe
chaussure à semelle compensée	platform shoe
chaussure de sport	sports shoe, sneaker, trainers
chauve-souris	bat
chef	chief, head, leader
chemin	way, path
chemin de fer	railway
cheminée (extérieure)	chimney
cheminée (intérieure)	fireplace
chemise	shirt
chemisier	blouse
chêne	oak tree
chenille	caterpillar
cher	dear
cher	expensive
chercher	look for, search, seek*
chercheur	researcher
chercheur d'or	gold-digger
cheval	horse

Chevalier de l'Ordre du Mérite	O.B.E. (Officer of the Order of the British Empire)
chevalier, faire chevalier	knight *(n.)*, *(v.)*
cheveux	hair
cheveux roux (qui a les …)	red-haired
cheville	ankle
chèvre	goat
chien	dog, hound
chiffre	figure
chimie	chemistry
chinois	Chinese
choc	shock
choisir	choose*, pick, adopt
choix	choice
chômage	unemployment
choquant	offensive, shocking
choqué, scandalisé	shocked, outraged
choquer	shock
chose	thing
chou	cabbage
chrétien, Christ	Christian, Christ
christianisme	Christianity
chronologie	chronology
chronométrer (se)	time oneself
chutes d'eau	falls, water falls
ci-dessous	below
cible, cibler	target
cicatrice	scar
ciel	sky
cil	eyelash
cinéma (aller au)	cinema, pictures (go to the)
cinéma (lieu)	movie-theatre
citadins	townspeople
citer	quote
citoyen	citizen
citron	lemon
citrouille	pumpkin
civilisation	civilization
clair	clear
clair de lune	moonlight
clairement	clearly
claquettes	tap-dancing
classe	class, year, grade (U.S.)
classe moyenne	middle-class
classique	classic
clavier d'ordinateur	keyboard
clé, clef	key
cliché	cliché
client	customer
clinique *(adj.)*	clinical
cliquer	click
clochard	bum
cloche, clocher	bell, bell tower
clonage	cloning
clouer	nail
coccinelle	ladybird
cocher	tick
cœur, noyau, centre	heart, core
coffre, coffre-fort	chest, safe
coin	corner
colère	anger
collaborateur	collaborator
collant	sticky
collants	tights
colle	glue
collectionner, ramasser	collect
collège, lycée	secondary school
coller	stick*
colline	hill
colombe	dove
colon, colonie	settler, colony

colonie de vacances	summer camp
coloré, multicolore	colourful
coloré (peau)	coloured
combattant	fighter
combien de temps	how long
combinaison d'astronaute	space suit
comédie	comedy
comédie musicale	musical
comme, semblable à	like
comme si	as if, as though
commencer	begin*, start
comment	how
comment se fait-il ?	how come?
commenter	comment
commerçant	shopkeeper
commettre	commit
Commonwealth	Commonwealth
communauté	community
communiquer	communicate
comparaison	comparison
comparer	compare
compétence, savoir-faire	skill
compétent	competent
compétition	competition, contest
complet, compléter	complete
complètement	completely
complice	accomplice
comporter (se)	behave
compositeur	composer, songwriter
compréhensible	understandable
comprendre	understand*, include
compte bancaire	bank account
compter	count
compter sur	rely (on)
comté	county
concentrer (se)	concentrate, focus
concerner	concern
concevoir	design
conclure	conclude
conclusion	conclusion
conducteur, chauffeur	driver
conduire	drive*
conférence	conference
confiance	confidence
confiant, sûr de soi	confident
confiance, faire …	trust
confirmer	confirm
conflit	conflict
conformer (se)	conform
confort	comfort
confortable	comfortable
confronter, affronter	confront
conique	conical
connaissance	knowledge
connecter	connect
connection	connection
connu	well-known
connu et aimé	popular
connu sous le nom de	known as
conquérir	conquer
conquête	conquest
conscience de soi	self-awareness
conscient	aware
conseil, tuyau	advice, tip
conseiller	advise
conservateur	conservative
considérablement	considerably
considérer, prendre en considération	consider
consignes de sécurité	safety instructions
consister	consist
consommateur	consumer
consommer	consume
conspiration	conspiracy
constamment	constantly
consternation	consternation

constituer, composer	compose, make up
construction	building
construire	build*, construct
contagieux	infectious
contaminer	contaminate
conte	tale
content	pleased, glad
continuer	go on, continue
contradiction	contradiction
contraire (au)	contrary (on the)
contrat	contract
contravention	parking ticket
contre	against, versus
contribuer	contribute
contribution	contribution
convaincant	convincing
convaincre	convince
conventionnel, classique	conventional
conversation	conversation
convoi	convoy
coopération	cooperation
coopérer	cooperate
copie	paper
copier	copy
coquille	shell
corde	rope
corne	horn
cornemuse	bagpipe
cornouaillais	Cornish
corps, corps humain	body, human body
correctement	correctly
corrompu	corrupt
corruption	corruption
corvées	chores
cosmique	cosmic
costume, tailleur	costume, suit
côté	side, edge
côte, côtier	coast, coastal
côte (os)	rib
cou	neck
coucher de soleil	sunset
coude	elbow
couloir	corridor
coup de pied	kick
coupable	guilty *(adj.)*, culprit *(n.)*
coupe	cup
coupe de cheveux	hair-cut
coupé ras	close-cropped
couper	cut*
coups de feu	gunfire
cour	yard
courage	courage
courageusement, avec courage	bravely
courageux	brave, courageous
coureur	runner
courir, faire fonctionner	run*
courir après	run after
couronne, couronné	crown, crowned
courrier	mail
au cours de/du	in the course of
course	race
court	short
coussin	cushion
coût	cost
couteau	knife (pl. knives)
coûter	cost*
coutume	custom
couverture	cover, blanket
couverture télévisuelle	TV coverage
couvrir, cacher	cover up
craie	chalk
crainte, doute	misgiving
crâne	skull
cravate	tie
créativité	creativity

créature	creature
créé par ordinateur	computer-generated
créer, créateur	create, creator
creuser	dig*
creux	hollow
crevaison	puncture
cri	cry (cries)
crier	scream, shout
crise	crisis
crise cardiaque	heart attack
croire	believe, think*
croisement	junction
croissance	growth
croître, croissant	increase, increasing
croix	cross
cru	raw
cruauté	cruelty
crucial	crucial
crucifier	crucify
cruel	cruel, bloody
cuir	leather
cuire (au four)	bake
cuisine (faire la)	cooking (do the)
cuisiner *(v.)*, **cuisinier** *(n.)*	cook
cuivre	copper
culotte	knickers
culture, culturel	culture, cultural
curieux	curious, nosy
cynique	cynical

D

d'abord	first
d'accord, bien	all right
d'occasion	second-hand
d'un seul coup	in one go
d'une façon ou d'une autre	somehow
dame	lady
danger	danger
dangereusement	dangerously
dangereux	dangerous
dans	in, into
dans ce cas	in that case
dans l'espoir de	in hope of
danser	dance
date limite, date butoir	deadline
de plus	moreover
de près	closely
de quelle manière ?	in what way?
de toutes façons	anyway
débarasser (se … de)	get rid (of)
débarrasser la table	clear the table
débat télévisé	talk show
débattre	argue
(se) débattre	struggle
débile *(n.)*	moron *(n.)*
débris	debris
début	beginning
(au) début de l'année 2003	in early 2003
débutant	beginner
décapiter	behead, cut someone's head off
décennie	decade
déception	disappointment
décevoir	disappoint
décharger	dump
déchets	waste
déchiré	torn
déchirer	tear*
décider, décision	decide, decision
déclaration	statement
déclarer	declare
(se) déclarer (guerre, feu)	break out
décliner	decline
décoller	take off

décolonisation decolonisation
décor setting, set
décourager discourage
découverte discovery
découvrir discover, find out
décret Act
déçu disappointed
défaite defeat
défaut bad point
défavorisé disadvantaged, underprivileged
défectueux deficient
défendre, défense defend, defense
défenseur de l'environnement conservationist
défi challenge
défilé procession, parade
définir define
définitif definite
dégâts damage
dégoûtant, écoeurant revolting, disgusting
dégradant, humiliant degrading
(se) déguiser dress up (as a...)
déjà already, ever, yet
délaissé neglected
délicat delicate
délit offence
demander ask, require
demander de l'aide ask (for help)
demander son chemin ask one's way
démarrer start
démocratie democracy
démodé unfashionable, old-fashioned
démolir knock down, wreck
démon demon
dénoncer (qqn) denounce, rat on
dent(s) tooth (teeth)
départ departure
dépêcher (se) hurry (up), rush
dépendre de, compter sur depend on
dépenser son argent en... spend money on...
déplaisant unpleasant
déprimant, déprimé depressing, depressed
depuis (ce moment-là), since (then)
depuis (+ durée) for
dernier, dernier en date last, latest
dernièrement lately
dès que (possible) as soon as (possible)
désagréable nasty
désagréable, pas sympa unfriendly
descendant descendant
descendre go*/come* down, get* off
désert *(adj.)* deserted
désert *(n.)* desert
desespérément desperately
désespoir despair
déshabiller (se) undress
déshumaniser objectify
désillusion disillusion
désirer long for
désobéissant disobedient
désordonné, mal tenu messy
désordre (en), dans un triste état mess (in a)
dessin, plan drawing, design
dessiner draw*
dessous, en-dessous, ci-dessous under, below
destabilisant unnerving
destin fate
détaché detached
détecter detect
déterioration degradation
déterminé, volontaire determined
détester, avoir en horreur loathe, hate, detest
détourner les yeux look away
détresse distress
dette debt

deux fois twice
dévastateur devastating
développement development
développer develop
devenir become*, turn into
deviner guess
devise motto
dévoué dedicated, devoted
Dieu God
différemment differently
difficile hard, tough
difficile, capricieux difficult, fussy
diffuser broadcast
diffusion, radiodiffusion broadcast
dignité dignity
dilemme dilemma
diligence stagecoach
diminuer decrease
diminuer, s'effacer diminish, fade
dinde turkey
dire say*, tell*
dirigeant ruler
diriger, conduire conduct, lead*
disagréable disagreeable, unpleasant
discours speech
discrimination discrimination
diseur de bonne aventure fortune-teller
disparaître disappear, pass away
disparaître, en voie d'extinction become* extinct
disponible available
disputer (se) quarrel, fight*
disque record
distrait absent-minded
distraitement absently
distrayant entertaining
distributeur automatique vending machine
divers various
diversité diversity
divertir entertain
divertissement entertainment
diviser divide
divorcé divorced
doigt finger
doigt de pied, orteil toe
dominer dominate
dominion, territoire sous domination dominion
don donation
donc therefore
donc, alors so
donner des conseils give advice
dont whose
doré, or golden, gold
dormir un peu get some sleep
dos back
dossier file
dot dowry
double duplicate
doucement gently, softly
douleur pain
douter doubt
doux soft
douzaine dozen
drapeau flag
drapeau britannique Union Jack
dresser put up
drogue drug(s)
droit, avoir le droit de right, have the right to
droits de l'homme human rights
droite (à) right (on the)
droite (à), côté droit right-hand
droits civiques civil rights
dur hard, tough
durée duration
durée de vie lifespan
durer last

E

eau (souterraine) (ground) water
écart discrepancy
échanger, échange swap, exchange
échanger, être en contact interact
écharpe scarf
échecs chess
échelle ladder
échouer, rater fail
éclair flash
éclater burst*, break* out
écologie ecology
écologique environmental
écologiste environmentalist
économie economy
économies savings
économique economic
économiser de l'argent save money
écossais Scottish
Écossais (personne, langue) Scot, Scots
Écosse Scotland
écouler (s'), couler flow
écran tactile touch screen
écraser run over
éducation sur la santé health education
effet effect
effet de serre greenhouse effect
efficace effective
efficacement efficiently
effrayant frightening, scary
effrayé scared, frightened
effrayer frighten, scare
égal equal
égalité equality
égalité des droits equal rights
église church
égoïste selfish
électricité electricity
électronique electronic
élève qui fait l'école buissonière truant
éliminer eliminate
éloigné remote, distant
éloigner de (s') turn away from
élu elected
embarquer (s') embark
embêter, ennuyer bother, annoy
emblème emblem
embouteillage traffic jam
embrasser kiss
émerger emerge
émerveillement wonder
émigrer emigrate
emmener qqn en voiture give someone a lift
émouvant moving
empêcher qqn de faire qqch. prevent/stop someone doing something
empoisonner poison
emporter (rapidement) take away, whisk away
empreinte de pied footprint
empreinte digitale fingerprint
emprunter borrow
en ce qui concerne regarding
en face opposite
en fait in fact
en grande partie largely
en outre besides
en pleine forme fit
en plus de ça on top of that
encore, à nouveau again
encore, toujours still
encourager encourage
endormi asleep
endroit place, area
enfance childhood

enfant gâté	spoilt brat
enfant(s)	child (children), kid
enfant unique	only child
enfantin	childish
enfer	hell
enfreindre la loi	break* the law
enfreindre le règlement	break* the rules
enfuir (s')	escape, run* away, flee*
enlever	remove
enlever	abduct
ennemi	enemy, foe
ennui	boredom
(avoir des) ennuis	be in trouble
(se mettre dans les) ennuis	get into trouble
(s') ennuyer, … à mourir	be bored, … stiff
ennuyeux	boring
énorme	huge, enormous, massive
enquête	survey, investigation
enquêter	investigate
enregistrement	recording
enregistrer	record
ensanglanté	bloody
ensemble	together
ensuite	afterwards
ensuite, après	then, after that
entendre	hear*
enthousiaste	enthusiastic
entier, tout	entire, whole
entièrement	entirely
entraînement	practice
entraîner (s')	practise
entre	between
entrepôt	warehouse
entreprendre	undertake*
entreprise, compagnie	company, corporation, business
(de l') entreprise	corporate
entrer	come* in
entrer (dans une pièce)	enter (a room)
envahir	invade
envelopper	wrap, envelop
(à l') envers	upside-down, face down
envers, vers	towards
environ, à peu près	around, about
environnement	environment
envisager, prendre en considération	consider
envoler (s')	fly* off
envoyer	send*
épais	thick
épaule	shoulder
épée	sword
épeler	spell*
épinard	spinach
épingler, coller	stick*
épique	epic
épouse, femme	wife (pl. wives)
épreuve	hardship
épuisant	gruelling
épuisé	exhausted
équipe, bande	team, crew
équipe de secours	rescue team/service
équipement	equipment, gear
équiper	equip
équitation	horse-riding
ère	era
errer	roam
erreur	mistake
escaliers	stairs
escaliers mobiles	gantry
escargot	snail
esclavage, esclave	slavery, slave
escrime	fencing
escursion	tour
Espagne	Spain
espagnol	Spanish
espèce	species
espèce en voie d'extinction	endangered species
espérer	hope
espion	spy
essayer	try, have a try
essence	petrol
essentiel	essential
est	east
estimer	estimate, esteem
estomac	stomach
établir	establish
étage, à l'étage	floor, upstairs
étagère	shelf(ves)
étant donné	considering
étape	stage
état, États-Unis	state, States, USA, U.S.
été	summer
éteindre (lampe)	switch off, turn off
étendre	expand
(s') étendre	stretch
étiquette, label	label, tag
étoile	star
étonnant	surprising, astonishing
étonné	astonished, puzzled
étonner, rendre perplexe, s'interroger	puzzle
étrange	strange, queer, curious, funny
étranger	foreign
étranger, inconnu	stranger
étrangler	strangle
être à court de	run* out of
être à la mode	be in, be trendy
être allongé	lie*
être d'accord	agree
être humain	human being
étroit	narrow
étude, bureau	study
étudiant, élève	student
étudier	study
européen	European
évanoui, inconscient	unconscious
(s') évanouir	faint
événement	event
éviter	avoid
évoluer vers, devenir	evolve (into)
évoquer	evoke
exagération	exaggeration
exagérément, de manière irréaliste	unrealistically
exagérer	exaggerate
examen	exam, test
examiner	examine, inspect
excessivement	excessively
excitation, agitation	excitement
exclure	exclude
exécuter	execute
exister, être là	be around, exist
expérimenter, tester	test, experiment
explication	explanation
exploiter	exploit
explorateur	explorer
explorer, étudier	explore
exploser	burst*, explode
explosif	explosive
exposé	talk
exposition	exhibition, exposure
exprimer	give voice to, express
exproprier	expropriate
extérieur	outdoor
extinction	extinction
extraire, extrait	extract
extraordinaire	extraordinary
extrêmement	extremely

F

fabricant de chaussures	shoe-maker
fabuleux, chouette	fabulous
fâché	angry, cross
facile	easy
facilement	easily
facile à vivre	easy-going
façon, manière	way
facteur	factor
facture	bill
faiblir, s'affaiblir, s'effacer, diminuer	fade
faim	hunger
faire attention	pay attention
faire attention à qqch.	mind something
faire de son mieux	do (one's) best
faire des expériences	experiment
faire du stop	hitch hike (hitch)
faire face à	face
faire l'expérience de	experience
faire la queue	stand* in line, queue
faire mal (se)	hurt*
faire pression en faveur de	lobby for
faire ressortir	bring* out
faire semblant	pretend
faire une pause	take* a break
fait	fact
fait maison	home-made
falaise	cliff
fanatique, intoxiqué	addict
fantôme	ghost
farce	practical joke, trick
farine	flour
fascinant	fascinating
fasciner	fascinate
fatigant, fatigué	tiring, tired
fauché, sans le sou	penniless
fauteuil	armchair
fée	fairy
félicitations	congratulations
femelle	female
féminité	womanhood
femme d'affaires	businesswoman
femme(s), épouse(s)	woman (women), wife (wives)
fenêtre	window
fer	iron
fer à cheval	horse-shoe
fermer	close (down)
fermer à clé, enfermer	lock
féroce	fierce, murderous
férocement	fiercely
(en) feu, … de joie	(on) fire, bonfire
feuilles	leaf (pl. leaves)
feux d'artifice	fireworks
fiche de renseignements	information sheet
fidèle	faithful, loyal
fier, fierté	proud, pride
fil	thread
fille	girl, daughter
filon	vein
fils	son
fin, dénouement	end, ending
finalement	finally
finir	finish, end
fioriture	flourish
fixer un but	set a goal
flambant neuf	brand new
flèche	arrow
fléchir	flex
fleuri	flowered, flowery
flipper	pinball machine
flou	blurred
foi	faith
fois	time

folie	madness
follement	madly
foncé, noir	dark
fonctionner, marcher	work
fond	bottom
fondamental	fundamental
fonder	found
fondre	melt
fonds (argent)	funds
forçat, prisonnier	convict
force	strength
forcer	force
forer	drill
forêt	forest, woods
forêt tropicale	rainforest
formation professionnelle	professional training
forme	shape
formel	formal
former	shape, form
formule	formula
fortement, avec force	strongly
fou *(adj.), (n.)*	mad, madman
fou (de)	crazy (about)
fouet	whip
foule	crowd
four (à micro ondes)	(microwave) oven
fournir	provide
fourrure	fur
fracasser	smash
fraise	strawberry
français	French, Frenchman
France	France
frapper	hit*
frapper avec le pied	kick
frayeur	alarm
fredonner	hum
frimeur	show-off
frisé	curly
froissé	rumpled
froncer (les sourcils)	frown
front	forehead
frustré	frustrated
fumée, fumer	smoke
fumées d'usine	fumes
furieux	furious
fusée	rocket
fusil à rayons (tirer avec ...)	ray-gun *(n.), (v.)*
fusillade	shooting
futur époux	husband-to-be
futuriste	futuristic

G

gâcher, gâter, pourrir	spoil*
gagner	win*
gagner (argent)	earn (money)
gaiement	gaily, cheerfully
gallois	Welsh, Welshman
galoper	gallop
gamin	kid
gant	glove
garde, gardé	guard, guarded
garde-forestier	ranger
garder	keep*
garder en tête	keep* in mind
garder en vie	keep* alive
gardien de zoo	zoo-keeper
gaspiller	waste
gâter, pourrir	spoil*
gauche (à)	left (on the)
géant	giant
geler	freeze*
gémir	moan, groan
gênant, embarrassant	embarrassing
générer	generate
généreux, qui a bon cœur	good-hearted, kind-hearted
génial	brilliant, great ,super
génie	genius
genou	knee
genre	genre, type
gens	people *(ind. pl.)*
gentil	kind, sweet, friendly, nice
gentillesse	kindness
gentiment	kindly
geste	gesture
gibier	game *(ind.)*
gifler	slap
gilet	waiscoat
glace, crème galcée	ice, ice cream
(en papier) glacé	glossy
glacial	freezing
glaçon	ice cube
glisser	slide*
gomme	rubber
gonfler	swell*
gourmand	greedy
goûter, sentir le goût de	taste
gouvernement	government
gouverner, dominer	rule
grâce à	thanks to
graine	seed
Grande-Bretagne	Britain
grandir (pour une personne)	grow* up
grange	barn
gras (lettre, caractère)	bold (letters)
gratte-ciel	skyscraper
gratter	scratch
gratuit	free
gravir	ascend, climb
grec	Greek
grenier	attic
grève	strike
grille	grid
grimper, escalader	climb (up)
gris	grey
grognon	grumpy
grondement	rumble
gros plan	close-up
gros titre	headline
grossier	crude
groupe de pression	pressure group
groupe jouant des tambours	drum band
Guatémala	Guatemala
guérir, guérisseur	heal, healer
guerre	war
Guerre Froide	Cold War
guerre mondiale (première/deuxième)	world war (first/second)
guerrier	warrior
guide , guider	guide, lead*, leader
guillemets	inverted commas

H

habiller(s')	get dressed, dress
habitant	inhabitant
habitude	habit
habituel	usual
habituellement , d'habitude	usually
hache	axe
hache de guerre	tomahawk
hâché, pilé	chopped
haie	hedge
haillons	rags
haineux, détestable	hateful
hameçon	fish hook
handicapé mental ou physique	mentally or physically handicapped/deficient
hanté	spooky, haunted
harceler	bully
harmonie	harmony
harpe	harp
haut niveau	high-level
haute technologie	high-tech
(à) haute voix	aloud
hauteur, taille	height
hebdomadaire	weekly
hérétique	heretical
héritier	heir
hésiter	hesitate
heureusement	happily
heureux	happy
heurt, opposition	clash
heurter (se)	clash
hic, piège	catch
hideux	hideous
hindou	Hindu
historique	historical
hit-parade	chart
hochet	rattle
homme d'affaires	businessman
honnête	honest
honnêtement	honestly
honnêteté	honesty
honneur	honour
honorer, honoré	honour, honoured
honte	shame
honteux , avoir honte	ashamed (be)
horloge	clock
huile	oil
humanitaire	humanitarian
humanité	mankind
humiliant	humiliating
hypnose	hypnosis
hypocrite	hypocritical

I

ici, présent	here
idéal	ideal
idéaliser	idealise
idéalisme	idealism
idée	idea
identification	identification
identifier	identify, pick out
identité	identity
idiot	stupid, fool, moron
idole	idol
ignorer	ignore
il y a combien de temps	how long ago
il y a (une heure, ...)	(one hour) ago
île	island
Ile de La Trinité	Trinidad
île déserte	desert island
îles Britanniques	British Isles
îles Caraïbes	Carribean islands
îles du Pacifique	Pacific Islands
îles Fiji (Fidji)	Fiji islands
illégal	illegal
illégalement	illegally
illustrer	illustrate
imaginaire	imaginary
imaginer	picture, imagine
imiter	imitate
immédiatement, tout de suite	immediately, right now
immensément	vastly
immigré	immigrant
immortalité	immortality
immortel	immortal
imperméable	raincoat
impitoyable, sans merci	merciless
implication	implication
impliquer	involve

implorer implore
impoli, grossier rude, impolite
impoliment, grossièrement rudely, impolitely
imposant massive
impressioner impress
impressionnant impressive
impressionné impressed
imprévisible unpredictable
imprimer print
impuissant, sans défense helpless
inacceptable unacceptable
inattendu unexpected
incandescent glowing
incapable unable
incertain unsure
incident incident
incident violent patch
inclure include
incohérent incoherent
incolore colourless
inconfortable uncomfortable
inconnu unknown
incontrôlé uncontrolled
incorporer incorporate
incroyable incredible, unbelievable
Inde India
indice clue
indiquer indicate
individu individual
individuellement individually
industrie industry
industriel industrial
inexpliqué unexplained
infecté infected
infecter (s') get infected
infiltrer (s') infiltrate
infini infinite
infirme disabled
infirmière nurse
ingénieur engineer
inhabituel unusual
inhumain inhuman
initiative initiative
inné inborn
inoffensif harmless
inoffensif, de manière inoffensive inoffensive, inoffensively
inquiet worried
inquiéter (s') worry
inquiétude concern
(avec) inquiétude uneasily
inscrire (s') enrol, sign up, join
insensé foolish
insistant insistent
insister insist (on)
insolent cheeky
inspirer inspire
installer install
installer (s') settle
institut institute
insuffisant insufficient
intégral integral
intégration integration
intégrer integrate
intellectuel intellectual
intelligent bright, clever, intelligent, smart
interdire forbid*
interdit forbidden
interdit de sortie (être) grounded (be)
intéressant, intéressé interesting, interested
intérêt interest, concern
(à l') intérieur inside
interprète (langue), (œuvre) interpreter, performer
interpréter, jouer perform
interroger qqn question s.o., interrogate
intoxiqué *(n.)*, *(adj.)* addict, addicted
inutile useless, pointless
invincible invincible
invisible invisible
invité guest
inviter qqn à sortir ask someone out
involontairement involuntarily
invulnérabilité invulnerability
irlandais *(adj.)*, *(n.)* Irish, Irish man
Irlande Ireland
Irlande du Nord Northern Ireland
ironie, ironique irony, ironic
irréaliste unrealistical
irréel unreal
islam Islam
isoler isolate
Italie Italy
italien Italian
itinéraire route

J

jalousie, jaloux jealousy, ealous
Jamaïque Jamaica
jamais never,ever
jambe leg
Japon Japan
japonais Japanese
jaune yellow
jeter un coup d'oeil take* a look at
jeter un sort cast* a spell
jeu game
jeu de mots play on words
jeune *(n.)* youngster
jeunes, jeunesse youth
jeux d'argent gambling
(se) joindre à join (in)
jonquille daffodil
joue cheek
jouer de l'argent gamble
jouer (film) star
jouer par équipe play in teams
jouer un rôle play a part
jouer (un rôle), agir act
jouet toy
joueur, espiègle, en jouant, d'un ton taquin playful, playfully
jour férié, vacances holiday(s)
jour J D-day
jour ouvrable working day
journal newspaper, diary, journal
journaliste reporter, journalist
joyeusement joyfully
joyeux cheerful, merry, gay
juillet July
juin June
jumeau, jumelle twin
jumelles binoculars
jupe skirt
jurer swear*
jus juice
jusqu'à ce que till, until
jusqu'à (+ moment) until
jusqu'à (+ nombre) up to
jusqu'à présent so far
juste (équitable, vrai) just, right
juste (seulement) just, only
justifier justify

K

kidnapper kidnap, abduct

L

labourer farm
labyrinthe maze, labyrinth
lac lake
laid ugly
laine, laineux wool, woolly
laisse leash
laisser leave*, let*
laisser tomber, quitter drop (out)
lame de rasoir razor blade
lancer throw*, launch
lancer dans (se), s'adonner à engage in
lancer un appel appeal (to)
langue language, tongue
lapin rabbit
large wide
larme tear
(faire un) lavage de cerveau brainwash
laver, (se) laver wash, have a wash
le long (de) along
leçon de conduite driving lesson
légendaire legendary
légende legend, tale
légende de photo caption
léger light
légume vegetable
lent, lentement slow, slowly
(se) lever get* up, stand* up, rise*
lèvre lip
libéral liberal
libéré, sorti released
libérer (qqn) set (s.o.) free, release
liberté freedom
libre, librement free, freely
lié à related to
lien link
(au) lieu de instead (of)
lieu de naissance birthplace
lieu de rendez-vous meeting-place
lieu de travail workplace
lieu, endroit place
ligne line
ligoter tie
limiter limit, restrict
lire rapidement scan
lisière fringe, edge
lisse, lisser smooth
littérature literature
livre (453 grammes) pound
livre (monnaie anglaise) pound (£)
livrer deliver
localiser locate
logiciel software
logique logic *(n.)*, logical *(adj.)*
loi law
loin far (away)
lointain, au loin distant, in the distance
loisir, activité de loisir leisure, hobby
long terme long-term
longueur, (tout au long de) length, (the … of)
lorsque, le temps que by the time
louange, louer, complimenter praise
louer, laisser let*
louer qqch. hire,rent
loup(s) wolf (pl. wolves)
loupe magnifying glass
lourd, lourdement heavy, heavily
lumière(s) light(s)
lune moon
lunettes (de soleil) (sun)glasses, spectacles
lutin Leprechaun
lutte contre la famine famine relief
lutter wrestle

M

mâcher	chew
machine à remonter le temps	time machine
mâchoire	jaw
magasin	shop, store
magazine de bandes dessinées	comic-book
magie	magic, wizardry
magique	magical, magic
magnétoscope	VCR
magnifique	magnificent
magnifiquement, à la perfection	beautifully
maigre	skinny, thin
maillot de bain fille	swimsuit
maillot de bain garçon	swimming trunks
main, (fait) à la main	hand, by hand
maire, mairie	mayor, Council
maïs	corn (U.S.)
maître	master
mal à l'aise	uneasy, ill-at-ease
mal *(adj.), (n.)*	bad, wrong *(adj.)*, harm *(n.)*
mal au ventre	stomach ache
mal de dent	toothache
mal de tête	headache
mal, le mal	evil
malade	ill, sick
maladie	disease, illness
maladoit	awkward, clumsy
maladresse	clumsiness
malchanceux	unfortunate
malgré, en dépit de	despite, in spite of
malheur, chagrin	woe
malheureusement	unfortunately
malheureux	unhappy, miserable
malicieux	mischievous
malin	clever, smart, cunning
maltraité	mistreated, abused
maltraiter	ill-treat
Manche (la)	Channel (the)
mannequin	model
manier	wield
manière	manner
manifestation	demonstration, rally, march
manifester	demonstrate
manipuler	manipulate
manquant, absent	missing
manque	lack (of)
manquer (l'école)	skip (school)
manquer, rater	miss, fail
manteau	coat
maquillage	make-up
marchand	dealer, trade, merchant
marchand de fruits et légumes	greengrocer's
marchand de journaux	newsagent's
marché	market
marché (contrat)	deal
marche, ... de protestation	walk, march
marcher	walk
marcher (fonctionner)	work
mare	pond
marécage	swamp
mari	husband
mariage	wedding
marié *(n.)*	groom
mariée	bride
marier (se)	marry
marmite	cooking pot
marque	brand, make
marquer	score
marraine	godmother
marre (en avoir)	fed up (be)
marron clair	light-brown
marteau	hammer
martien	Martian
martyr	martyr
masque	mask
masquer	screen
massacre, massacrer	massacre, slaughter
massivement	massively
matière	subject
matin, faire la grasse matinée	morning, sleep in
mec	guy
méchant	mean, cruel, bad
méconnaissable	unrecognisable
médaille	medal
médicament	medicine
mélanger	mix
membre de la convention constituante (USA)	Founding Father
même (le)	same (the)
même (si)	even (if)
mémoire, souvenir	memory
menaçant	threatening
menace, menacer	threat, threaten
mener, conduire (à)	lead* (to)
meneur, dirigeant	leader, ruler
menteur, mentir	liar, lie
mentionner	mention
menton	chin
mer, mer agitée	sea, rough sea
mérite	merit
mériter	deserve
merveilleux	wonderful
mesure, temps(musique)	beat
mesurer	measure
méthode	method
métier, travail	job, trade
métro	underground, tube, subway
mettre	put*
mettre en danger	endanger
mettre en route (se)	set off
mettre hors-la-loi	outlaw
mettre la pression sur	put pressure on
mettre la table	lay the table
mettre qqn mal à l'aise	make someone feel stupid
meurtre	murder, killing
meurtrier	murderer
mexicain	Mexican
microbe	microbe
microscopique	microscopic
midi	midday
miel	honey
milieu	middle
militant, militer	campaigner, campaign
mille (≈1,6 km)	mile
mille, milliers	thousand, (-s)
milliard	billion
million	million
mimer	mime
mince	slim, thin
minorité	minority
minuscule	tiny
miroir	mirror
mobiliser	mobilize
mode	fashion
mode (à la mode)	cool, trendy
mode de vie	way of life
modèle	model, pattern
modérer	moderate
modifier	modify
moins	less, fewer (+ n. pl.)
mois	month
moitié	half
moment, à un moment	moment, at one point
monarque	monarch
monde	world
(dans le) monde entier	worldwide
mondial, global	global
moniteur	instructor
monstrueux	monstrous
montage sonore	sound mix
montagne	mountain
montant	amount
monter dans	get* into
monter (une entreprise)	set* up
montrer	show*
se moquer	laugh at, make fun of
moralité	morals
morceau (de)	piece, bit of
morceaux, bidules, machins	bits and pieces
mordre	bite*
mort *(adj.), (n.)*	dead, death
mortel	deadly
mortel, pas mortel	lethal, non lethal
moteur	engine
motiver	motivate
mots croisés	crosswords
moucharder	rat
mouche	fly
mouchoir	handkerchief
moulin	mill
mourir	die
mourir de faim	starve to death
moustique	mosquito
mouton	sheep
mouvement	movement
moyen	average
Moyen Âge	Middle ages
moyens de transport	means of transport
municipalité	borough
mur, mural (graffiti)	wall, mural
musée	museum
musicien	musician *(n.)*, musical *(adj.)*
musique	music
musulman	muslim
mutuel	mutual
mystère, mystérieux	mystery, mysterious
mythique	mythical

N

nager	swim*
nain	dwarf (pl. dwarves/dwarfs)
naissance	birth
narration	narrative
nature	nature, wildlife
nature(dans la)	wild (in the)
nature sauvage	wilderness
naturel	natural
naturellement	naturally
naval	naval
navigation	navigation
naviguer sur le web	surf the Internet
ne pas être d'accord	disagree
néanmoins	nevertheless
nécessaire	necessary
nécessairement	necessarily
nécessiteux	needy
négligé, délaissé, abandonné	neglected
négligent	careless
négocier	negociate
nettoyer, effacer	clean
neutre	matter-of-fact
nez	nose
nid	nest
niveau	level
noble	noble
Noël	Christmas

noeud papillon bow tie
noir comme dans un four pitch dark
noisette, noix nut, walnut
noix de coco coconut
nominer nominate
nommer name
non-croyant non-believer
non identifié unidentified
non-officiel, officieux non-official
nord north
nostalgie nostalgia
nostalgique nostalgic
note de bas de page foot-note
noter mark, note down
nounours teddy bear
nourrir feed*
nourrir de (se) live on something
nourriture food
nourriture exotique ethnic food
nouveau, tout nouveau new, brand new
nouvelle short story
Nouvelle-Zélande New Zealand
nouvelles news
noyau, centre core
noyer (se) drown
nu naked, bare, nude
nuage, nuageux cloud, cloudy
nuit night *(n.)*, dark *(adj.)*
nul, très mauvais (être … en) rubbish (be … at)
nulle part nowhere

O

obéir obey
obéissant obedient
objet object
obscène obscene
obscurité (dans l') dark (in the)
obsédé obsessed
observateur watcher
observer watch, observe, scan
obstacle obstacle
obtenir get*, obtain
occasion, opportunité opportunity
occidental Western
occupé busy
occuper de (s') look after
Océan Atlantique Atlantic Ocean
Océan Pacifique Pacific Ocean
odeur smell
odieux horrible, hateful
odorant, qui sent bon sweet-smelling
œil eye
œuf egg
oeuvre d'art art work
oeuvre de bienfaisance, organisation caritative charity
officiel official
officier de police police officer, marshall
offrir give (a present), offer (propose)
offrir (s'), avoir les moyens afford
oiseau bird
ombre shadow
omniprésent omnipresent
oncle uncle
opposer oppose, contrast
oppresseur oppressor
opprimer oppress
orage, tempête storm
orageux stormy
ordinaire ordinary
ordinateur portable laptop
ordonné tidy
ordre order
ordures garbage
oreille ear
orgueil pride
originaire, natif native
original original
origine (à l') origin, originally
orphelin orphan
os bone
ou bien, sinon, autrement or else
oublier forget*
ouest west
ours bear
outré outraged
ouvertement openly
ouverture opening
ouvrier workman
ouvrir, ouvert open
ouvrir/fermer (robinet) turn on/off

P

pacifique, en paix peaceful
pacifiste pacifist
pagayer paddle
page d'accueil home page
paiement pay
paisible untroubled
paisiblement peacefully
paix peace
Pakistan Pakistan
pakistanais Pakistani
panier basket
panneau sign
panorama view
pantalon trousers, slacks
pantalon taille basse hipsters
pantalons pattes d'éléphant bell-bottomed trousers
panthère panther
pape pope
Papouasie-Nouvelle-Guinée Papua New Guinea
Pâques Easter
paquet packet
par, à travers through
par exemple for instance
par (jour / semaine) a (day / week), per
paradis paradise
paralyser paralyze
parapluie umbrella
parcourir des yeux scan
(entre) parenthèses (in) brackets
paresseux lazy
parfait perfect, fine
parfaitement perfectly
parfum perfume
parfum, essence flavouring
parier bet*
parlement parliament
parmi among, amongst, out of
parodie, parodier parody
parrain godfather
partager share, split*
partager la douleur de qqn sympathize with someone
parti away, gone
participation involvement
participer participate
particulier particular
particulièrement especially, in particular, particularly
partie de, faire partie de part of, be part of
partie, match game
partir leave*, be off, go away
partisan follower
partition (musique) score
partout everywhere, all over
pas step, footstep
pas en sécurité unsafe
pas encore not…yet
passager passenger
passé past
passer des heures spend hours
passer, donner (qqch.) pass (something)
passer l'aspirateur hoover
passer (se), arriver go on, happen
passer (se) (histoire, film) be set (story, film)
passer (un certain âge) turn
passif passive
passioné de, amateur de be keep on, be fond of
patrimoine heritage
pause break
pause (faire une) pause
pauvre, pauvreté poor, poverty
pavillon (hôpital) ward
payer pay*
Pays de Galles Wales
pays en voie de développement developing country
pays enchanté fairy land
paysage scenery, landscape
peau mate (ayant la) dark-skinned
peau, peau (d'animal) skin, hide
peau-rouge redman
pêche, pêcher fishing, fish
peigne comb
peindre paint
peindre au rouleau roll over
peinture pour visage face paint
peinture vaporisée spray paint
pèlerin pilgrim
pelle spade
pellicule (photo) film
pelouse lawn
pencher (se) bend*, lean* over
pendant during
pendant ce temps in the meantime, meanwhile
pendant (des heures) for (hours)
pendant que while
pendre, suspendre hang*
pénétrant penetrative
pénétrer penetrate
pénétrer par effraction break* into
pénible, enquiquinant (être) (be a) pain
pensée thought
penser think*
penser à qqch. give* a thought
perche pole
percuter crash into
perdre lose*, waste
Père Noël Santa Claus
perle bead
permettre allow, enable
permis de conduire driving test
permission, (armée) permission, furlough
perplexe puzzled
persécuter, s'en prendre à persecute, victimize
personnage character
personnalité personality
personne âgé elderly
personne sondée, interrogée respondent
personnel personal
personnellement personally
perspective perspective
peser weigh
petit little, small
petit à petit gradually

pétition, adresser une pétition	petition *(n.)*, *(v.)*
petits boulots	odd jobs
pétrifié de peur	petrified with fear
pétrole	oil
peu de	few (+ n.pl.)
peu de, un peu de	little , a little
peuple	people (dén.)
peur	fear, fright, scare
peut-être	maybe, perhaps
peut-être bien mais…	maybe so but…
pharmacien	chemist
phénomène	phenomenon
physique	physical
pièce de théâtre	play
pied (à)	foot (on) (pl. feet)
piégé	trapped
pierre	stone
pieu	stake
pilote de chasse	fighter-pilot
pilule, médicament	pill
pinceau	brush
piqûre	injection
pire, le pire	worse, worst (the)
pitié, avoir pitié de	pity *(n.)*, *(v.)*
pittoresque	picturesque
pizzeria	pizza parlour
placard	cupboard
place de (à la)	instead (of)
place, espace	space
placer	set, put, place
plafond	ceiling
plage	beach
plaindre (se)	complain
plaine	plain
plainte	complaint
plaire à	appeal (to)
plaisanter	joke
plan	map
plante, planter	plant
plaque numéralogique	number plate
plaqué or	gold-plated
platine	platinum
plein d'espoir	hopeful
plein (de)	full (of)
plein de préjugés	prejudiced
pleurer	cry
pleuvoir	rain
pleuvoir à verse	pour (with rain)
plombier	plumber
plonger	dive
pluie, pluvieux	rain, rainy
plume	feather
pluralisme	pluralism
plus loin	farther
plusieurs	several
plutôt	rather
poche, (marsupiaux)	pocket, pouch
poésie	poetry
poids	weight
poignard	dagger
poignet	wrist
poilu	hairy
poing	fist
point	point, spot
point de départ	starting point
point de repère	landmark
point de vue	point of view
pointu	pointed, sharp
poli	polite
police d'assurance	insurance policy
poliment	politely
politesse	politeness
politicien	politician
politique	policy
politique étrangère	foreign policy
polluant	polluting
polluer	pollute
pomme, pommier	apple, apple tree
pompier	fireman
pont	bridge
portable (téléphone)	mobile
portail	gate
porte arrière	back door
porte d'entrée	front door
portefeuille	wallet
porter	bear*
porter, transporter	carry
porter (un vêtement)	wear*,have* … on
posséder	own
postuler	apply
pot-de-vin	bribe
poubelle	dustbin, bin, garbage can
pouce	thumb
poule	hen
poumon	lung
poupée	doll
pour cent	percent
pour toujours	forever
pourcentage	percentage
pourri	rotten, spoiled, spoilt
poursuivre	chase
pousser	push, shove s.o.
poussiéreux	dusty
pouvoir	power
pouvoir d'achat	buying power
pouvoir, être capable de	be able to , can
pratique	practical
précéder	precede
précurseur	precursor
prédire	predict
préface	foreword
préféré	favourite
préférence	preference
préférer	prefer, like best
premier plan	foreground
prendre en voiture	pick (someone) up
prendre le contrôle	take over, take control
prendre note	jot down
prendre part à	take part in
prendre plaisir à, aimer	be fond of, enjoy
prendre racine	take root
prendre soin de	take care of
prendre un bain de soleil	sunbathe
près de	near, nearby, next to, beside
présenter	introduce, present
préservation	conservation
presque	almost, nearly
pressé	in a hurry
prétendre, affirmer	claim
prêter	lend*
prévenir	warn
prévention	prevention
prévoir, projeter	plan
comme prévu	as planned
prier	pray
principal (n.)	headteacher
principal (adj.)	main, leading
principalement	mainly, mostly
printemps	spring
prison	jail
prisonnier	prisoner
privation	deprivation
prix (argent), prix (cadeau)	price, prize
Prix Nobel de la Paix	Nobel Peace Prize
probablement	probably
problème, affaire	matter, issue, problem
procédé	device
procès	case, trial
prochain, prochainement	next
proche, près de	close (to), next to, beside
procurer	provide, procure
produire	produce
produire, faire surgir	come up with
produit	product
produit chimique	chemical
produit de beauté	cosmetic
profane	unholy
profession	occupation
professionnel	professional
profond	deep, profound
profondément	deeply
proie	prey
prolongation	overtime
promettre, promesse	promise
promouvoir, faire la promotion de	promote
promouvoir, faire la publicité	advertise
proposer	offer, suggest
propre, à soi	own
propriétaire	owner
propriétaire de ranch	rancher
prospérité	fortune
protection	pad, protection
protéger	protect
protestant	Protestant
protestataire	protester
protestation	protest
protester	protest
prouver	prove
provenir de	spring*
provision	supply
provocateur *(adj.)*	provocative
provoquer	provoke
prudent	careful
psychologique	psychological
psychologue	psychologist
public, spectateurs	audience
publicité	advertising
publicité, petite annonce	advertisement advert-ad
publier	publish
puis, ensuite	then, after that
puissant	powerful, mighty
puits	well
punir	punish
pureté	purity

Q

qualité	good point, quality
quantité	quantity, amount
quart, quartier, quart-temps	quarter
quartier	neighbourhood
quartier général	headquarters
quelqu'un d'autre	someone else
quelque part	somewhere
quelque peu	somewhat
quelquefois	sometimes
quelques	a few (+ n. pl.)
question, problème	issue, matter
quête	quest
queue	tail
quitter	leave*, quit*
quotidien	daily

R

raconter	tell*
raconter une blague	crack a joke
radiation	radiation
radioactif	radioactive
raid, faire ou lancer un raid	raid
raison	reason

raisonnable	sensible
ramasser	pick (up), collect
rameur	rower
ramper	crawl
rangée, à la suite	row (in a)
ranger	tidy (up)
rapidement	rapidly
rappeler	remind
(se) rappeler	recall
rarement	seldom, rarely
rasage, se raser	shave *(n.)*, *(v.)*
raser (se)	have a shave
rater	miss, fail
rater tout, faire rater	mess up
ratifier	ratify
ravissant	enchanting, lovely
réaliste	realistic
réalité	reality
reapparaître	reappear
rebelle	rebel *(n.)*, rebellious
rebeller (se)	rebel
rébellion	rebellion
récapituler	recapitulate, sum up
recette	recipe
recevoir	receive, get*
recherche, chercher, rechercher, à la recherche de	search *(n.)*, *(v.)*, in search of
rechercher une information	look something up
recherches (faire des)	do research
récolter des fonds	do fund-raising, raise money
récompense(argent)	reward,
récompense (prix)	award
réconforter, consoler	comfort
reconnaissance	acceptance
reconnaissant	grateful
reconnaître	recognize
reconquérir	reconquer
récréation, pause	break
recruter	recruit
récupération	recovery
rédaction	essay
référer à (se), faire référence	refer
réfléchir	think about
refléter	reflect
reformuler	rephrase
refroidir	cool
réfugié	refugee
refus, refuser	refusal, refuse *(v.)*
regard	look
regarder	look (at)
regarder autour de soi	look around
regarder, jeter un œil	have a look
regarder (TV), surveiller	watch
règles/règlement	rules, regulation
régner	reign
regret, regretter	regret
régulier	regular
regulièrement	regularly
réimplanter	relocate
reine	queen
réintroduire	reintroduce
rejeter	reject
rejoindre	rejoin
relation, lien	relationship
relier	link
remarquable	outstanding, remarkable
remarqué	noticed
remarquer	notice
remonter le moral	cheer up
remplacer	replace
rempli de	packed with
remplir	fill in
remuer	stir
renard	fox
rencontrer	meet*
rendre	give* back, return
rendre compte (se), réaliser	realise
rendre conscient	make aware
(se) rendre à	get* to
(se) rendre, se livrer	turn oneself in
rendre (un devoir)	hand…in
renforcer	reinforce
renommée	fame
renoncer à	give* up
renouveau	revival
rentrer	get in
rentrer (en voiture)	drive back
renverser	knock over
renverser	spill*
répandre	spread*
réparer	repair, fix
repas	meal
repasser	iron
repère (animal)	den
repérer	spot
répondre	answer, reply, respond
réponse	answer, response
reposant	relaxing
(à maintes) reprises	repeatedly
reprocher, faire porter la faute à	blame
requin	shark
réserve	reservation
réserver	book
résigné	resigned
résister	resist
résorber, réduire	reduce
résoudre, pénétrer	solve, crack
resource	resource
respect de soi	self-respect
respecté	well-respected
respecter qqn	respect, look up to s.o.
respectueux	considerate, respectful
responsable	responsible
responsable (de)	charge (in … of)
responsable *(n.)*	official
ressemblance	similarity
ressembler	look like
restaurant qui fait des plats à emporter	take-away restaurant, carry-out-place
rester	stay, remain
rester à distance de	keep* off
rester à la maison	stay home, stay in
rester calme	stay cool
résultat	result
résumé	summary, recapitulation
retirer, emporter	take* away
retour	return
(de) retour à	back (to)
retourner	go* back, return
retourner, revenir	return
rétracter	retract
retraite	retirement
réunion	meeting
réunir	gather
réunir de l'argent	raise money
(se) réunir	get* together
réussir	succeed
réussir, avoir du succès	successful (be)
réussir (examen)	pass (test)
réussir, se débrouiller	manage
réveil	alarm clock
(se) réveiller	wake* (up)
révélation	revelation
revenir	come* back
rêver, rêve	dream
réviser	revise
révolte	revolt
Révolution Industrielle	Industrial Revolution
révolutionnaire	revolutionary
révolutionner	revolutionize
revolver, arme à feu	gun
rez-de-chaussée	ground floor
rhume	cold
riche	rich, wealthy
ridicule	ridiculous
ridiculiser	ridicule
rien, rien du tout	nothing, nothing at all
rimer	rhyme *(v.)*
rire	laugh
risible	ludicrous
risque, risqué	risk, risky
rituel	ritual
rivaliser, être en compétition (avec)	compete (against)
rive	bank
rivière, fleuve	river
riz	rice
robe	dress
roc, rocher, rock (musique)	rock
roi	king
rôle	part, role
romain	Roman
roman	novel
rond	round
rond-point	roundabout
rongeur	rodent
rose	pink
rôtir	roast
rouge vif	bright-red
rouler	roll
route de campagne	country road
royaume	kingdom
Royaume-Uni	United Kingdom
royauté	kingship
ruban	ribbon
rue, route	street, road (Rd)
ruée vers l'or	gold rush
ruiner, abîmer, gâter	spoil*
ruisseau	stream
rumeur	rumor/rumour
ruminer	ruminate
rusé	cunning

S

s'en prendre à	pick on
s'entendre avec qqn	get along with s.o.
sable	sand
sabot	hoof (-ves)
sac à dos	backpack
sacré	sacred
sacrifier	sacrifice
sage, sagement	wise, wisely
sagesse	wisdom
sain et sauf	safe and sound
saint	holy
saint patron	patron saint
Saint-Graal	Holy Grail
salaire	earnings, salary
sale	dirty
salle des professeurs	staff room
sang	blood
sans	without
sans abri	homeless
sans espoir	hopeless, hopelessly
sans importance	unimportant
sans risque	risk-free
sans travail	jobless
sans valeur	worthless
santé	health
satisfaisant	satisfactory
satisfait	contented

saturation saturation
sauf, excepté except
sauter jump, hop
sautiller skip
sauvage wild, savage
sauvagement savagely
sauver save
sauveteur rescue worker
savoir-faire expertise
saxon Saxon
scandaleux scandalous, outrageous
scarabée beetle
scénario screenplay
scène, lieu scene, stage
scientifique scientist
scruter du regard peer, scan
sculpter carve
séance session
sec dry
secouer shake*, jerk
secourir rescue
secrètement secretly
sécurité security, safety
seigneur lord
sel salt
selon according to, depending (on)
semblable similar (to), like
sembler, avoir l'air seem, look (+ adj.)
sembler, paraître sound (+ adj.)
sénat senate
sens de l'humour sense of humour
sensible sensitive
sentier trail
sentiment feeling
sentir smell*
sentir (se) (+ adj.), ressentir feel* (+ adj.)
séparer (se) separate, part
série télé TV series
sérieux, sérieusement serious, seriously
séro-positif HIV-positive
serré tight
serrer clench
serrer (la main), secouer shake* hands
serviable helpful
servir (de) serve (as)
seul, solitaire lonesome, solitaire
seul, tout seul alone, on (one's) own
seulement just, only
sévère strict, severe
shampooing shampoo
si, si seulement if, if only
si, tellement such, so (+ adj.)
SIDA AIDS, HIV
siècle century
siège, siège arrière seat, back seat
sieste nap
sifflet, siffler whistle
signer sign
significatif meaningful
signification, sens meaning
silencieusement silently, quietly
silhouette figure
simple simple, mere
simplement merely
singe monkey
sinistre sinister
sirène siren
situer la scène set the scene
soi-disant supposedly
soi-même oneself
soie silk
soigneusement carefully
soins, attention care
sol floor, ground, soil
soldat, simple soldat soldier, private
solde (en) sale
solitaire lonely, lonesome
solstice solstice
sombre dark
somme amount
sommet, haut (en), en premier top (at the)
somnolent drowsy
son sound
sonate sonata
sondage d'opinion poll, survey
sonner ring*
sorcellerie witchcraft, wizardry
sorcier wizard
sorcière witch
sorte de sort, kind of
sortie exit, release
sortir (film-CD) release
sortir qqch. de take out
sou penny
soucoupe volante flying saucer
soudain suddenly
souffle breath
souffler blow*
souffrance suffering
souhait, souhaiter wish
soûl drunk
soulager, soulagé relieve, relieved
soulever lift,raise
souligner underline
(se) soumettre submit
soumis submissive
soumission submission
soupçonner suspect
source source
sourcil eyebrow
sourire smile
souris mouse (pl. mice)
sous, dessous, ci-dessous under, below
sous-marin submarine
sous-payer, sous-payé underpay, underpaid
sous-vêtements underwear
soutenir (une équipe) support
souvenir *(n.)* memory(ies)
souvenir (se) remember
souvent often
souverain sovereign, ruler
souveraineté sovereignty
soviétique Soviet
SPA RSPCA
spectaculairement, de manière spectaculaire dramatically
sponsorat sponsorship
sportif (adj.) sporty
sportif *(n.)* sportsperson
sports, jeux games
spot publicitaire commercial
station (balnéaire) resort
statut status
Ste Lucie St Lucia
stéréotypé stereotyped
stimulant challenging
stimuler stimulate
stocker store
strictement strictly
stupéfait astonished, puzzled, amazed
stupéfiant, étonnant amazing
stupide silly, brainless
style de vie lifestyle
subir suffer
submerger overwhelm
subsister subsist
succès success, hit
succés (avec) successfully
sud south
suffisant sufficient
suffocant boiling hot
suggérer suggest
suicider (se) kill oneself
suivre, suivant follow, following
suivre la mode keep up with fashion
suivre (une rue) go along
sujet, thème topic
superstitieux superstitious
supporter, tolérer stand*, bear*
sûr, certain sure, positive
sûr, en sécurité safe
sûr, sur qui on peut compter dependable
sur une période de over a period of
surnaturel supernatural
surnom nickname
surpris, surprendre surprised, surprise
surveillance watch
surveiller watch, monitor
susceptible touchy
suspendre suspend, hang*
suspendu hanging
symbolique symbolic
symboliser symbolise
sympa fun, good fun, great fun, cool
sympathie sympathy
système immunitaire immune system

T

tabac tobacco
taille size, height
taille (corps), taille (robe) waist (body), midriff (dress)
taire (se) keep quiet
talent skill
taper knock
taper dans ses mains clap (one's hands)
taper des pieds stamp (one's feet)
tas, des tas de heap, pile, piles of
tatouage tatoo
technologique technological
teindre color/colour, dye
teint dyed
tel que such as
téléphone rouge hotline
téléphoner phone
témoin witness
temps libre free time
temps (météorologique) weather
temps partiel part-time
tenailles pliers
tendance tendency
tendre hold* out
tendrement dearly
tenir hold*
tenir à value
tenir compagnie à qqn keep someone company
(se) tenir immobile stand* still
(se) tenir debout stand*
tenter try, tempt
tenter sa chance try one's luck
tenue outfit
terrain, champ field
terre land
terre, la Terre earth, Earth
terreur terror
terrible terrible, awful
terriblement terribly, awfully
terrien earthling
terrifiant terrifying

terrifié	terrified, scared to death
territorial	territorial
tête	head
têtu	stubborn
texto	text message
texture	texture
thérapeute	therapist
thérapie	therapy
Tiers-Monde	Third-world
tige	stem
timide	shy, timid
timidité	shyness
tirer des conclusions	draw conclusions
tiroir	drawer
tisser	weave*
tissu écossais à carreaux	tartan
tomber	fall* (down)
tomber amoureux de	fall* in love with
tomber en panne	break* down
tomber raide mort	drop dead
torchon	towel
tordre	twist, wring*
torturer	torture
tôt	early
totalement, complètement	totally, completely, entirely
totem	totem pole
toucher, produire un effet	affect
toujours	always, all the time, still
tour	tower
tournage (film), fusillade	shooting
tourner	turn
tourner (film)	shoot* (film)
tournoi	tournement
tournure, chute (d'une histoire)	twist
tous les deux, à la fois	both (and)
tousser, toux	cough
tout	everything
tout au long de	throughout
tout d'abord	at first, first of all
tout de suite	right away
tout le long (du chemin)	all the way
tout le monde	everybody, everyone
tout le temps	all the time
tout, tous, toutes	all
toute la journée	all day
toutefois	however
toxique	toxic
trace, marque, vestige	mark, trace
traditionnel	traditional
traduction	translation
trahir	betray
trahison	treachery
traîner	drag
traîner, passer son temps	hang* out
traité	treaty
traitement	cure
traiter	treat
traiter de, avoir affaire à	deal* with
trame d'une histoire	plot
tranchant	sharp
transférer	transfer
transformer, se transformer en	transform, turn into
transpirer	sweat
travail des enfants	child labour
travail des métaux	metalwork
travailleur, qui travaille dur	hardworking
traverser	cross, go across
trèfle	shamrock
tremblement de terre	earthquake
trembler	shake*
trésor	treasure
tribu	tribe
tricher, tricheur	cheat
trimestre	term
triste, tristement	sad, sadly
tristesse	sadness, sorrow
tromper, duper	fool
trompette	trumpet
tronc	trunk, bole, caber (Scottish)
trottoir	pavement
trou (prison)	stockade
troubler	trouble
troupeau	herd
trouver	find*, pick out
trucs	stuff
tuer	kill, murder
tueur	killer, murderer, slayer
tuyau, canalisation	pipe
type bizarre	weirdo
typique	typical
tyran, brute	bully

U

un peu	a bit, slightly
un peu plus de	a little over
unifier	unify
unir (s')	unite
unir ses forces	join forces
unité	unity
urbain	urban
urgence	emergency
urgent, de manière urgente	urgent(ly)
usé	worn-out
usine	factory, mill (19thc.)
ustensile (de cuisine)	utensil (cooking)
utile	useful
utiliser, utilité	use

V

vacances	holiday(s), vacation
vague *(n.)*	wave
vaincre	defeat
vaisseau spatial	spaceship
valeur	worth, value, preciousness
valise	case, suitcase
vallée	valley, glen
valoir	be worth
vaniteux	conceited
vantard	boastful
vaporiser	spray
varié	diverse, varied
variété	variety
vaste	vast, large
véhicule	vehicle
veille de Noël	Christmas eve
vélo, bicyclette	bike, bicycle
velours	velvet
vendeur de drogue	drug-dealer
vendre	sell*
venimeux, vénéneux	poisonous
vent, venté	wind, windy
verger	orchard
vérifier	check
véritable, réel, authentique	real-life
vérité	truth
vers (poésie)	rhyme *(n.)*
vers sa maison/son pays	homeward
verser (sang)	spill*
vertueux	upstanding
vêtement de sport	sportswear
vêtements	clothes
viande	meat
victoire	victory
vide, à moitié vide	empty, half-empty
vie	life (pl. lives)
vie après la mort	afterlife
vieillesse	old age
Vietnam	Vietnam
vieux	old, elderly
vif, éclatant, clair	vivid
vilain	naughty
ville	town, city, borough
violemment	violently, hotly
virilité	manhood
visage pâle	pale face
viser	aim (at)
visqueux	slimy
vite, rapide	fast, quick
vite, rapidement	quickly
vitesse *(n.)*, **à toute vitesse** (exp.)	speed *(n.)*, in a hurry (exp.)
vivant	living
voisin	neighbour
voix	voice
vol	robbery, theft
vol à l'étalage	shop-lifting
vol (avion)	flight
voler	fly*
voler, dérober	rob, steal*
voleur de bétail	cattle-thief
voleur(s)	thief (pl.-ves), robber
volontaire	volunteer
volontaire, déterminé	strong-willed
vorace	voracious
voter	vote
vouloir dire	mean*
voyage	travel, trip, journey
voyage d'affaires	business trip
voyage dans l'espace	space travel
voyage dans le temps	time travel
voyage scolaire	school trip
voyager, voyageur	travel, traveller
vrai, juste	true, right
vrai, véritable	real
vraiment	really
vue	sight
vue, panorama	view
vulgaire	loud, vulgar, rude, crude
vulnérable	vulnerable

W

webcam (caméra)	webcam
whisky	whisky
wigwam	tepee

Y

y compris	including
yeux	eyes
yeux bleux (qui a les)	blue-eyed

Z

zèbre	zebr
zone urbaine	urban area

The Commonwealth and its Members

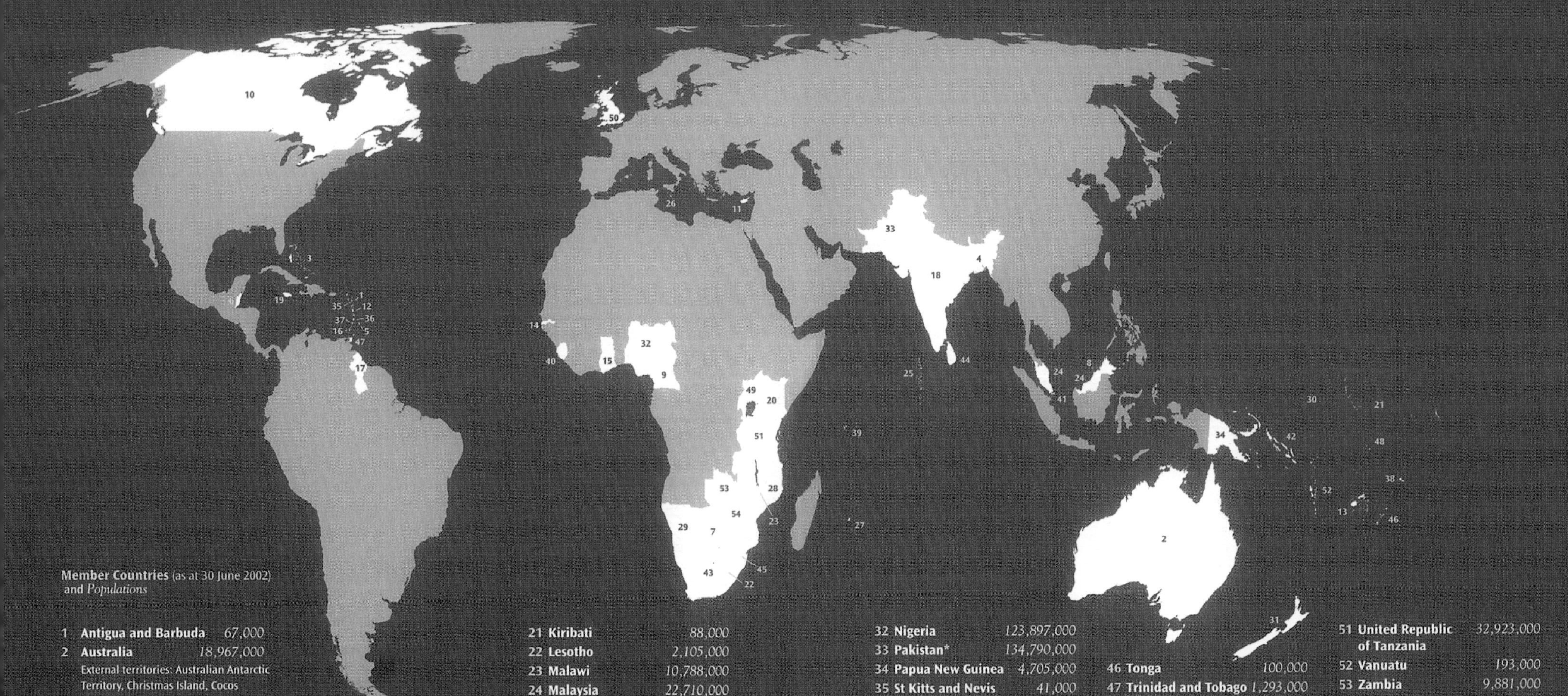

Member Countries (as at 30 June 2002) and *Populations*

1 **Antigua and Barbuda** *67,000*
2 **Australia** *18,967,000*
External territories: Australian Antarctic Territory, Christmas Island, Cocos (Keeling) Islands, Coral Sea Islands Territory, Heard Island and McDonald Islands, Norfolk Island, Territory of Ashmore and Cartier Islands
3 **The Bahamas** *298,000*
4 **Bangladesh** *127,669,000*
5 **Barbados** *267,000*
6 **Belize** *247,000*
7 **Botswana** *1,588,000*
8 **Brunei Darussalam** *322,000*
9 **Cameroon** *14,691,000*
10 **Canada** *30,491,000*
11 **Cyprus** *760,000*
12 **Dominica** *73,000*
13 **Fiji Islands** *801,000*
14 **The Gambia** *1,251,000*
15 **Ghana** *18,785,000*
16 **Grenada** *97,000*
17 **Guyana** *856,000*
18 **India** *997,515,000*
19 **Jamaica** *2,598,000*
20 **Kenya** *29,410,000*
21 **Kiribati** *88,000*
22 **Lesotho** *2,105,000*
23 **Malawi** *10,788,000*
24 **Malaysia** *22,710,000*
25 **Maldives** *269,000*
26 **Malta** *379,000*
27 **Mauritius** *1,174,000*
28 **Mozambique** *17,299,000*
29 **Namibia** *1,701,000*
30 **Nauru** *11,000*
31 **New Zealand** *3,811,000*
Includes the territories of Tokelau and the Ross Dependency (Antarctic). Self-Governing Countries in Free Association with New Zealand: Cook Islands and Niue
32 **Nigeria** *123,897,000*
33 **Pakistan*** *134,790,000*
34 **Papua New Guinea** *4,705,000*
35 **St Kitts and Nevis** *41,000*
36 **St Lucia** *154,000*
37 **St Vincent and the Grenadines** *114,000*
38 **Samoa** *169,000*
39 **Seychelles** *80,000*
40 **Sierra Leone** *4,949,000*
41 **Singapore** *3,952,000*
42 **Solomon Islands** *429,000*
43 **South Africa** *42,106,000*
44 **Sri Lanka** *18,985,000*
45 **Swaziland** *1,019,000*
46 **Tonga** *100,000*
47 **Trinidad and Tobago** *1,293,000*
48 **Tuvalu** *11,000*
49 **Uganda** *21,479,000*
50 **United Kingdom** *59,501,000*
Overseas Territories: Anguilla, Bermuda, British Antarctic Territory, British Indian Ocean Territory, British Virgin Islands, Cayman Islands, Falkland Islands, Gibraltar, Montserrat, Pitcairn, Henderson, Ducie and Oeno Islands, St Helena and St Helena Dependencies (Ascension and Tristan da Cunha), South Georgia and the South Sandwich Islands, and Turks and Caicos Islands
51 **United Republic of Tanzania** *32,923,000*
52 **Vanuatu** *193,000*
53 **Zambia** *9,881,000*
54 **Zimbabwe**** *11,904,000*

* Pakistan was suspended from the councils of the Commonwealth in October 1999 following a military coup.

** Zimbabwe was suspended from the councils of the Commonwealth in March 2002.

1999 population figures from *2001 World Bank Atlas*, except for Nauru and Tuvalu

International capital
Country capital
Important city
+ 1 000 m
500 to 1 000 m
0 to 500 m
International boundary
Country boundary
Shetland Islands
Orkney Islands
Hebrides
Northwest Highlands
Loch Ness
Grampians
Aberdeen
SCOTLAND
Ben Nevis 1343
ATLANTIC OCEAN
Dundee
Perth
Edinburgh
Glasgow
Tweed
Southern Uplands
Londonderry
Hadrian's Wall
Newcastle upon Tyne
Tyne
NORTH SEA
NORTHERN IRELAND
Belfast
Isle of Man
Ouse
York
Bradford
Leeds
REPUBLIC OF IRELAND (EIRE)
IRISH SEA
Manchester
Liverpool
DUBLIN
Galway
Shannon
ENGLAND
Snowdon 1085
Nottingham
Limerick
Cambrian Mts.
Severn
Birmingham
Great Ouse
Blackwater
Cambridge
WALES
Cork
Oxford
St George's Channel
Swansea
Cardiff
LONDON
Bristol
Thames
Dover
Strait of Dover
Calais
Portsmouth
Brighton
Isle of Wight
Plymouth
The English Channel
Falmouth
Scilly Islands
Channel Islands
Scale
100 km
62.15 miles

ARTIC OCEAN
GREENLAND
Ellesmere Island
Parry Islands
Devon Island
Beaufort Sea
Baffin Sea
Banks Island
Somerset Island
Prince of Wales Island
Victoria Island
Boothia Peninsula
Baffin Island
Davis Strait
Melville Peninsula
Endicott Mountains
Michelson 2816
Yukon
Porcupine
ALASKA
Alaska Mountains
Dawson
Mackenzie Mountains
YUKON
TERRITORY
Great Bear Lake
Mackenzie
NORTH WEST
TERRITORIES
Back
NUNAVUT
Hudson Stait
Thelon
Crater of New Quebec
Juneau
Cassiars Mountains
Great Slave Lake
Coast Mountains
Hudson Bay
New Foundland
Lake Athabaska
Peace
LABRADOR
BRITISH
COLOMBIA
Athabaska
Reindeer Lake
Nelson
ALBERTA
SASKATCHEWAN
MANITOBA
Fraser
Mt Robson 3954
CANADA
QUEBEC
Gulf of Saint Laurent
Waddington 4042
Mt Colombia 3747
Edmonton
Saskatchewan
Attawapiscat
Lake Mistassini
Saint Laurent
Lake Winnipeg
ONTARIO
Calgary
Victoria
Vancouver
Lake Manitoba
NEW BRUNSWICK
NOVA SCOTIA
Regina
Fredericton
Quebec
Olympia
Seattle
Winnipeg
MAINE
Halifax

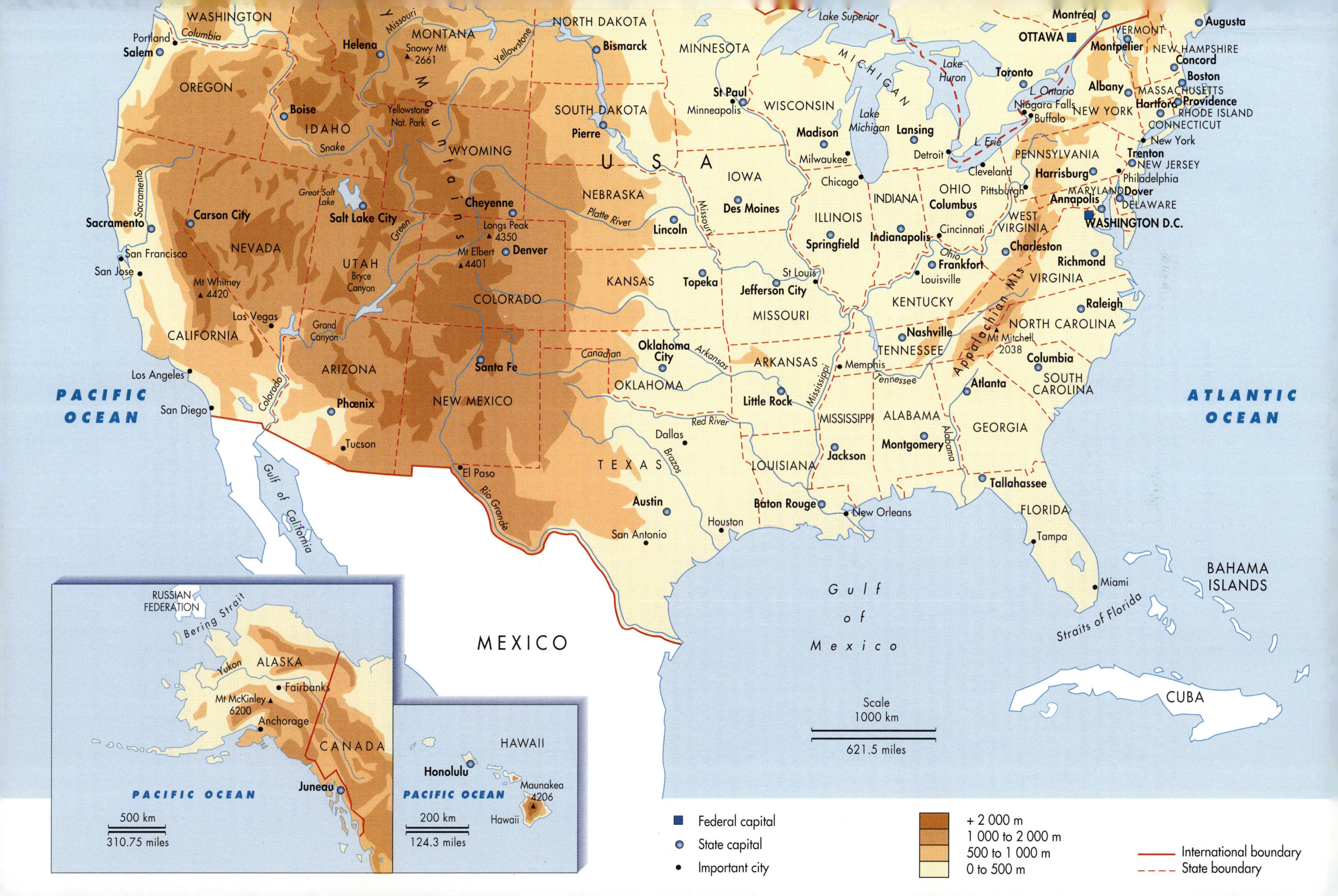

WASHINGTON
OREGON
CALIFORNIA
NEVADA
IDAHO
MONTANA
WYOMING
UTAH
ARIZONA
COLORADO
NEW MEXICO
NORTH DAKOTA
SOUTH DAKOTA
NEBRASKA
KANSAS
OKLAHOMA
TEXAS
MINNESOTA
IOWA
MISSOURI
ARKANSAS
LOUISIANA
WISCONSIN
ILLINOIS
MICHIGAN
INDIANA
OHIO
KENTUCKY
TENNESSEE
MISSISSIPPI
ALABAMA
GEORGIA
FLORIDA
SOUTH CAROLINA
NORTH CAROLINA
VIRGINIA
WEST VIRGINIA
PENNSYLVANIA
NEW YORK
MARYLAND
DELAWARE
NEW JERSEY
CONNECTICUT
RHODE ISLAND
MASSACHUSETTS
VERMONT
NEW HAMPSHIRE
U S A
Rocky Mountains
Appalachian Mts
Portland
Salem
Boise
Helena
Snowy Mt 2661
Yellowstone Nat. Park
Sacramento
San Francisco
San Jose
Carson City
Mt Whitney 4420
Las Vegas
Los Angeles
San Diego
Great Salt Lake
Salt Lake City
Bryce Canyon
Grand Canyon
Phœnix
Tucson
Cheyenne
Longs Peak 4350
Mt Elbert 4401
Denver
Santa Fe
El Paso
Bismarck
Pierre
Lincoln
Topeka
Oklahoma City
Dallas
Austin
San Antonio
Houston
St Paul
Minneapolis
Des Moines
Jefferson City
St Louis
Little Rock
Baton Rouge
New Orleans
Jackson
Memphis
Madison
Milwaukee
Chicago
Springfield
Indianapolis
Lansing
Detroit
Cleveland
Columbus
Cincinnati
Frankfort
Louisville
Nashville
Mt Mitchell 2038
Montgomery
Atlanta
Tallahassee
Tampa
Miami
Columbia
Raleigh
Richmond
Charleston
Pittsburgh
Harrisburg
Annapolis
WASHINGTON D.C.
Dover
Philadelphia
Trenton
New York
Hartford
Providence
Boston
Concord
Augusta
Montpelier
Albany
Buffalo
Niagara Falls
Toronto
OTTAWA
Montréal
Columbia
Snake
Missouri
Yellowstone
Green
Colorado
Sacramento
Platte River
Canadian
Arkansas
Red River
Brazos
Rio Grande
Mississippi
Ohio
Tennessee
Alabama
Lake Superior
Lake Michigan
Lake Huron
L. Erie
L. Ontario
PACIFIC OCEAN
ATLANTIC OCEAN
Gulf of California
Gulf of Mexico
MEXICO
CUBA
BAHAMA ISLANDS
Straits of Florida
Scale
1000 km
621.5 miles
RUSSIAN FEDERATION
Bering Strait
ALASKA
Yukon
Fairbanks
Mt McKinley 6200
Anchorage
CANADA
Juneau
PACIFIC OCEAN
500 km
310.75 miles
HAWAII
Honolulu
Maunakea 4206
Hawaii
PACIFIC OCEAN
200 km
124.3 miles
Federal capital
State capital
Important city
+ 2 000 m
1 000 to 2 000 m
500 to 1 000 m
0 to 500 m
International boundary
State boundary

Table de références documentaires

Couv. : Express Newspapers/Sipa (hg) ; Boondocks © Aaron McGruder. Dist. by Universal Press Syndicate, Reprinted with permission, All rights reserved (hd) ; Stringer Rich Pedroncelli/AP-Sipa (bg) ; John Harris/Report Digital-REA (bc) - **p. 9 :** Richard Turpin/Aspect Picture Library - **p. 11 :** Photo © John Murphy, graphic/irelandseye.com and Appletree Press - **p. 12 :** The National Wallace Monument leaflet, © Argyll, The Isles, Loch Lomond, Stirling & The Trossachs Tourist Board - **p. 13 :** ARJ-Photos12.comARJ - **p. 14 :** Central Bank of Ireland (hc) - **p. 15 :** Express Newspapers/Sipa (h) ; Ancient Art and Architecture Collection Ltd/The Bridgeman Art Library-Giraudon (mhg) ; Roman Baths, DR (mbg) ; British Tourist Authority (mbc) ; Hulton Archive (bg) ; Covent of the Holy Name, Malvern Link/The Bridgeman Art Library-Giraudon (bd) - **p. 16 :** © Wales Tourist Board (hg) ; C. Vaisse/Hoa-qui (hd) ; Ian Hodgson/Reuters/Maxppp (mc) ; John Harris/Report Digital-REA (bg) ; Report courtesy of the South Wales Evening Post, Swansea, Wales (bd) - **p. 17 :** R.Weir/Scotland in Focus (hg) ; Gerry McCann/Report Digital-REA (hd) ; Buss Wojtek/Hoa-qui (md) ; Patrick Ward/ANA (bd) - **p. 18 :** Hervé Champollion/Top (hg) ; Richard Turpin/Aspect Picture Library Ltd (hd) ; Will & Deni McIntyre/The Image Bank-Gettyimages (mg) ; J.J. Sommeryns/ANA (md) ; Claude Thibault/ASK Images (bc) ; Central Bank of Ireland (bd) - **p. 19 :** Ian Waldie/Reuters/Maxppp (h) ; Paul McErlane/Reuters/Maxppp (mg) ; D. Lefranc/Explorer (bg) ; Jeffe J. Mitchell/Reuters/Maxppp (bd) - **p. 21 :** The Corries Music - **p. 23 :** Robin Allison Smith - **p. 24 :** Calvin and Hobbes © Watterson. Reprinted with permission of Universal Press Syndicate. All rights reserved (hd) ; Nadia/www.bullyingnoway.com.au (md) - **p. 25 :** Reproduced with permission from Child Abuse Prevention Services, Roslyn, N.Y./www.kidsafe-caps/bullies.html (hd) ; Peta-Maree/www.bullyingnoway.com.au (bd) - **p. 27 :** From Scholastic Early Childhood Today © reprinted by permission of Scholastic Inc - **p. 28 :** Alliance for Justice's Drawing the Line on Gun Violence Student Poster Contest/Max Drzewinsky, Killingworth, CT (hd) ; George Eastman House/Lewis W. Hine/Archive Photos/Hulton Archive (bd) - **p. 29 :** Mary Evans Picture Library/Keystone Photos (hg) ; Popperfoto/Cosmos (hd) ; CARE® and CARE Package® are registered marks of the Cooperative for Assistance and Relief Everywhere, Inc. (CARE) (md) ; International Programme on the Elimination of Child Labour/International Labour Organization (bd) - **p. 30 :** Robin Allison Smith (hg) ; Santa Barbara County District Attorney's Office (hd) ; © Volunteer Reading Help. Reprinted by permission (md) ; BBC (mg) ; Picture The Evening Press, York (bg) ; Courtesy of Metropolitan Police, U.K. (bd) - **p. 31 :** Alliance for Justice's Drawing the Line on Gun Violence Student Poster Contest/Max Drzewinsky, Killingworth, CT (hg) ; Kim Kulish/REA (md) ; Sandy Huffaker/Gamma (bg) ; Bob Daemmrich/Corbis-Sygma (bd) - **p. 32 :** Center for the Prevention of Scool Violence, North Carolina Department of Juvenile Justice and Delinquency Prevention, USA (hg) ; Illustration by Sean Dillon (age 8), courtesy of the Scottish Anti-bullying Network (bd) - **p. 33 :** *The logical Song*, paroles et musique : Richard Davies, Roger Hodgson © Almo Music Corp./Delicate Music/Rondor Music - **p. 37 :** Charly Franklin/Taxi/Gettyimages - **p. 38 :** James Neff-2003, http://www.rense.com (hg) ; Charly Franklin/Taxi/Gettyimages (hd) ; Rue des Archives (bd) - **p. 39 :** © 1997 TIME Inc. Reprinted by permission - **p. 40 :** Images courtesy of the SETI Institute (hg) ; Seth Shostak/SETI Institute (hd, md) - **p. 41 :** Roger-Viollet (hg) ; Roger Ressmeyer/Corbis (m) - **p. 42 :** The Topps Company Inc/Coll. Maison d'Ailleurs/Agence Martienne (hc) ; Collection Christophe L (bd) - **p. 43 :** H.G.Wells, «The Time Machine» & «The War of the Worlds», published by Victor Gollancz, SF Masterworks (hg) ; Coll. Maison d'Ailleurs/Agence Martienne (hc) ; Les Archives du 7^{e} Art (mc) ; Rue des Archives (md) ; Henry Thomas/Stills (bg) - **p. 44 :** Rue des Archives (hg) ; Coll. Maison d'Ailleurs/Agence Martienne (hd) ; Les Archives du 7^{e} Art (mg) ; Reprinted with special permission of King Features Syndicate/Coll. Maison d'Ailleurs/Agence Martienne (md) ; Coll. Maison d'Ailleurs/Agence Martienne (bc) ; Corbis-Sygma (bd) - **p. 45 :** The Topps Company Inc./Coll. Maison d'Ailleurs/Agence Martienne (hg) ; Ballantine Books, a division of Random House Inc. (hd) ; 1996 by Warner Bros./Coll. Cinestar/Archives du 7^{e} Art (m) ; Rue des Archives (bd) - **p. 46 :** Images courtesy of the SETI Institute - **pp. 48-49 :** John Wyndham, «The Day of the Triffids», published by Penguin Books - **p. 51 :** Staff Reed Saxon/AP-Sipa - **p. 52 :** Historical Picture Archive/DG/Corbis (hg) ; Fototeca/Leemage (b) - **p. 53 :** Bettmann/Corbis - **p. 54 :** TheAmericanWest.com, DR ; Johnston Frances Benjamin, New York, Museum of Modern Art,»An American History Lesson,» taken from a Hampton Institute album, 1899-1900, © Photo SCALA, Florence (bg) - **p. 55 :** Corbis (hd) ; «Drawing Rations, San Carlos Apache Reservation» by K. Dodge, 1899, copy neg. 76-6091, National Anthropological Archives, © Smithsonian Institution (bg) ; Jan Butchofsky-Houser/Corbis (bd) - **p. 56 :** DG/Corbis-Sygma (hd) ; Coll. Cinestar/Archives du 7^{e} Art (bd) - **p. 57 :** Photos12.com (hg) ; © Keep America Beautiful, Inc. (md) ; DG/Corbis-Sygma (bd) - **p. 58 :** Ilkka Uimonen/Magnum Photos (h) ; Charles E. Rotkin/Corbis (mg) ; Handout/AP-Sipa (md) ; Patrick Zachmann/Magnum Photos (bc) ; Spooner/Gamma (bd) - **p. 59 :** Earth First ! (hg) ; Stringer Rich Pedroncelli/AP-Sipa (hd) ; © Diné CARE, http://dinecare.indiginousnative.org (md) ; Staff Reed Saxon/AP-Sipa (bg) ; Peabody (bd) - **p. 60 :** Woolaroc Museum, Bartlesville, Oklahoma (hg) - **p. 61 :** © SONY/ATV ACUFF ROSE Music - **pp. 62-63 :** From Key Stage 3 , English Letts Educational by John Barder, D.R. - **p. 65 :** Salifu Idriss/Redferns-Dalle - **p. 66 :** Boondocks © Aaron McGruder. Dist. by Universal Press Syndicate, Reprinted with permission, All rights reserved (hg) ; Jeremy Bembaron/Corbis-Sygma (bd) - **p. 67 :** Salifu Idriss/Redferns-Dalle (m) ; Neal Preston/DG/Corbis (bg) - **p. 68 :** «Vandals Breach Airport Defences» by Neale Maynard, 1998, Photograph by Glenn Barnes/The Courier Mail, Brisbane, Australia - **p. 69 :** Rex Features/Sipa (hd) ; Lewis Durham Kent News Pictures/Imapress (bc) ; Joe Tarr/Metropulse (texte) - **p. 70 :** The Advertising Archive Ltd. (hc) ; Hulton Archive (bd) - **p. 71 :** The Advertising Archive Ltd. (hd, mg) ; PPCM (bg) ; Henry Diltz/Corbis (bc) ; Hulton-Deutsch Collection/Corbis (bd) - **p. 72 :** The Advertising Archive (hg) ; Elliott Erwitt/Magnum Photos (hd) ; Photos12.com (mg) ; AP-Sipa (bg) ; Universal, DR (bd) - **p. 73 :** The Advertising Archive Ltd (hc) ; Mike Cameron/Redferns-Dalle APRF France (mg) ; Clark Bill/Corbis-Sygma (md) ; S.I.N./Corbis (bg) ; Keith Bedford/Getty-Sipa (bc) - **p. 74 :** McGraw Hill, DR - **p. 76 :** Boondocks © Aaron McGruder. Dist. by Universal Press Syndicate, Reprinted with permission, All rights reserved - **p. 79 :** Robin Allison Smith - **p. 80 :** Isaac Hernandez/Mercury Press - **p. 81 :** Photodisc Vert/Gettyimages (hd) ; Wally McNamee/Corbis (mg) ; Collection Cinestar/Les Archives du 7^{e} Art (bg) - **p. 82 :** Courtesy of www.adbusters.org - **p. 83 :** Courtesy of www.adbusters.org (hd) ; Danna Vajda and Willie Brisco (bd) - **p. 84 :** Robin Allison Smith (hc) ; Wojtek Buss/Hoa-qui (bd) - **p. 85 :** Robin Allison Smith (hd, mg, md) ; Photo © Pantene Pro-V, Reprinted with permission (bd) - **p. 86 :** © Motorola U.K. (hg) ; The Advertising Archive Ltd. (hd, bg, bd) - **p. 87 :** Roy Castle Lung Cancer Foundation (hd) ; The Advertising Archive Ltd. (mg) ; Robin Allison Smith (md) ; Royalty-Free/LD/Corbis (b) - **p. 88 :** The Advertising Archive Ltd./Moshino, DR - **p. 92 :** George Mikes, DR - **p. 95 :** John Harris/Report Digital-REA (hg) ; Commonwealth Youth Programme : Asia Centre (hd) ; Chris Young/PA Photos (m) ; R. Celentano/Laif-REA (mc) ; Rota/Camera Press/Gamma (md) ; Heiko Specht/Laif-REA (bg) ; AKG Paris (bd) - **p. 96 :** Musée des Beaux-Arts du Canada, Ottawa (hd) ; Georgia Lowell/Corbis (bd) - **p. 97 :** Printed by permission of the Norman Rockwell Family Agency, Copyright © 1926 the Norman Rockwell Family Entities/The Curtis/The Curtis Publishing Company (mg) ; The Bridgeman Art Lybrary-Giraudon (md)- **p. 98 :** Geoffrey & Scott Stirling and Danny Bulanadi (hg) ; © 2002 Mark Shainblum and Gabriel Morrissette. All rights reserved (hd) ; © 1998 by Arthur Slade and Owen Gieni. Reprinted by permission of S©ott Treimel NY (b) - **p. 99 :** © 2002 Mark Shainblum and Gabriel Morrissette. All rights reserved (hg) ; © Inuit Broadcasting Corporation, Reprinted with permission (hd) ; © 1998 by Arthur Slade and Owen Gieni. Reprinted by permission of S©ott Treimel NY (b) - **p. 102 :** The Commonwealth Secretariat (hd) ; Heiko Specht/Laif-REA (bg) - **p. 103 :** Bodleian Library Oxford/The Bodleian Library/The Art Archive (hg) ; Swim Ink/DG/Corbis (md) ; R. Celentano/Laif-REA (bc) ; The Commonwealth Secretariat (bd) - **p. 104 :** Martin Sasse/Laif-REA (hg) ; Shehzad Noorani/Still Pictures/Bios (mg) ; Explorer (md) ; Adil Bradlow/Reuters/Maxppp (bd) - **p. 105 :** Commonwealth Youth Programme : Asia Centre (hd) ; Heiko Specht/Laif-REA (mg) ; © The Commonwealth of Learning, COL (mc) ; The Commonwealth Secretariat (bg) ; Rota/Camera Press/Gamma (bd) - **p. 106 :** AKG Paris (hd) ; John Harris/Report Digital-REA (mg) ; Aroma Spice, DR (mc) ; Robin Allison Smith (bg) ; Christophe L (bd) - **p. 107 :** Ted Spiegel/Rapho (hg) ; Kim Myung, Jung Kim/PA Photos (mg) ; Robin Allison Smith (md) ; Chirs Young/PA Photos (bd) - **pp. 108-112 :** «Long Walk to Forever», from WELCOME TO THE MONKEY HOUSE by Kurt Vonnegut, Jr, copyright © 1961 by Kurt Vonnegut Jr. Used by permission of Dell Publishing, a division of Random House, Inc. - **p. 120 :** Article " Keep the cool in school " by Dr. Bruce Perry/From Scholastic Early Childhood Today © reprinted by permission of Scholastic Inc (bg) - **p. 155 :** Calvin and Hobbes © Watterson. Reprinted with permission of Universal Press Syndicate. All rights reserved (b) - **p. 204 :** RH Publications.